D1242468

"*Woman on Fire* is simply a smart, fierce, step-by-step guide by which we can finally name and actualize a meaningful and satisfying sexuality for ourselves, far beyond the limits of hetero or homo. That's a big wow."
—Kate Bornstein, author of *A Queer and Pleasant Danger* and *Gender Outlaws*

"There is not a woman I know who will not find part of her story, her sexual journey, her genuine concerns answered in *Woman on Fire*. Amy Jo Goddard, trailblazer and pioneer with deep wisdom and knowledge, understands that, for us, sex is exponentially greater than what our culture defines. By naming a myriad of possibilities and honoring you where you are, *Woman on Fire* is your guidebook where you can cast off shame and dare to take back your birthright as an ecstatic woman who is at home within herself."
—ALisa Starkweather, founder of the Red Tent Temple Movement and Women in Power

"Amy Jo is a warm and wise guide you can trust to support you on your journey to authentic erotic empowerment. Her work is brilliant, offering an intimate and inspiring path to not just more pleasure but to true sexual integration."
—Sheri Winston, award-winning author of *Women's Anatomy of Arousal* and founder of the Center for the Intimate Arts

"*Woman on Fire* is a passionate, empowering, game-changing guide for femme-identified people around the globe who want to break through the sex-negative garbage that has kept women playing small. Brava, Amy Jo Goddard!"   —Barbara Carrellas, author of *Ecstasy Is Necessary* and *Urban Tantra*

"Amy Jo Goddard is a pioneer in sexual empowerment and her extensive real-world experience sparkles throughout this book. This is a delightful journey toward better, richer, more fulfilling sex, for women who want more joyful, creative, pleasurable lives."   —Marcia Baczynski, cofounder of Cuddle Party

"All women deserve to read this book! Amy Jo writes an intelligent and inspiring manual, steeped in practical wisdom, to catalyze the rise of feminine power. With twenty years of leading her field, she is a luminary of sexual empowerment. *Woman on Fire* is a bold, lucid, and necessary work of courage. We all rejoice! Bravo!"   —Eva Clay, MSW, LCSW, psychotherapist

"Amy Jo Goddard knows that fear, shame, guilt, and lack of understanding around sex keep people from enjoying one of our greatest gifts and forms of expression. She leads you into the joy and power of your sexuality with her groundbreaking *Woman on Fire*. This is a must-read for all people."
—David Neagle, author of *The Millions Within*

"Amy Jo Goddard understands that creating a passionate, empowered sex life takes more than trying a new trick or wearing lingerie; she guides women to tune into their deep desires, ignite their sensuality, and maximize pleasure. If you are ready for discovery and to step into sexual empowerment, this book will definitely help you make it happen."
—Charlie Glickman, author of *The Ultimate Guide to Prostate Pleasure*

"This book is chock-full of savvy, sexy, and smart advice for every woman who's ever contemplated connecting with the deeper layers of herself to gain pleasure, self-expression, and more joy. Amy Jo Goddard is a generous writer and teacher, giving the reader an easy-to-access guide that will surely become a longtime staple in your success library. It's a must-read."
—Deborah Kagan, founder of the Rock Your Mojo system and author of *Find Your ME Spot*

"For any woman who wants to awaken to her sexual power, passion, and pleasure—*Woman on Fire* will open your eyes to greater satisfaction and erotic possibility!"
—Jaiya, author of *Cuffed, Tied, and Satisfied*

"If you're looking for the tools to build a grown-up sexuality that's radiant, empowered, playful, hot, and authentically yours, then Amy Jo's *Woman on Fire* is the spark that will ignite and fan the flames of who you are destined to become."
—Reid Mihalko of ReidAboutSex.com

WOMAN ON FIRE

WOMAN ON FIRE

9 Elements to Wake Up
Your Erotic Energy, Personal Power,
and Sexual Intelligence

AMY JO GODDARD

AVERY
an imprint of Penguin Random House
New York

an imprint of Penguin Random House LLC
375 Hudson Street
New York, New York 10014

Most Avery books are available at special quantity discounts for bulk purchase
for sales promotions, premiums, fund-raising, and educational needs. Special
books or book excerpts also can be created to fit specific needs. For details,
write SpecialMarkets@penguinrandomhouse.com.

Library of Congress Cataloging-in-Publication Data

Goddard, Amy Jo.
Woman on fire : 9 elements to wake up your erotic energy,
personal power, and sexual intelligence / Amy Jo Goddard.
p.   cm.
ISBN 978-1-59463-376-8
1. Sex instruction for women.   2. Women—Sexual behavior.   I. Title.
HQ46.G63   2015   2015014779
306.7082—dc23

Printed in the United States of America
1 3 5 7 9 10 8 6 4 2

Book design by Tara Long

For all of us who seek the fire

MORE, PLEASE!

I absolutely love my tribe, and I'm so glad you are a part of it. I would love to connect with you further.

Your place to go for everything about this book: womanon firethebook.com

I write and produce weekly articles and videos about sexuality and relationships at amyjogoddard.com and would love for you to join the juicy conversation there. There are tons of free resources for you.

Find me on Facebook at facebook.com/amyjogoddard
Talk to me on Twitter at @amyjogoddard
Use the hashtag #womanonfire

Sexual empowerment is a process, a practice, and an experience. You'll want some tools and juicy resources to help you along your journey. At womanonfirethebook.com, find all kinds of goodies to keep your fire blazing, including:

- **Your Sexual Empowerment Workbook:** your own downloadable copy of all the worksheets and assignments to fill out and keep, along with some extras that are not in this book
- **Free audio classes** to help you deepen your understanding and take the work further
- A step-by-step guide on how to create a **Woman on Fire book club** so you can work through the nine elements with a group of juicy women who are ready to claim their sexual power

CONTENTS

STARTING THE FIRE

This book is birthed from my desire to help you come home to yourself and live a sexually empowered life. I hope this book will inspire you, be a harbinger guiding you toward the sexual wholeness you dream of, and help you live the fulfilling sexual life you deserve.

I believe that having healthy, nonviolent relationships and working toward a pleasure-filled, creative life for all are the keys to changing the world. This vision comes from a place of knowing the world can be so much better, so much sexier, and more beautiful. And what peace, magic, and joy we can experience when we live in this more delightful, loving place. Healthy relationships are essential.

Sexual empowerment has to be holistic. It can't be partway. Your sexuality exists inside of a larger life and a larger world. A person does not become sexually empowered because they start having good sex, although good sex can be a very good start. Plenty of women know how to "have good sex" without fully realizing their own power. You've got to look at the whole package to become empowered sexually, emotionally, and spiritually.

I want to see us stop defining ourselves by forces outside ourselves, forces that tell us what to like, rather than defining ourselves by our own internal desire. I want us to embrace our desire fully without fear and to wholly express our own erotic being. I want women to demand healthy, mutually satisfying, fully lived relationships and to stop settling for less than they want or deserve. I want women to inhabit their bodies, take back their power, and claim their birthrights of pleasure, passion, and desire. I want each of us to be a Woman on Fire.

IT'S NEVER TOO EARLY OR TOO LATE

Women are the focus of my current work as a sexual empowerment coach. I have coached women via video conferencing from Switzerland to New York and Jamaica to Ohio. I've worked with women of different cultural backgrounds, class backgrounds, and sexual orientations. I've worked with women in countries where gender and sexual norms are very different from those in the United States. I've coached women in their early twenties who want to heal, women in their thirties who are feeling a dissatisfied itch telling them they need to focus in on their sexuality, women in their forties who are ready to address the famine in their sexual lives and the post-divorce women who are dating again and re-creating their sex lives, and women in their fifties, sixties, and seventies who want to do the work before it's "too late."

I've coached so many women who are single and know they must unlock the buried treasures in their own sexuality—and that they must do it for themselves. It's a tremendous honor when they show up. I've coached women who are married/partnered and don't want to have sex with their partners, women who are partnered and desperately want to have sex with their partner who can't or won't, women who are about to get married and are scared they'll never get to have the sex life they dream of. I've worked with women who are pregnant and are opening the capacity of their bodies to new experience, who are excited and also fearful of losing something they haven't quite found yet. Women who are lesbian or queer and refuse to succumb to the lesbian stereotype of companionate-not-sexual love, women who are becoming aware of their attraction to other women and want to explore it—and who know that something about exploring that love of other women is about learning to love themselves more fully. I also work with women who have big sexual wounds, who feel like they lost something at an early age and are saddened that now, in their thirties, forties, even fifties or sixties, they are working to get it back—or to have it for the very first time. I have worked with many powerful women who are doing extraordinary work in their lives, who are power players in the world, yet nearly mute in sex. They want to find their sexual voice and experience their sexual power. They want more pleasure.

In this book, I am honored to be able to share some of these women's stories with you, in their own words. I know you will appreciate if not relate to their tender, vulnerable, and honest tales. I work with creative, self-aware women who speak eloquently about their processes and growth, so I will quote them as much as possible to privilege their voices. This book is for all women—however you identify with your womanhood. We are not all the same kind of woman and I honor that. My perspective comes from my experience as a queer, white woman from the United States, with a middle-class, military family upbringing. I will speak to women directly in this book and talk about the socialization of girls and women, although people of other genders may also find it powerful.

THE NINE ELEMENTS

It is out of this intensely personal and powerful work with women that a framework for sexual empowerment revealed itself to me—growing organically from something unformed taking form, as a tribe of women expanded in this work. I teach with frameworks to make it more easily understood, accessed, and integrated into one's life.

In this book, I detail what I have found to be the nine essential elements of sexual empowerment. In chapter 1, I define what it means to be sexually empowered, which is the foundation and my approach to sexuality. In chapter 2, I lay out my Core Energy Model of Sexuality, which helps to organize sexuality as the powerful force it is in our lives. In the chapters that follow, I detail my Nine Elements to wake up your erotic energy, personal power, and sexual intelligence, which to me are the core components we each have to develop in order to make our sexuality as powerful as it can be. These elements are the ways we can animate, expand, and dance with sexuality. They are:

ELEMENT 1. VOICE:
Excavate and Rewrite Your Sexual Story

ELEMENT 2. RELEASE:
Make Space for the Sexual Self You've Been Waiting For

ELEMENT 3. EMOTION:
Show Up as Emotionally Powerful

ELEMENT 4. BODY:
Know and Radically Accept Your Body

ELEMENT 5. DESIRE:
Activate Desire and Create a Sexual Practice

ELEMENT 6. PERMISSION:
Give Yourself Permission to Be Erotically Authentic

ELEMENT 7. PLAY:
Develop Sexual Skills and Remember How to Play

ELEMENT 8. HOME:
Build Sexual Confidence and Come Home to You

ELEMENT 9. FIRE:
Use Your Dynamic Sexual Energy to Live Vibrantly

I believe we can use these elements of ourselves to develop our erotic energy, improve our sexual intelligence, and step fully into our own personal power. We can and should approach sexual intelligence the way we approach emotional intelligence: as something that requires knowledge, understanding, and the development of skills. Most of us are missing the information we need about the things we don't discuss. We need to ramp up our emotional skills in order to have the fully blossoming lives and relationships we most want. Our erotic energy is often our most untapped resource, and yet it is there inside us as a wellspring of juice we can use to direct our lives, and as we do, step more and more into our personal power. In the modern world, it's easy to spend the entire day in our heads in front of a computer, almost entirely disconnected from our bodies, eroticism, and desire, and then we want to turn back on when we are with our lovers. Our well-being and sexual fulfillment depend upon taking seriously improving our sexual intelligence and lighting up our core erotic energy.

HOW TO USE THIS BOOK

I have created an online portal for you with play sheets, exercises, and resources that will help you to get the most out of this book. Go to the portal at womanonfirethebook.com now to get a sense of what is available to assist you on this journey. I like to think of assignments as "home play." There are play sheets for all of the exercises that are included in this book and additional exercises and resources you won't see here. I RECOMMEND THAT YOU PRINT OUT THE DOWNLOADABLE PDF OF THE WHOLE WORKBOOK. All of it is designed to help you go deep into your sexual exploration, expansion, and healing.

You might choose to do some of the exercises or all of them as you go, taking in each aspect of the work and exploring it deeply. You may want to read the whole book through and then go back and do all of the home play. You might read the chapters in order or you can skip around. I have put them in the order that made the most sense, as one will build on others; however, they are not linear, so you can read them in the way that works for you.

I suggest you read this book with a friend, partner, therapist, or group of people so that you can have live conversations about the material and what it brings up in you. This journey is yours, and you can do it in community and with guides. Many of us are used to doing things alone. Not having been mothered properly, or busy caretaking everyone else, we often feel isolated in our own internal process and crave the support we typically give to others. The learning can often be deeper when you grow in a community. You have an opportunity to give your sexuality the attention it deserves, bring others into your journey, and find a new tribe. Even if you choose to read the book solo, know that many other women are on this powerful journey too. However you choose to do it, there is no wrong way. Engage with this book in the way that works best for you.

You picked up this book because there is a desire in you, in your sexual being. Your desire could be to figure out what you want, and to learn to get it. Your desire might be to go deeper in your relationships and in your life. It might be to become a sexually self-actualized being who lives her life in unapologetic ecstasy. Your desire might be to heal and develop a new relationship to sexuality. Your desire might be to more fully understand your sexuality and how to express it in powerful ways. Your desire might be to experience pleasure more wholly.

I can help make some sense of the vast terrain of sexuality. I'm going to define sexuality and sexual empowerment in a useful and practical way. I will give you tools. And a lot of encouragement and permission to explore your sexuality, to claim the sexual power that is yours to claim, and to live vibrantly at full capacity. I'm going to do my best to make it relevant to your life, and to share all of the things I wish someone would have shared with me when I was feeling pain and searching for answers. I hope that the framework of sexual empowerment I use in this book is powerful for you. I hope that it will allow you to see many of your blind spots, to heal your wounds, and to take on a new way of being that allows you to have the sexuality and life you desire.

1

THE BIG
ROUND BALL

All of us have a desire inside of us for more. We want to experience more, to grow more, to have more, to be more fulfilled, to be more of who we are meant to be. Women come to me in this place of wanting more, knowing it is intrinsically connected to their own sexual being. I am a guide. It is their journey. This is your journey.

You know there is more. Sexuality is at the core of the longing in us all. It *is* the core. It is the seduction of life itself, the texture of rain on your face, or the dry, cold air you feel in your nostrils on a winter walk. It is the creation of beauty and the meeting of the divine in you, in life itself. It is the enjoyment of being, the pleasure of creating your dreams, and it's there in the expansive space when you pause to appreciate your process. So many women have this hunger inside of themselves, this magic wanting to birth itself into life. To have your "more," you will have to claim your sexual power or there will always be a gap between what you want and what you have.

THE FEAR

I hear many of the sentiments I experienced at a young age from so many women: that fear of being *the only one*. The only one to experience shame, to have unfulfilled desire, to have deeply ingrained fears of being "broken," of never having experienced orgasm, or of being the only one who needs "this" particular form of healing (whatever "this" might be).

So many people fear they are sexually broken. Unfixable. It's a tremendous fear—that their sexual history, sexual functioning, sexual problems, or sexual trauma is so bad, so impossible to fix, that they must be permanently damaged. Yet I have watched client after client change her life entirely—change her experience of sex, her sexuality, her body, and her relationships dramatically—because she committed to the process and worked through those parts that made her feel hopeless and lost.

You are powerful and nothing is impossible for you no matter what your experience has been. Your journey might look different from everyone else's, yet it is possible to achieve your vision. You may have gotten messages from your family, friends, or culture that something about you is broken, because we live in a society that likes to tell us how imperfect we are (gasp!) so we stay stuck feeling bad, buying products to help us fix ourselves, and choosing not to rise up and use our power to challenge the systems that oppress us. You are whole and capable of healing the things that you are not at peace with.

In my two decades of teaching sexuality I have witnessed the transformations of many people. I have developed an understanding of the sexual and emotional devices that keep women from coming home to themselves, of the struggles and heartbreaks that keep them feeling alien to their own sexuality. I have listened to and learned about the stories and secrets women keep—the ones they are terrified of other people discovering or of showing to themselves. The stories I hear over and again are each precious and unique and yet so many threads of similarity are woven into this collective sexual herstory.

In this collective vision, I hear many of the same wants. Women tell me that they want more sexual confidence, the ability to get their needs met, to explore, to be more playful, to have more orgasms and pleasure, to have deeper intimacy, more emotional connection, more desire, and more time for their sexuality. They want to feel more alive, vibrant, and juicy. They want freedom.

THE POWER

We have a deeper idea about the power of sexuality. We know there is something more to it than our glossy sexualized media world has shown us. This power can feel like a secret that has been kept from us because they didn't know how to talk to us about it. After all, how would we teach the magnitude of this powerful force in school? Its true grandeur is so big, so beyond this mundane world and what we can see with our eyes, that it scares many people—so that's what they end up teaching children. Be afraid. Don't get this disease or be *that* girl. Don't let them "take it away" from you. Hold on tight.

And if you feel pleasure, you might like it far too much, so don't feel too much of that, because then you'll go too far and we won't know how to help you. Don't trust boys. Don't trust your body.

Don't trust anyone who is interested in you sexually. Don't trust this terrain of sexuality because it's a scary, complicated place, and since we can't explain it to you, let's just not talk about it.

A lot of women ask whether true power and pleasure is really possible, and fear that it's not—not for them, anyway. If you've had the thought that "maybe it's just not going to happen for me" or that maybe what you want is not really possible, let me assure you.

It is.

I can tell you with confidence that you are not the only one. Whatever your story, whatever your experiences—you are not broken, you are not "unfixable," you are not going to be left out of having the things you desire or the healing you need because of your history, desires, body, size, age, identity, or any of the other untruths they reinforced. If you want these things, they are here for you.

It's possible you might not even know exactly what you want, but you know it's not what you have right now. Most women are socialized to be led sexually, to be chased and to follow the desires of their partners rather than to tap into their own wants and express them. That paradigm has to shift, and it begins with identifying your own desires and figuring out what skills you could develop to make them real. You won't magically know what to do when you feel a great big attraction, land yourself in a sexual situation, and declare you are ready.

THE BIG ROUND BALL

I remember one day speaking to a woman who had been in conversation with me for several years about doing some work on her sexuality, and she said, "It's like my sexuality is a big round ball and I don't know what to grab on to or how to get in."

I think a lot of people feel that way about their sexuality. It's complex. Where do you begin? What is the first thing to touch? How do you make it concrete? How do you explain some of the feelings you have that are so profound or intangible you aren't sure how to access them using human words and emotions; or the longing that feels like such an amorphous craving and yet feels so important and rich, the one that would transform your experience of life itself if you could meet it? How do you share with a lover or a partner how magical and big you know this energy to be—and how do you go *there* with them? How do you access the orgasm that you know is waiting to be born inside of you? And once you do access it, how do you bring this energy into your everyday mundane life and make your life extraordinary?

ADULTS NEED SEX ED TOO

Many adults anguish in the myths about all we "should" know and the kind of sex we "should" be having and the sexual lives we "should" be living. The reality is that our culture chronically under-prepares us for fulfilling sexual lives. Since most young people never get adequate sex education, we all grow up into adults who think that just because we are grown, we are "supposed to know" how to have sex, how to do it well, how to orgasm, and how to not have any hang-ups. We're supposed to have a ravenous sexual appetite, healthy desire, and clear sexual communication. We should be confident in our bodies and sexual abilities. A tall order if you've never had any real sex education or developed your sexual intelligence. How exactly are people supposed to learn how to be sexually healthy adults? Even if you were lucky enough to get quality sex education in primary or secondary school, it's likely that the word *pleasure* was never even mentioned. Sex ed is too often taught in that fear-based model of everything you need to avoid and with little about what to pursue besides abstinence and "virtue."

GIVING IT UP

As girls, we are taught to fiercely guard our virginity, this thing we barter with and will "give away" to someone—almost always assumed to be a male. And many of us have a story of it being "taken away" by someone we didn't consent to "give it" to. This idea divorces us from our sexuality and our bodies as an intrinsic part of who we are, as if one act of sexual intercourse is more important than a whole lifetime of discovering what this body and heart is capable of and what it really desires. Again, there is this deficit model: we think we *lose* our sexuality to someone else, and then we wonder why we grow into adults who think we are *broken*. There are pieces that have gone *missing*.

Marry and you are "given away" again. Is it any wonder so many women don't feel like they have agency over their own sexuality? We continually put it in the hands of men. The system was set up that way a long time ago. Many women enter sexually blind into marriage because they've "been saving it." We think the choice to say "I do" will automatically give us the ability to have a functional and fulfilling sexual relationship. You aren't any more ready to have a marriage without relationship education and self-examination than you are ready to have a child without any birth preparation or child-rearing education. The same goes for sex.

As an adult, you have all sorts of new aspects of your sexuality that you are discovering and new sexual situations and dynamics to work with, so the need for adult sex education remains paramount. For instance, how do you negotiate safer sex in an adult dating world? What do you do if your partner doesn't know how to please you? What do you do when you partner with or marry someone with whom you do not feel sexually compatible? What if you haven't had an orgasm? How do you explore new sexual territory or introduce a new idea into a relationship like a new toy, a threesome, an open relationship, or some erotic power play?

SEX ED FOR ADULTS

We need ongoing sexual education for every stage of our lives. Everyone needs sex education. And I mean *everyone*. In general, people do not treat sex and sexuality as something to work on or put effort into. The assumption is that sex will just happen. This is a harmful myth. Optimal sex and sexuality require awareness, skills, and practice. If you want to cash in on the best sexual pleasure possible to you, you have got to put in the time and energy. You've got to cultivate your sexual intelligence. There are many ways to feel supported on your journey and some essential things you can do. Understand that becoming sexually empowered is not magic . . . it's about dedication to parts of yourself you may have neglected because you didn't know you needed to do something different. There are no enchanted pills or shortcuts to make it all better. Good thing, because it is one of the most enlivening, beautiful, expanding journeys a person can take. You really want to enjoy the ride.

Simply becoming an adult does not make you ready for a sexual relationship or mean you will automatically have good sex. Becoming an adult does not empower you as a sexual person. What it does do is give you more freedom to make your own choices and to act on your desires. What you do with these desires is entirely up to you. How well you do it is related to your knowledge, skills, self-awareness, and commitment to growth. The fact that you picked up a book about sexual empowerment indicates that you are well ahead of most of your peers on this path. Welcome to the journey.

CLARIFY YOUR "MORE"

Take a moment now to start defining your "more" that you want. You'll see throughout these chapters just how excited and refined your answers will become. What is the desire in you that made you pick up this book? What needs to happen for you to give yourself permission to want it?

KATHIE'S STORY

Kathie came to me at sixty-five years old wanting to work on her sexuality but was really nervous and in some disbelief that it would change anything. We had many conversations before she decided to step into my women's sexual empowerment program. I knew she needed it and I wanted it for her. I wanted her to know it is never too late.

> *Right out of college, I joined a religious order as a nun—a lifestyle that meant giving up two key things: sexuality and money. After two decades in the ashram, I realized I wasn't happy or fulfilled, so I left. As I moved into normal life, I gradually had to face all I had not done, and sexuality and a money-making career were the two biggest things.*
>
> *During my forties and fifties, I went back to school and earned a master's degree, traveled and studied, and opened a small business as a solo entrepreneur. I was surviving, but I still wasn't successful and fulfilled any more than I had been as a monastic. Something still was wrong, so I started digging—inside.*
>
> *I did all kinds of therapies. I was always attending workshops, seminars, coaching. I found that old grief and emotional pain from things that happened to me in early childhood were holding me hos-*

tage. Underneath all that pain, I discovered the core belief that I was not lovable, not deserving. When I was a teenager, this belief had run through my conscious mind as "I'm not pretty enough." The body shame and insecurity connected with that had been severe enough to stop me from being social or dating.

My mother had left when I was a toddler, and I had built a shield around myself. I shut down strongly, disconnected from my capacity to love and from my desire. I had a fear of abandonment. As I grew older I disconnected from my capacity to experience sexuality with another person, although I had discovered masturbation when I was eleven or twelve. I dated a little bit as a teenager but didn't do anything sexual. In college I got made fun of. I had not had any sexual intercourse, and that was part of the shame I carried. I just avoided sexuality. As a young adult I discovered the spiritual life— it was a way of contacting an absolute level of love without it having to be with a person. I fell in love with the universal, you might say.

I still have not had intercourse at sixty-five. A story like that is so far off the cultural bell curve (people make jokes about forty-year-old virgins, right?) that I've had people laugh at me when I share it. That's painful, and it reinforced my own shame about it. In that respect, doing this work where the approach to sexuality is big and broad enough to include even someone with a story like mine has been a lifesaver.

By the time I started working with Amy Jo, I was determined to reclaim my sexuality. I had realized that I must connect with and rescue this part of myself no matter what. I can't help but run into things that prompt regret." What if I'd done this sooner, when my hormones were on board?" I see younger women who are confident and beautiful and think, "If only I'd been where I am now when I was at that age." It does hurt. It does sting. You can't undo time. But I find that every step I take toward my sexuality overrides those regrets. It's more powerful to have the experiences I can have in this body now than to dwell on what I could have done.

Amazingly, a partner walked into my life just about the time I started working with Amy Jo. Early on, we would sit on the couch and he would lean over to kiss me and this "No!" would pop up from somewhere inside me. It was shocking, like I didn't have control over it. So I decided one day to override that, to overstep my resistance and kiss this guy. That was a breakthrough point for me. I redefined myself to myself in that moment. As we began to make out more often, I began to find that I could trust my body's response to things like his hand on my back. I felt my sexuality waking up in my pelvic area and hips, and I could follow it. I felt like I was following my desire. We've had some fun. We're talking about intercourse now—another point where I will have to overstep resistance and fear.

I now believe that accessing the sexual self and tapping into sexual, creative energy is vital to a woman's thriving physically, emotionally, creatively, even financially, no matter what her age or lifestyle or life story. Who's to say that confidence, pleasure, and what the hell, joy, too, can't be ours right up to our last days on the planet?

DEFINING SEXUAL EMPOWERMENT

The more whole we are as sexual beings, the more fulfilled we are as human beings. I believe this with every ounce of my being. This core belief is what has driven me in my life's purpose for twenty years and gotten me out of bed every day as a change agent ready to make the world a more sexually healthy place. Sexuality and, in turn, sexual fulfillment is a deeply important wellspring for happiness in all of life.

Sometimes it is easier to know what something is *not* than to know what something *is*. We learn to deal with sexuality in deficits. What's *not* there. What we *don't* have. What we *can't* be. What we can't do. What we need to stay *away* from.

In the case of sexuality and sexual empowerment, because we lack role models and positive images, it's hard for many people to describe what sexual empowerment is. We often know what it's not when we see it or experience it. We can just feel that somehow, *this isn't it*. Sometimes that looks like making poor sexual choices or using sex to get approval from others. It might be a person who doesn't take care of herself sexually or emotionally. It could be a lack of understanding or knowledge of sexuality. Sometimes it's when you settle for less than what you want that you realize how much more you desire. Most people stop here, telling themselves they don't deserve more or can't have it.

Sexual empowerment is what we *do* want. What we *can* be. What we *can* have. What we *can* do. What experiences we *can* create for ourselves. What kind of lovers we *can* be. What types of lovers we *can* draw to us. It's how we can *expand* who we are exponentially when we develop, nurture, heal, and explore our sexuality.

The concept of *empowerment*, while overused, is an important one. There is no other word that means what empowerment means: *to embody power*. To live from a place of personal strength, autonomy, and integrity. To hold, embrace, and employ one's personal power for the highest good. To make choices and take action and feel an impact. It is to be the independent agent of your own life, the architect of your destiny.

Maybe you've felt moments of sexual empowerment—times when you tapped into the power and pleasure of your body, clarified a desire and experienced it, or had the best sex of your life. Maybe you've also felt moments when you settled, when your desires were unrequited, when you had sex you weren't into or experienced that disturbing place of self-betrayal. This book is about creating a life filled with moments of power.

In this book, I aim to contribute a clear picture of what sexual empowerment looks like, how to live it, and how it can impact every other part of your life. I want it to touch you, help you to cherish your time, to know that, like sex and pleasure, life is immediate: it's right now, and you can't afford to wait any longer to give it the attention it deserves. I hope to help you affirm and to step into your big, bold, dreamy, sexy, on-fire self.

Empowerment is action, and it's a state of being. There are many essential parts to living a truly powerful sexual life. I want to talk about these essential elements on three levels: our relationship with our self, with others, and with our culture. After all, sexuality does not exist in a vacuum.

Our Relationship with Ourselves

PEOPLE WHO ARE AUTHENTICALLY SEXUALLY EMPOWERED:

... Are intimately connected to their sexual selves

... Accept their bodies and are educated about how their bodies "work"

... Understand and acknowledge that changes in sexual function or desire are a normal part of aging, and that they can work with those changes to create a satisfying sexual life at each new phase of life

... Know that they do not have to have sex to be a sexual person

... Feel fully sexually expressed, and when not in full expression, they have tools to help them get there, utilizing available options for sexual expression and erotic experience

... Make pleasurable, satisfying, fulfilling sex their norm and experience pleasure regularly and as a norm in their lives

... Attain sexual agency by thoughtfully exploring sex and sexuality and making authentic decisions about what is right for them and what is not

... Develop healthy coping skills for managing difficult emotions like loss and pain

... Explore and develop an authentic sexual identity and do not need to hide or shift that identity to feel comfortable and safe in their lives (also impacted by culture)

... Live in alignment with their desires and know they never have to settle for less than what they really want

... Commit to heal and release any shame, guilt, or trauma about their sexuality

... Develop their confidence and sexual self-esteem

... Feel at home in themselves and move through the world from a place of self-intimacy

Our Relationships with Others

PEOPLE WHO ARE AUTHENTICALLY SEXUALLY EMPOWERED:

... Communicate needs, wants, and desires without blame or shame

... Set clear boundaries and identify and experience their wants and desires without crossing the boundaries of others

... Accept rejection without taking it personally

... Express a range of emotions in healthy ways that do not harm themselves or others

... Identify defensive patterns in relationships and work to overcome them by replacing the patterns with healthy ways of connecting to others

... Minimize the need to be competitive with others and release patterns of lack, deprivation, or feelings that they can't have what others have

Our Relationship with Our Culture

PEOPLE WHO ARE AUTHENTICALLY SEXUALLY EMPOWERED:

... Critically examine cultural messages about sexuality, gender, and sex

… Reject and challenge sexual stereotypes, assumptions, false ideas, and cultural myths that hinder, impair, squash, or dim their sovereign sexuality

… Identify and experience erotic authenticity even when social pressure or popular ideas push them to do or like something else

… Examine how the values and beliefs of their culture impact their personal experience of gender, sexuality, and power

It may feel like a tall order. Do not be overwhelmed—be inspired! Your sexuality is vast. There are many parts of it, and different aspects of your sexual self will be prominent at different stages of your life. That's the good news. You never need to stop growing as a sexual person, or forsake your sexuality for security, a relationship, a new phase of life, or for any other reason. There is always more to learn, room to grow, and a choice to experience your life *now*.

Sexual empowerment is a way of living life fully, with passion and creativity, and in deep love. We are meant to be expansive as sexual and creative beings, and many gender roles and other expectations limit and diminish our expansiveness. Subscribing to limiting roles is the opposite of empowerment. Breaking roles and rules to be who we really are will bring us to an authentically powerful place.

In this book we are going to talk about the things on the above list and why they are important. We are also going to address what gets in the way of having the sexually empowered life you deeply desire and deserve. We are going to talk about sex and how to create a fulfilling sexual life. And know that when I talk about "sex," I am not saying intercourse—they are not synonymous. Intercourse is one form of sex, and there are many more ways to have sex. I'm talking about the whole pie. The enchilada with the sauce and the guacamole.

TOOLS FOR BUILDING THE FIRE

Sexual empowerment is not only for people who are having sex or want to have sex. Whether you are in a heterosexual marriage or several relationships at once; identify as heterosexual, gay, lesbian, bisexual, or queer; are young or old; are asexual; are celibate; or pay for sex, you are a sexual person who can experience sexual empowerment. Your core energy is sexual energy. You do not leave your sexuality at home because it doesn't match today's outfit, you are having a night out with your girlfriends, or because you don't have a sex date planned.

No matter who you are, there are means of support we all need on this journey if we are committed to our fullest sexual expression and expansion:

RESOURCES—Everyone needs accurate resources about sexuality. Books, honest information, websites, and places you can go to get the support you need for your sexual journey. This book is one such resource.

SKILL BUILDING—Remember, sex requires skills. You have got to *learn* skills. And how do you get better at them? Practice. There is much to say about sexual skills, and we'll discuss this in depth in chapter 9.

TEACHERS/EDUCATION—You deserve educators who have studied sex and can share information to help you grow and understand the things that confuse you about sexuality. Teachers can be both formal and informal. Some of my greatest teachers were lovers (informal), yet my formal teachers were pivotal for my own development.

RELATIONSHIPS—Relationships are our greatest teachers. That means lovers, friends, coworkers, family—every relationship in your life is a teacher.

ROLE MODELS—Role models of healthy sexuality are important. Some examples of my sexual role models: my sexuality professors, Madonna—powerful woman, unabashedly sexual—was a role model for me growing up in the eighties; my mentor Betty Dodson became a powerful role model; and I had peers who accepted and embraced their sexuality and became role models to me. Who are your sexual role models? If you don't have any, keep looking.

OPEN DIALOGUE—If you don't bring sex out of the closet, you cannot actually work on it, and you will stay alone with it on your journey. Everyone has to overcome the messages they have internalized that tell them not to talk about sex and that it should stay private. You will have to learn to talk about it, even if you only talk about it with your partner or lovers. Open dialogue diminishes any shame associated with the subject.

RITUAL—Ritual is a tool that helps human beings enjoy life. Ritual makes experiences special. We have rituals around marriage and death, but how about rituals for our own developing sexuality? In some cultures, there are puberty rituals that can be very empowering for young people. Developing rituals for yourself around your body and sexual expression, pleasure, sex, and other parts of your sexuality is a very helpful way to bring more meaning and honor to your sexual journey. There are more details about ritual in chapter 7.

HEALING WORK—Most people have some healing to do around their sexuality. How we do our healing looks different for everyone. It can be some type of therapy, energetic healing work like Reiki, bodywork, shamanistic ritual, women's circles, workshops, or being guided by any number of gifted practitioners who can help you to heal physically, spiritually, and emotionally.

LIFE EXPERIENCE—Exposing yourself to new sexual ideas or ways of being and trying new things expands your sexuality. Not everything is right for everyone, but there are new experiences that may well open and expand you at your core.

SELF-INTIMACY—This means to know who you really are, how to tap into your own desires or need for boundaries, how to be with yourself, and how to feel at home. Your self-possession reverberates outward to others. True self-intimacy is a deep self-love and comfort in being you, and being *with* you. That is a great gift in any relationship. Developing your self-intimacy is vital for this journey.

COMMIT TO A SEXUALLY EMPOWERED LIFE

When I talk to people interested in working with me as a coach or participating in one of my educational programs, I often ask, "Are you committed to working on this?" Commitment is such a big part of the equation; it determines who really empowers themselves and who continues to stay exactly where they are, having the same conversations, the same pain, the same bad relationships, the same frustrations.

Ask yourself, "Am I committed?" How will you push yourself when it gets challenging or when you have to face the parts you've avoided? Because these moments of reckoning are a normal and important part of the process.

Get Clear on Your Commitment to Yourself

Before you go any further, visualize who you want to be as a sexual being. I invite you to download my guided visualization on becoming your sexually empowered self. You can find it in the *Woman on Fire* online portal at womanonfirethebook.com.

LISTEN TO THE VISUALIZATION
AND GET AN IMAGE FOR YOURSELF

What does it feel like to step into your sexual power? How do you walk in the world, express yourself with lovers, experience your body and pleasure? What do you want from this journey? What will it look like and feel like when you have it? How will you know you have it? What are you committed to?

TAKE A FEW MINUTES
TO FIRST SEE IT IN YOUR MIND'S EYE,
AND THEN WRITE IT ALL DOWN

Make a list, or draw pictures, write a story, or even make a collage. Whatever works best for you. It might simply be the top five things you want to focus on creating and developing. Keep this image, list, story, description, or collage where you can see it to remind yourself of what you are working to create as you read this book.

This is a journey, and there will be times when you'll need reminders about why you started on this journey to begin with. Your commitment is the most powerful reminder you have. Your image and ideas of what is possible will evolve throughout your process. This is a starting point meant to inspire you and to act as a reminder if you find yourself feeling muddled.

As you begin, allow yourself to want. Stop pretending about the things you really do know. Dream the seemingly impossible dream and live full-out now. There is no other time but now. Your path to a place of true sexual empowerment (which is also creative empowerment and life empowerment) is one you cannot ignore or avoid. You know sexuality is important and valuable. You know there is work to be done and things to be examined. You know there is space to be made and passion to be lived. You know you have a personal power to claim. You know there is a fire that burns inside of you.

Once you know, there is no going back to not knowing.

2

CORE ENERGY MODEL OF SEXUALITY

THE PURE STATE
OF PLEASURE

By nature, human beings are fully in their bodies in infancy—in a state of natural joy. Ever seen an infant flirt? They smile, giggle, look away, look back, giggle more, flap their arms. They engage in joyful flirtation with the world. Unadulterated glee. It's pure. It's beautiful.

For many of us, that ability doesn't last long. Soon enough we hear: "Why are you laughing?" "Don't touch me!" "Don't touch yourself!" "Stop playing!" "You think you're so cute!"

All creation holds a kernel of pleasure and joy in it. Conception comes in a variety of ways. No matter the how, within that tiny cellular creation is the joy of life. We start in a combustion of cells and energy that grows and we come into this world open and ready to be all we are meant to be here as human beings.

Sexuality is the nucleus of all life. Before we have any physical form, our humbly magnificent inception emerges from an energetic desire for life. Our very being desires birth, love, and connection. It wants to thrive and to live. This erotic impulse that creates us all—even before conception—gives us a preformed desire for more life. That core erotic impulse is the nucleus of who we are from the very beginning. Within the melding of those two nascent cells that birth us are the requisite components of creation and connection. What is more powerful than that? What is more sexual than that?

The universe gave us this well of energy so that we could fully live and love all of who we are as human beings. It gave us a body so that we had a place to hold this energy and a vehicle for exaltation and pleasure. We would not have been given such a wondrous capacity to feel pleasure through our senses and our body if we were not meant to experience it. Our sexuality is our spirituality in physical form. Stepping into true sexual power is part of the spiritual journey.

SEXUAL AGENCY IN A SEX-NEGATIVE WORLD

Committing to live a pleasure-filled, sexually healthy life is not easy in a culture that often condemns sex, pleasure, and full sexual expression. The United States is an incredibly sex-negative place. We are born into it, live in it, and are steeped in this sex-negative environment. We are bombarded with its pejorative and conflicting messages from the get-go. We learn the antiquated "sex is dirty, don't talk about it" messaging, and yet we can't look at a magazine, billboard, or mass-marketed video without being bombarded with sex—and a very specific version of what a sexy woman looks like.

I believe sex-negativity refers to the cultural, social, and psychological view that sexuality is by nature shameful, harmful, or vile, and therefore that it should be repressed, policed, or otherwise controlled. This repression, control, and policing happens within families and other interpersonal relationships, in schools, hospitals, places of worship, retirement homes, and other institutions, and is perpetuated in powerful ways via legislation and law enforcement. It serves to preserve and promulgate control of women, gay, lesbian, bisexual, and other queer people, and those whose sexual expression or identity is outside the dominant norm. Why is a person's sexuality still a reason for us to be denied services, rights, and privileges?

Sex-negativity uses shame, guilt, fear, and stereotyping to harm people sexually and disconnects us from the pleasure, joy, and acceptance that is our natural-born state. How could this not result in violence? It is already violence because it disconnects us from our birthright. It is a way of shaming and denying people. It often reproduces itself over and over in people's lives.

Sexual agency means to have control and dominion over your own sexuality. You are a free agent. You are the agent of your body, your sexuality, your sexual choices, your sexual expression, and your sexual pleasure and power. The power over your sexuality is in your hands. You have true independent sexual choices. As a sexual agent, you are susceptible to many conflicting influences as you work to stand in your own place of power as a sexual being. It can feel as if sexuality has been hijacked by the beautiful when we look at the mass media sexual narrative. The oversexualized, youthful storyline that directs women to be "perfect" at everything teaches us that perfection equals sexy. If you aren't young and perfectly beautiful, you aren't sexy or you won't have access to sexuality. It leaves a lot of people out.

If no one sent us sex-negative and confusing sexual messages, our natural state would be one of sexual agency and empowerment. But that power and agency gets condemned, taken away, judged, squashed, and shamed and we are left feeling unhealthy or broken. Yet that kernel of a pure empowered state is in there. You just have to peel away the layers and reconnect to it.

CREATING A SEX-POSITIVE WORLD

There is a common term in the sex educator world that many people strive for or purport to be: "sex-positive." There is some variation and many assumptions about what it means to be sex-positive. At its basic root, to be sex-positive is to acknowledge sexuality as a natural and healthy part of our lives and of who we are. It is to create space for people to make the sexual choices that are right for them, without pressure or judgment that they should be or should like something else. It firmly acknowledges our sexual diversity, that we are the agents of our own desire, and that everyone has rights as sexual beings.

A true sex-positive world is the antidote to all of that negativity we are bombarded with about sexuality. I invite you to consider what it would mean for you to really shape-shift toward a sex-positive way of living and being—and if you have children, parenting. How would you think about and talk about sex differently? How would you reframe some of your sexual judgments?

Women and girls are taught so many false ideas that keep our sexuality limited and in someone else's hands. We learn that sexuality is about losing something or giving something away. The concept of virginity as a bartering chip and something outside of our bodies is disempowering and often hurtful. We learn that it's our job to be pretty and sexy and not to rock the boat. We learn to be a glossy two-dimensional version of sexual—not an authentic sexual that comes from a place inside of us. We are constantly taught to mimic the oversexualized version of what and who to be sexually. This is a disfigured sexual agency.

ANN'S STORY

Ann came to me after her third divorce. She was about to turn fifty and had four children.

I was living in sexual unfulfillment because of religious shame for my whole life. I was shamed by my parents' post–Depression Era middle-class upbringing of "not talking about it," and the shame was both overt and unspoken. If we didn't talk about it, then it must be awful, right? I ran from that, trying to explore, and was shamed for it by our misogynistic society. Being a wild child didn't work, so I went to the extreme end of the spectrum and joined the Mormon Church in order to be a "good" woman. That led to my loss of self-expression and internal anger for not having power of my voice, my body, my career, my mind, and my desires.

For a long time the Mormon Church and its doctrine shamed me in so many ways as a divorced woman and a woman who stood up for what was right. I was made to feel guilty and ashamed about how I dressed, how my makeup and hair looked, and even about wearing jewelry by some members of the Mormon Church. Unseen or unnoticeable was virtuous, and bigness was shamed, shunned, or gossiped about. I realized that sexuality is a power, that if it is open and an integrated part of us as women, it freaks men out because they can't control it.

I got permission from watching others in their own power. I wanted what they had and was afraid to allow myself to have it. Their power was magnificent and I was afraid of it. When I thought long and hard about it, I realized it was my right to have it and I realized I had given my power away and had to reclaim it immediately. I gave myself permission to not feel shame or guilt for my desire and preferences.

This work [on my sexuality] has allowed me to love my body and to seek pleasure in whatever way serves my highest purpose without shame. Understanding my own sexuality has opened my eyes and heart to myself and others with compassion for our human-ity in a tough world of shame, darkness, and disempowerment. I became gentler and compassionate rather than judgmental with my-self and others. The deepest part of this healing work is my soul healing and my work on recognizing how religion had taken away my ability to see my spirit and my spirituality. I have sexually evolved into knowing that I deserve pleasure and it is my divine right. Pleasure without the price of pain.

To become sexually empowered, we must learn to question our beliefs. You must excavate those that limit you and don't work for you. There may be lots of beliefs that you like and want to keep. Not all of your learned messages about sexuality are bad. It's almost al-ways a mixed bag. The key is to figure out what supports you in your sexual growth and which beliefs you need to let go of or reframe, as Ann did.

SEXUAL ENERGY

We cannot talk about sexual power without talking about sexual energy. I believe our sexuality is, at its root, an energy. This energy is our own powerful core, the fire we use to flirt, connect, explore, fantasize, and express our power in a multitude of ways.

When your energy is strong and you are aligned with it, you have a powerful way of attracting to you the things you want. This is an ideal state. This core sexual energy is essentially your gas tank; it keeps you going, but it's not mere fuel. There is a quality to it that is fundamental to your having a dynamic, ecstatic life.

When your core sexual energy gets depleted, it impacts you on multiple levels. You become dulled to life, sometimes even depressed.

The joy, poetry, and allure of everyday life dissipates. You find it harder to appreciate your life and the details that make it gorgeous and worth living. You forget the power you have to create a life with the people, relationships, experiences, and things you want. You stop experiencing pleasure.

Most people do not work with their sexual energy consciously. An essential step in living a sexually empowered life is to acknowledge that this energy exists, to nurture it like the friend it is, and increase it. Then you have more fuel and power to experience pleasure and desire and to express your sexuality with the fervor that makes your life vibrant and joyous.

Your core energy is your life force. It's that part of you that tingles with excitement and spreads through your body when you orgasm. You can keep it for yourself and you can share it. You can funnel it in many different directions. You can use it for creativity, to make art, or to make love. You can use it as the fuel for developing your career or professional pursuits. You can use it to create strong communities or to make and raise children. You can use it to work toward social justice and change in the world. This energy wants to express itself.

Sexual energy is incomprehensibly expansive, so it will take a while to meet its edges. So get in and put your goggles on. Once you experience its power, there is no going back. Audre Lorde, a celebrated black lesbian, feminist writer, said in her classic and extraordinary essay "The Uses of the Erotic: The Erotic as Power":

> *The erotic is a measure between the beginnings of our sense of self and the chaos of our strongest feelings. It is an internal sense of satisfaction to which, once we have experienced it, we know we can aspire. For having experienced the fullness of this depth of feeling and recognizing its power, in honor and self-respect we can require no less of ourselves.*

THE SPIRITUALITY OF
SEXUAL ENERGY

Spiritual energy is creation energy is sexual energy. It all comes from the same source. There are many false divisions between spirituality and sexuality. Our spiritual and sexual paths provide us with tools to reach our greatest good. And both spirituality and sexuality can be misused, abused, misrepresented, and manipulated.

The core of sexuality is energy. The core of spirituality is energy. Energy is the beginning of all creation. It grows and expands as it comes to life because that's what it's meant to do: it's meant to reproduce. We often separate sexual energy and spiritual energy, yet they come from the same well. We all have that well within us. Our core energy is the source for creation: whether for art-making, love-making, baby-making, community-building, or project development, we use it for things that are important to us and the world. That same core energy is the well we tap into to orgasm, to fall in love, to love God/Goddess/Spirit, to meditate, to feel pleasure, to feel divinely inspired. It all comes from the same deeply rich life force that is creative source energy, that is our higher self, that is our capacity to heal and love, that is the erotic core of our very being.

People have ecstatic experiences with "God/Goddess," the universe, the cosmic, creator—whatever you choose to call it. There is an enlivening, a quickening, sometimes a powerful surge of energy that comes from connecting to the universe or the greater creative energy that is all around us. You can have a similar energetic surge when you have ecstatic partner sex, or when you connect with yourself when you masturbate and drop in deep.

OUR EROTIC CORE

At our core where this energy or fire lives is that desire toward more, toward being, toward growth, toward becoming what we are here to become. It is a desire to experience pleasure and joy in the magnificent matter our bodies are made of, in living a fully expressed life. Our souls are determined to live vibrantly in this world—which reflects this core eroticism in all things: it whispers in the wind and radiates in the warmth of the sun on our faces. It is the pure bliss of a cat basking in sunshine. It is the glisten on the rhythmic waves of the ocean. It is the softness of skin and the sound of your lover's voice in your ear. It is a baby's full-bellied laugh. It is the texture of the strawberry as you bite into its flesh. It is the heat of breath in sexual ecstasy. It is a bee that plumes a flower for nectar. We all seek that nectar of life itself, which is in and wholly of itself enough. A complete experience. That nectar is joy and bliss and orgasm. It is making love to the natural world as well as we would a lover. It is playing with the eroticism in others through hearty laughter, sharing memory, appreciating beauty. It is the core of life. Life would not exist at all without this powerful energy.

True north is there in your erotic core, and it will always lead you to the promised land of a life fully lived, of breathtaking edges explored, and dreams lavishly realized. When you are tapped into this energy, when you embrace it and love it and get to know it, this energy allows you to create more, to become more. When you deplete it, you deplete your core self, you smolder your fire, and you dim the lights on possibility. You agree to what might at one time have been unacceptable and give in to mediocrity, accepting less than you want of life.

OUR NEED FOR A NEW MODEL OF SEXUALITY

I have spent years looking for a good definition of sexuality, and I have been shocked at how few real definitions exist. I've got a bookshelf full of sexuality textbooks and I have poured through them seeking a good, solid definition for what sexuality actually is, only to find that nearly all of them fail to define sexuality at all, even though they are each entire tomes on this important subject. When I have found definitions of sexuality, they are either so broad and vague or so specific and related to sex itself that none of them really do justice to the magnificence and magnitude of sexuality.

The women I work with know sexuality is bigger than the larger culture acknowledges. They ask good questions: Where is the nature, the magic, the energy of sexuality? Where is art and music and creativity? Where is the aliveness I feel when I'm sitting in a beautiful place against an old tree? Where is the image I see of my own genitals that shows up in the natural world, on tree bark, in cliffs, and in flowers? Where is the ecstasy I feel when I'm dancing, that ecstatic connection to the power of my own body? Where is the breadth of sexuality that deeply connects me to all that is, the storm inside me that feels the rush of water when I bring a vision to life?

I began to play with this idea, and I wanted to create a model that held the magic of sexuality that these women know, and that I know, exists. I developed the Core Energy Model of Sexuality as a way of expressing what sexuality is capable of and what it encompasses in the wholeness of our creative lives and erotic selves.

CORE ENERGY
MODEL OF SEXUALITY

In my Core Energy Model of Sexuality, I see sexuality as more like a ripple where the core is our energy or fire, and from that energy we move into connection, on which we build identity and, finally, power. I think the impact of each part is like a breath, taking in and strengthening at its core, and then flowing out in a ripple like water does when a pebble is dropped into it. And it's a two-way street . . . your power impacts your identity development and expression, which impacts your ability to make connection and build intimacy, and ultimately affects your own core energy vibrancy.

Sometimes your core energy is depleted or not in a healthy place, and that will impact everything else adversely. It all begins with that core of energy you have within you. This model depicts sexual power and its functioning, and the Nine Elements in the rest of this book are how we can amplify, develop, and support the growth of this core power in each person.

CORE ENERGY MODEL OF SEXUALITY

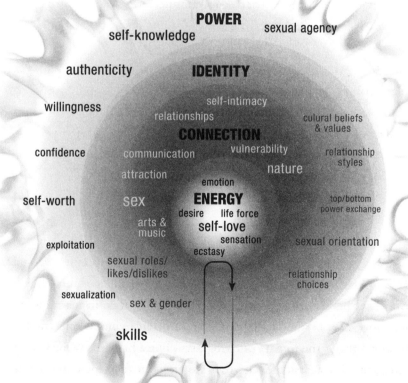

Energy

There is a powerful well of energy at the core of your being, and you have many choices for how you will develop and use that energy. Energy is the beginning of all creation. It is a fire that builds in you and expresses itself in many forms. It comes alive when it is creating because that's what it's meant to do: it's meant to expand and multiply.

WHAT YOU FEEL/EXPERIENCE:

Self-love	Arousal
Breath	Libido
Desire	Orgasm
Senses/sensuality	Ecstasy
Pain/pleasure/sensation	Bliss
Pulsation	

HOW YOU EXPRESS IT:

Voice	Play
Creativity	Laughter
Emotion	Fantasy
Body movement	Divinity
Strength	Intention

You use your core energy to experience desire, bliss, pain, or pleasure, to breathe and invigorate your body, to become aroused and to have orgasms, to feel sensation and experience your senses. You use this energy to create a work of art or a delicious meal, to dance or sing, to play, laugh, and cry, to feel deep emotion, to entertain a fantasy, and to express your own divinity. When you are feeling most vibrant and alive, your core energy is fueled with the life force that propels you in your life and helps you to feel the depths of emotion and heights of ecstasy. You have so many different ways you can choose to use this well of energy.

You can choose to connect to yourself or your world in some way, or to deepen your experience of intimacy and *connection*.

Connection

Sexual energy is the fuel that is capable of building connection. We are meant to connect. We are not designed to be alone here. We never are actually alone, and yet our path is decidedly solo. Along the way we are supposed to connect—to commune—to have intercourse of many kinds with one another, to have companionship, to play. You connect to many things in many ways and create intimacy using your powerful well of energy. You might even be a person who does not actually desire strong connection with other people, but you might desire connection with yourself, or with nature, with art, or with the divine. Connection can be about many things:

Self-intimacy and intimacy with others	Attraction and crushes
Sex and masturbation	Skin hunger and affection
Relationships	Merging and boundaries
Caring/sharing	Sexual communities
Loving/liking	Reproduction/birth/ making family
Experimentation and exploration	Nature
Trust	God/Universe/Cosmic/Creator/ Divine
Vulnerability and risk-taking	Art and music
Communication and emotional expression	Self-development and growth

If you are working on developing your human relationships, you are going to do a dance with expressing your caring and sharing of yourself by making yourself vulnerable and taking risks. Any meaningful relationship will be founded on attraction, communication, loving and liking, trust, and exploration. When people become intertwined and begin to lose their boundaries, they may experience what is known as merging—not always healthy, and the crux of codependency. You might experience skin hunger and share affection or explore and express your emotionality terrain. You will express your own boundaries and you might explore sex, and even pursue reproduction, birth, or creating a family with others. You might also be someone who feels enlivened by experiences of profound connection to nature, art, and music. You might be highly spiritually inclined and cultivate relationship to what you consider divine. And your own masturbation practice and self-development is part of your relationship to self that is so critical to how you relate to others.

The greater your sense of yourself, your values, and who you are in this world, the more you may take on *identities* that are important to you.

Identity

From and within connection we are able to identify ourselves as a sexual being. We express and define ourselves in reference to our environment, our world, and the people in our lives. Our identity is very much based on culture and our place in history. It actually changes with time and place. Humans have a need to categorize and create identities for ourselves and sometimes, nonconsensually, for others (more aptly known as "labeling"). Those identities relating to our sexuality are varied, and they give us power in many ways—and sometimes we feel disempowered around identity as well. It depends on how we use identities and what messages we've internalized about each one. We can also get very attached to certain identities and they can limit us or be very ego-driven. Identities can give voice to who we are, allowing us to create community and to be more visible in the world. This is not a book about identity, so I am going to focus here on sexual identity, but other identities around race, class, culture, ethnicity, and disability are also really important. Many sexual identities are also racialized, and that can add important layers of meaning to them.

WE CREATE SEXUAL IDENTITIES ABOUT MANY ASPECTS OF WHO WE ARE:

Biological sex	Cultural archetypes
Gender identity	Sexual communities
Gender roles	Sexual likes/desires
Gender attribution	Vanilla/kink/BDSM
Sexual orientation	practices
Sexual roles	Top/bottom power exchange
Relationship status/ID	Relationship styles/choices
Cultural beliefs/values	Choosing non-identity

Your identities can be related to your biological sex or gender. Who you are as a woman, man, transgender, trans*, or intersex person might be very important to you. Your biological sex is your body (genitals, chromosomes, hormones), and your gender is culturally learned, evolved, or chosen. People play with gender and express it in so many ways. There are literally hundreds of gender identities now, from high femme, butch, trans*, boi, grrrl, genderqueer, drag queen, drag king . . . the list goes on. For many people sexual orientation of heterosexual, bisexual, gay, lesbian, queer, pansexual, heteroflexible, or asexual might be very important. Relationship status like single, married, divorced, or widowed might be something we strongly identify with, or relationship styles like polyamorous, monogamous, nonmonogamous, or monogamish can be important for how we organize our relationships. Sexually, people take on many identities: top, bottom, dominant, submissive, service boy/girl, vanilla (sex that is rich without a kinky twist), kinky (enjoys playing with power, control or sensation, fetishes, or BDSM in some way), and so on. We might even choose cultural archetypes to wear proudly as identities like virgin, slut, wild woman, or femme fatale.

We may choose to become part of (or create) communities organized around a particular identity. The value in this kind of community-building is having others with shared interests, qualities, and desires in our lives, garnering support and visibility and a way to meet other like-minded individuals who may have shared values. For people who are largely unseen in mainstream culture, this can be really important and can create power. For instance, we have gained power and acceptance of gay/lesbian/bisexual/trans* people via organized communities and people willing to speak out and be seen.

From that place of connection, knowing and naming who we are, we either step into our power and claim it, or we feel powerless. To look at how sexual *power* shows up, ask:

... How do I animate my sexual agency?

... How do I actually take action around my sexuality in my relationships and in the world?

... How do I utilize my sexuality as a source of strength for my life?

Power

Sexual power is about how we exercise our own personal power and agency sexually and in the world at large. Women often get really uncomfortable with the idea of power. When I talk about "sexual power" I am talking about your confidence, your expression of agency over yourself, your desire and your body, your internal sense of personal power, and how you use all of it to create the world and life you want. It's *power-within* and *power-with*. Not *power-over*.

**POWER (OR THE LACK OF IT) AROUND OUR SEXUALITY
COMES FROM:**

Self-awareness	Confidence
Self-knowledge	Eroticism
Sexual agency	Sex education
Decision-making and choices	Safer sex practices
Authenticity	Sexual health
Gender expression	Sexual and spiritual practice
Body image	Self-worth
Body knowledge	Capacity for pleasure and
Skills	intimacy
Willingness	Shame and guilt
Flirtation and seduction	Assault/abuse/trauma
Self-care and self-nurturing	Exploitation and sexualization

As an individual, your deepening self-awareness, self-knowledge, and confidence will give you a big sense of power. Likewise, not having these things will deplete your power or make it hard to build. You can develop more skills and knowledge through sex education. You can empower your body image and your sexual health through body knowledge, sex education, and self-love. You can develop your ability to care for yourself, your sexual and spiritual practices, and your capacity for pleasure and intimacy, which will lead to greater self-worth and happier relationships. Flirtation and seduction are ways you express power, as are your eroticism and gender expression. Your power of choice is actualized via your decision-making. Your willingness is a root of your own agency. When any of these things are deficient or out of alignment with your true desires, you will experience a loss of power or a sense of powerlessness. More acute disempowerment might come from abuse, assault, sexualization, sexual shaming, trauma or guilt, or any other way your sexual agency feels taken away. You might also give away your own agency in the choices you make.

MY SEXUAL POWER

The preceding power list is a glimpse of what constitutes sexual power, and is by no means exhaustive. Your sexual power has many vehicles of expression and expansion. What creates power for you? When do you feel sexually powerful?

This Core Energy Model of Sexuality is another way to view the wholeness that is sexuality. Given its complexity, there is not one all-encompassing, perfect, all-knowing way of defining it. What I hope to share in this model is that sexuality is far more than sex and it is a core part of who we are that impacts us on so many levels and in so many areas of our lives. I can often hear the inner knowing in many women I speak with that there is something much greater—a bigger payoff—that working on their sexuality will mean for them. They often cannot put their finger on it, but they know that connecting more deeply to their sexuality is the key. This model is the closest way I can explain sexuality and its potential ripple effects for a powerful life.

In the next nine chapters, I share with you the Nine Elements to wake up your Erotic Energy, Personal Power, and Sexual Intelligence that have changed so many people's lives. They can do the same for you.

Whether you are in a relationship or are enjoying a solo life, you are the architect of your experience. You are the seductress of life itself. Birthed from the core of your sexuality, your desire is the nucleus of your dreams, driven by your inner fire, and it will always guide you back to true north. So better to tap into it and begin to befriend it rather than see it as an enemy combatant, a need you will never fulfill, or an ember you can't find the oxygen to ignite. It's there, and it wants you to bring form to your dreams, motion to your sexy life, and passion to your relationships. It wants you to stop settling for less. It will light you up and guide you to live your most magnificently dynamic and powerful life—if you turn up your pilot light and let it burn. Your sexual energy is the raw fuel for your own becoming.

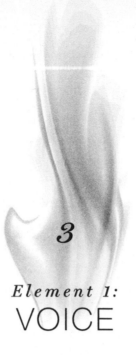

3

Element 1:
VOICE

EXCAVATE AND REWRITE YOUR SEXUAL STORY

You have an internal and external sexual voice. Internally, you have a sexual story. It's one of the most private and precious parts of your history, and you probably do not share it with just anyone. You are careful with how you share your story, making assessments about your own safety and risks as you contemplate to whom and how you talk about it.

And that's smart. It's important not to make yourself vulnerable to the point of real harm. Your sexual story is a major undercurrent of your life. It is your intimate herstory, and holds the keys for why you do the things you do in your relationships, in sex, in creating intimacy, in loving your body, and whether you take risks or play it safe. It directs whether you speak up, use condoms, stay quiet, feel shame, go mute, rage loud, make demands, or ask for a need at just the right pitch. Your sexual story is a part of you.

You have an internal personal risk manager in your subconscious who refers to your story—that herstory—to assess what choices you will make today based on your past experiences and the narrative you have created around them. It's prudent of your risk manager to do that. But here's the thing: some of your narrative is outdated. It doesn't represent you anymore. Some of the ways you've developed an understanding of your own sexual life are no longer serving you to be the sexual person you are becoming. And where that's true, it's time to excavate, rewrite, or let go of your stories. Even the funny ones that you can haul out at a party.

Sometimes you tell your own stories so many times they become mythologized. Sometimes you are so attached to the way things happened that you keep yourself a victim. You can't be a victim if you want to be empowered. Victimhood and empowerment are antithetical. It's time to take a hard look at the story you've been telling yourself and see if there is a more powerful one you can tell.

This is not to say you need to deny what has happened to you. In fact, as part of your own healing you may need to acknowledge your experience, say it out loud, and find peace with it. It's part of the fabric of what made you who you are, and because of that, it's important.

What I want you to know is how grateful I am that I learned what it was to have my sex and desire directed entirely by someone else, that I know what it is to feel my voice wanting to speak requests and boundaries that are stuck deep in my esophagus, suffocating my agency as they beg to be born, and that I am not now, nor was I ever, a victim. What I want you to know is that every one of those subjugating or powerless moments brought me to this place of vision, on a mission as a sexuality advocate, a fierce woman on fire who has come with this message to support you in your own sexual awakening. It was out of those moments when I couldn't speak my truth that I birthed the woman who would. That is the story I am going to tell you. I made it through, and so can you, no matter the trauma, the exile from your own pleasure, the disconnection from your own desire or the ability to voice it, the disbelief that it can be different, or the stories that aren't the ones you want to live.

FINDING YOUR VOICE

A voice is a human gift; it should be cherished and used, to utter fully human speech as possible. Powerlessness and silence go together.
—MARGARET ATWOOD

One of my mentors, Janene Sneider, used to say that in the gender wars, women lost their voices and men lost their ability to emote. It's a broad stroke, but it's in large part true. I know many powerful women who are not afraid to speak up for themselves at work or in life or demand justice in the world but lose their voice sexually. Otherwise powerful women will morph into nervous, coy girls in front of men (especially ones they are attracted to), not speak up during sex if they want something or if something hurts, and become afraid to assert themselves or be who they really are in sexual situations. Powerful women can become mute and submissive around potential partners. One woman wrote to me recently, "When I'm really sexually attracted to someone I lose my voice, and that surprises me."

To be sexually empowered, the first element is your voice. You've got to find and uncage it. If you never learned to talk about sex or utter your desires, there is a voice that wants to be unlocked. There are conversations to have. If you are silent during sex and do not even allow yourself to make sounds as a free part of sexual pleasure, you are amputating your own ecstasy. Your voice is a tool for pleasure and it enhances sex tremendously. It is an intrinsic part of your own sexual expression and power. This is the external sexual voice.

We learn to have sex silently. Don't get caught (whether you were masturbating or with someone else). Don't let them hear you. We learn to hold our breath, stifle our own voice, and then we wonder why it's hard to have an orgasm.

I spent years not knowing how to have orgasms because I lacked resources, information, and role models that could assist me to learn how. And I learned to keep a lid on it and be very quiet. I never had sex education at all until I went to college, but in my first year the Baldwins walked into the lecture hall and my world changed.

John and Janice Baldwin were legends at the University of California at Santa Barbara, where I was an undergrad. They taught what was easily the most popular class on campus: SOC152. It was in Campbell Hall, and the Baldwins packed the house every quarter with roughly nine hundred students. Their classes were always brimming with those eager and nervous to learn about that hushed, undiscussed topic that impacted every one of our late-adolescent lives: *sex*.

I had never been taught to touch my own body, and I didn't know how to talk about sex. In fact, I'd been taught *not* to. I had attended three different high schools and had strategically avoided taking health class because I thought I was "healthy," which meant I unwittingly skirted my way out of any sex education whatsoever. And even if I had gotten some sex ed, it would be unlikely it would have encouraged healthy attitudes toward sex and masturbation.

John and Janice Baldwin actually encouraged me to touch my genitals, to get to know them, and to learn how to pleasure myself. They even assigned it! Being an overachiever, I took it on, and that act of self-possession completely changed my relationship to my body, my sexuality, my pleasure, and my power. There, as a first-year student in SOC152, a whole world began to open up for me—a world that was shut down from a young age.

I read my Masters and Johnson sexuality textbook cover to cover—I don't believe I ever did that again in my entire student career. I was hungry for the information—so many of the questions I'd had for years about my body and sex and what was normal were being answered. I finally had role models for how to talk about sex, and I began to find my voice.

The Baldwins asked us to turn in a short application if we were interested in their advanced sexuality course, SOC152B. It was a seminar open to only fifteen students. After the way SOC152 had changed my life, I was determined to be a part of it.

The summer after my freshman year I got a letter in the mail from the Baldwins inviting me to take their advanced seminar. I was out of my mind with excitement. An opportunity to sit in a small room with these two smart sex educators and discuss sexuality issues in depth? Heaven!

I was already becoming an advanced sexuality student. My passion for sexuality had been lit and I was learning to talk about it in a way not many people around me could. I was in, and though I didn't know it at the time, I had already begun to live my life's purpose. I knew I wanted to work to empower women and girls, and I just wasn't sure how. I wanted to impact people's lives, to usher them toward their own sexual self-knowledge, self-actualization, and sexual empowerment.

My personal growth from my own places of shame, confusion, and pain about sexuality led me to become more powerful—more powerful as a woman, more powerful in my relationships, more powerful as an educator, and more powerful as a sexual being. More powerful in the world.

Ultimately, I came home to myself on a deep level. Several times. Coming home is like that. We do it over and over. Sometimes we disappear and leave something precious behind. Then something happens, something opens up, something urgent calls us back to our roots. And we go home again.

In SOC152, I got permission for the first time to enjoy and explore sex. I was finding my voice and my orgasm. First, I figured out how to have orgasms with myself. I'd never done that before, and it shifted my perspective about my sexuality, pleasure, and what my body was capable of dramatically. Next came the communication with my then boyfriend so it could happen with him. I remember the joy I felt when I first had an orgasm with him. Before him, my high school sweetheart and first true love had tried for years to help me have an orgasm, and though we were deeply in love, we were sexually ignorant, and our uneducated but passionate sex life left us both feeling frustrated and dissatisfied. I enjoyed sex then, but I knew there was more.

My own process gave me compassion for the frustration many women feel in not being able to have orgasms or figure out the complex puzzle of how their sexual bodies work. I changed my experience and changed my story. Sometimes you have to change your story first in order to change your experience. We can identify so strongly with our own stories that they keep us from moving forward.

I found my voice. Like me, many women lose it in sex. Stuck in a good-girl prison, we don't express ourselves sexually. It's not proper. Or we feel shy about it because we have had no practice speaking openly about sex without fear of experiencing shame. Or we are so confused about what we want sexually that we don't know what to ask for. So we don't. Many women follow the desires of men who are taught to lead and initiate sex, and through whose lens we experience sex via film, pornography, lawmaking, legislation, sexual research, and personal heterosexual contact. Follow someone else's desire map long enough and you won't know what yours is or that you even have one. No wonder talking about it is so hard. No wonder so many women freeze when asked by a partner about their fantasies and desires.

THE PIVOTAL FIRST TIME

As a young teen, I had premature sexual experiences and faced my budding sexuality in fear and isolation. No adult ever talked to me about sex. Not one. Zero. Radio silence. I never even heard a fear-based abstinence message about sex, much less a healthy one. I certainly had not had a conversation *with myself* about sex or what I wanted to do about it, when, or with whom, because I didn't even know there was a conversation to have. How we start with sex will impact who we will be in it.

My relationship to sex started when I was a neophyte menstruator, periods all wacky, new and unreliable. I had only "dated" a couple of boys and had no sexual experience at all. I had a new boyfriend who was two years older than me. On a snowy February afternoon, he and I were making out after school on the quilt-covered couch in my living room. Suddenly my corduroys were unzipped and in an instant I felt something completely foreign, warm, and soft between my legs. If I tried to release any words, I choked. We'd just had sex, but before I could process what had happened, it was over. I zipped up my pants and we finished our visit as if we'd simply been drinking Coke and playing Atari. And so began my relationship with sex.

The next day at school, he stopped by my locker to check in. The check-in consisted of: "Do you have any regrets?"

Again, I was unprepared. How do I answer this question? I didn't know what to feel. Regrets? *That's* the question? Not, "Tell me about that experience. Is it what you wanted? How did it feel in your body? Did it feel good? What are you feeling now?" Of course, those questions come from my mature adult voice. I wouldn't have thought of them then any more than he would have. We had no language for talking about sex, pleasure, or desire or for understanding the grandiosity of it all.

"Regrets? No, no, of course not," I lied. In truth, I didn't understand what was happening. I played it cool and pretended everything was okay, but it was most definitely not okay.

That's how so many of us learn to treat sex—no problem, everything's cool with me, I'm good, nothing to see here, let's just not talk about it. Somehow, in the midst of my inexperience, I knew to put on my game face so I didn't reveal the shame, fear, and confusion I felt. And I stayed silent. Many of us do, and then we might start a pattern of not talking about it at all, for years, or for most of our lives. But your voice is there inside you, and sex needs a voice.

For me, a process had begun. A coming of age. A relationship to a part of myself I didn't know was there. A way of relating to boys, and later, to men. A painful process of trying to find resources to help me deal with my terror and my silence when I had pregnancy scares on an isolated air force base at the northern tip of Maine. A compassionate process of healing from a lonely place of shame for doing something I thought I shouldn't have been doing, and for somehow forsaking myself. A disempowering entry into sexual life that would eventually lead to self-empowerment through a career choice that was birthed right there on that quilt-protected couch. In that ignorance. Sexual ground zero.

My first sexual experience, at a primal level, was a rape. It took me years to call it that. Many sexual assaults happen like that. Some people could judge it as something else. It took years more to look at the complexity of that experience, the gender role conditioning that made my boyfriend do what he did, and why I couldn't stop it or speak up for myself with my lack of skills, knowledge, or support, and how alone and scared I felt afterward. It was not an empowered way to inaugurate my sexual life with partners. But it happened, and that's my story, right?

Not necessarily. There are so many stories within the story.

I would guess that if I could talk to that boyfriend today, he probably remembers it very differently. I'm sure he probably has a different narrative about how we began that early sexual relationship and what it meant for him. He, too, was a victim of sexual ignorance and a total lack of sexual vocabulary or communication skills. He wouldn't be able to explain the idea of consent. For me, I suddenly found myself in a sexual relationship at thirteen years of age that I didn't have the emotional capacity to comprehend, that I was unprepared for and didn't want, yet I didn't know what to do about it. None of my friends talked about sex, and all of the girls made it seem like they weren't having it. I was sure I was the only one. My emotions were in a storm, and my teen dating war with my protective military dad was on. Since I had almost no experience in my young life and I didn't know any better, I rationalized the relationship in all sorts of ways, ultimately telling myself that this must just be what boyfriends and girlfriends do.

That experience was pivotal for me and remains important to my life experience. Everyone has a "first time" story. Firsts can be so fun . . . yours might have been. Mine was confusing and painful. How do your stories of "the first time" impact how you view sex today? Or yourself? Or your lovability? I've turned my experience around. I don't feel like a victim, because I have an educated, adult understanding of why that first time went down the way it did. I'm actually grateful for all it taught me. That's my story today.

Today I enjoy toying with new sexual firsts as a way of reclaiming agency over "my first time." Sometimes we need to do that for ourselves. There are always more firsts to have and new stories to write. You have many firsts that inform who you are sexually. Who you are as a sexual person developed over time with your experiences in becoming aware of your body, experiencing pleasure, orgasm, first love, first sex, understanding gender and your sexual identity, and so much more. These are the tales that make up your collective sexual story, your sexual lifeline.

HOW AND TO WHOM YOU TELL

If we can share our story with someone who responds with empathy and understanding, shame can't survive.

—Brené Brown

Share It

As I mentioned, it's important to assess how and to whom you want to tell your story. You might choose to share it with a friend or a lover whom you trust as you test the waters and see how it feels. Maybe you process a lot out loud, as I do. For me, it has been essential that I express my story to people with whom I felt emotionally cared for in a context where I can talk about it and gain deeper understanding. If this is the case for you, find the right people to be your confidants, therapists, and healers.

Write It

Writing about your story is another important way to tell it. You might write in a personal journal just for yourself, giving yourself space to lay it out. Some people come to a place where they are comfortable blogging or even publishing their stories. Not everyone will choose to come out about their story in a public way as I am doing here in this book. I could not have shared my story so openly years ago. It was a process to be able to do so. I would advise that you use caution if you decide to blog or write publicly about your sexual story. You may indeed find you are not ready for your story to be forever in print for the world to read. You may never be, and that's okay.

WRITE YOUR SEXUAL STORY

Just write it for yourself, not for an audience. You can start it with "My first memory of my sexuality was . . ." and just go. Let it all out. See what is revealed. For some people, their sexual story is painful and this is not an easy task. Part of healing the painful parts is bringing them out and not staying alone with them. Often, as you dig deeper, you will find the golden parts and the joy.

CONSIDER WRITING ABOUT: sexual firsts, how you learned about desire, arousal, what you discovered about sex and how, meaningful relationships, your relationship to your body, family beliefs about sex that you had to work through, places of sexual shame, your sexual identity, your experience of gender, sexual power, attraction, pleasure, and orgasm.

Tell It through Art

Some people have intense sexual stories that are hard for people to hear or even believe. I worked with a woman who had a multilayered sexual story of abuse that touched me deeply. I've heard a *lot* of stories, and hers was troubling on many levels. She was committed to her process of healing and was using art to do it. This had been a lifelong process for her. She used her photography and dance to heal her stories, sharing them through photographic portraits that allowed art to tell the story. Art changes people's lives, and it was this woman's lifeline. She built her life around her art and was committed to finding her voice through art because her story was hard for people to hear and believe and she needed this outlet for it. She was slowly finding her way in real-life relationships and working on finding ways to trust—herself first, and then others. I admired the way she cared for herself in her healing process. Art is a great healer. How might you use your favorite art form (visual art, music, dance, drama, writing, performance) to explore or share your story?

Testimonials and Witnessing

There are many events that have succeeded in giving people the space to actually speak about their violations—the "unspeakable things"—publicly. Take Back the Night (TBTN) is an event that uses the testimonial model to give survivors of sexual assault and abuse a platform where their stories can be spoken and heard. I co-founded Take Back the Night at New York University in the nineties and have attended many TBTN events over the years. I have seen the profound impact storytelling has on both the people who speak and the listeners. I've seen many people tell their stories for the very first time because they felt supported to do it, a first step in their healing process: witnessing.

I've also seen people who tell their stories over and over, year after year, wearing them as badges of honor. In these cases, the act of storytelling ceases to be empowering. A person can begin to identify so strongly with the role of victim that it keeps them in a perpetual state of victimhood that does not allow for growth. Your story may need to be processed further and retold. Tell it as many times as you need to work through it, but at some point, boldly redefine it so your story can change to one that empowers you.

Perform It

The Vagina Monologues is a play that has been very popular for more than twenty years, produced all over the world. I believe its popularity stems from the fact that it breaks the silence about our sexual bodies and the history that goes with that oppressive silence. It dares women to utter words like *vagina* and *cunt* with pride, tell stories they'd never dared tell and to do so with confidence—even if the stories are not their own. The actors almost always connect with something personally in each monologue. Often the experience of revealing these stories theatrically gives the actors more courage to tell their own stories.

I traveled for years teaching workshops around *The Vagina Monologues* and V-Day events (designed to raise awareness about sexual violence at Valentine's Day), in which I got people talking about the issues raised in the play. My favorite workshop was "My Own Vagina's Monologue," in which I helped women write their own version of their vagina's monologue, giving them a platform on which to tell it—which most of them welcomed. It is a courageous act for any woman to break her silence about her own sexual body and herstory.

Today one of my favorite and most recommended storytelling events is Bawdy Storytelling, organized in several U.S. cities by Dixie De La Tour, in which real people tell real stories about sex, relationships, desire, and the body. It is powerful both to witness and be witnessed in the humor, pain, frustration, angst, and celebration of our sexual stories. There are other similar events too, so if one comes to your area, go. It's a treat.

MY OWN VAGINA'S MONOLOGUE

Write a monologue from the perspective of your own vulva/vagina. What would she say? What does she want us to know?

Try freewriting using any or all of the following prompts:

... My favorite word for vagina/vulva is . . .

... My vagina/vulva desires/craves/wants . . .

... I want more than anything for my vagina/vulva . . .

... My connection to my vagina/vulva is . . .

... My vagina/vulva makes me feel powerful because . . .

... When my vagina/vulva heals, I will . . .

... An important memory I have about my vagina/vulva is . . .

PILAR'S JOURNEY TO
HER SEXUAL VOICE

Pilar was an accomplished woman from the Caribbean. When she came to work with me she told me what many women do: that she had done a lot of self-development work and felt powerful in her life and as a businesswoman in so many ways, yet she had not tackled her sexual power. It was time.

When I started this work I had no sexual voice—I was unable to express my wants and needs in both physical and emotional contexts. Although I perceived myself, and was always perceived by the public, as an accomplished, fulfilled, and confident woman, behind closed doors I was still shy, afraid, and believed that I was undeserving and unworthy of recognition and acknowledgment. Accordingly, in the bedroom, and by extension in relationships, part of me still reverted to the meek child from middle school who never asked for what she wanted, never expected to get it anyway, and was always willing to compromise and accept less than I deserved. I began to recognize my passive-aggressive tendencies and realize that I never seemed to get what I wanted because I was afraid to ask for it. The resentment I would feel as a result of this immobilized me— throwing me back into a cycle of feelings of unworthiness, depression, anger, and self-blame/pity. Despite years of therapy, counseling, spiritual work, yoga, and meditation, I did not realize that at a core level of my being, this was my default mode in all of my relationships. Mind you, not that anyone else would have seen that—in romantic or sexual relationships I was always perceived as cold or unfeeling, when I actually was simply immobilized by fear.

I realized through my work that this fear stemmed from an inability to claim my voice (sexual or otherwise) and speak my truth. I now identify my sexual/creative energy, and my ability to tap into that to identify my needs and then go after them, as the main source of my power. I learned to release my fear of rejection and to make empowering choices in my personal and sexual relationships, like walking away when I need to and always speaking my truth no mater how people respond.

I literally found my voice "between the sheets"—to ask for what I wanted, talk dirty, play around, and be completely open with my feelings and needs. This was very new territory for me—I was no prude by any means and I had experienced some very enjoyable and pleasurable sexual relations throughout my life—but this work led me to a place where I was able to experience true *pleasure, bliss, and ecstasy; for the first time I was revealing my true self with no shame, no judgment, no blame, and no fear of rejection. I began to allow myself to be vulnerable—a place I had avoided all my life by shutting down and not revealing certain aspects of myself. I remember Amy Jo saying to me one day—and this was a huge revelation for me: "People around you love you, they want to help you—maybe you need to try letting them." And she gave me an assignment to ask three people for help in the upcoming week. That was the hardest and scariest assignment I ever got from her—because for me I did not know how to ask for what I needed.*

Learning the language to express myself sexually and ask for what I needed in the most intimate and vulnerable situations in my life gave me the tools and the courage to do that everywhere else as well. This has led me to deeper places of self-discovery than I ever thought possible. It revealed to me parts of myself that I never even knew existed—I discovered fantasies that I never knew I had, and I learned how to voice those fantasies. Exploring my sexual fantasies in turn encouraged me to dig deeper into exploring my life fantasies, which has ended up being transformational for me and completely shifted my career, home life, friendships, and partnerships. I realized how truly essential our sexual energy is to who we are, to how we function, and to the space we inhabit in this world. I knew then that by finding my sexual voice I had been able to shift into my truest and highest self.

RELIGION, CULTURE, AND SEXUAL BELIEFS

I have known many women who have internalized the story that the only way to be in a sexual relationship is through a monogamous marriage. Of course, you can be wildly sexual and totally fulfilled in a monogamous marriage. Yet some women keep themselves sexually closed off, and hold themselves back from sexual experiences they

EXAMINING BELIEFS ABOUT SEXUALITY

1. IDENTIFY BELIEFS ABOUT SEXUALITY

On a sheet of paper, write "Beliefs about my sexuality that I've learned based on my story," and make a list of them.

What have you believed about your sexual identity, your sexual ability, your sexual body, your relationships, love, intimacy, your power, your ability to make good choices, and so on. What are the beliefs you've been operating from?

Some will be positive, empowering keepers, and some will be disempowering beliefs.

2. ASSESS AND REWRITE YOUR LIST OF BELIEFS

Ask yourself what no longer serves you that you'd like to change. For every belief that is no longer serving you, write out the new belief.

Even if you aren't totally on board yet.

What beliefs do you now want to have about your sexuality?

have wanted as married women. All of it based on a belief that it is somehow wrong or a sin to explore, or that they would be a "certain kind" of woman they don't want to be.

Oftentimes such stories are attached to religious or cultural beliefs that can be very limiting to our sexuality. As we grow up and develop our own belief systems, sometimes we need to leave behind some of our religious beliefs in order to free ourselves. This can be a charged subject. I can't always say this to my clients. I respect a cli-

Some Examples

1. **BELIEF ABOUT SEXUALITY:** A woman who makes the first move will be seen as a "slut" and, therefore, undesirable.

   MY NEW BELIEF: A woman who makes the first move knows what she wants and goes for it, and that's powerful and highly desirable.

2. **BELIEF ABOUT SEXUALITY:** Fat women won't find good sex partners, and I'm fat so I won't get to have great sex.

   MY NEW BELIEF: Many great sex partners are attracted to larger women, and there are great partners out there for me. My body is beautiful.

3. **BELIEF ABOUT SEXUALITY:** I don't deserve a good relationship/good sex because I cheated on my partner.

   MY NEW BELIEF: I learned a lot from my affair and it was an important experience for me. I do not have to keep paying for it by punishing myself.

ent who is devoutly committed to her religious life. It's not for me to steer her otherwise. And sometimes people realize they have to make some choices.

It's important to acknowledge the role of religion and family culture in creating our belief systems because we are often at odds with these ingrained beliefs, and it can be difficult to extricate ourselves from them. So many clients have come through my programs needing to free themselves from limiting religious doctrine about sexuality. It can be an extended process depending on the depth of those beliefs and how attached a person is to them.

Excavate your own sexual story and create beliefs that are supportive of your own growth and who you are today. Rewrite the parts that don't work and accept your own agency in deciding how and to whom you want to tell those stories that are meaningful.

FUNCTIONS OF YOUR SEXUAL STORY

Your sexual story can play many functions for you in your life and relationships. Some of these functions are beneficial, while many are not. It's important to ask yourself how any given story is functioning for you. What is it holding in place? What need is it meeting? And is it in alignment with who you want to be?

Intimacy and Community

Some of your stories can help you develop intimacy as you share the deeper parts of who you are with lovers, close friends, or family members. I sometimes share a personal story with a client if I think it will help her gain some understanding or not feel so alone in her journey. Your stories can also connect you to others with shared experiences. I gave the example of Take Back the Night, which is a space where people can create community for healing. There are coming-out support groups for young lesbian, gay, bisexual, and transgender youth. There are couples' groups and asexuality support groups. Our stories and experiences often bond us to a community. Be willing to let go of a community that once served you but no longer does because you've healed or learned what you needed to learn. You could choose to keep the community members in your life in other ways without having to continue to identify with an outdated identity.

Victimhood

I already mentioned that many people will use their story to maintain their own victimhood. If you are using your stories to maintain your identity as a victim, it might be time to change your perception of your story and tell it differently, or stop telling it altogether. Many people keep their victimhood firmly in place for their entire lives and never choose to move beyond it. You can choose to have a different narrative. It doesn't change that maybe what happened to you was painful, but how you decide to relate to it is what becomes empowering. Maintaining an identity as a victim will never get you the empowerment you seek. Sometimes it's difficult to see how our victim self shows up. Everyone has one, and it's a part of ourselves to get to know and understand, yet we don't need to let that victim self be the core part of who we are nor of our story.

Self-Awareness and Self-Intimacy

Our stories deepen self-awareness, understanding, and self-intimacy. I remember in graduate school having a deep cry after meeting a friend's thirteen-year-old daughter who looked a lot like me when I was her age. Seeing her tiny body and seeing her as an image of who I had been at the time of my early painful sexual initiation made me really mourn that experience. My own self-awareness was heightened, I saw new parts of my story, and I moved into a much more powerful place of peace about my history. As I moved into working with others, my own self-awareness helped me to relate, and yet avoid projecting my experiences onto them, which wouldn't be helpful. Our stories often evolve as we do.

Maintaining Standards

Sometimes you might use stories to hold yourself to particular standards. For instance, maybe you hold a standard of virginity or of what "good girls do." You have stories about yourself that keep that standard in place or help you to depict yourself as a certain type of sexual person. "I'm not the type of girl to have sex on a first (or even a third) date." "I can't have too much sexual enjoyment or it might mean I'm a slut." Maybe you have an image of yourself as sexually adventurous, so to be that sexual globetrotter, you tell yourself you have to be into everything under the sun. "Anal sex? Of course. Fisting? Sure! Threesomes, foursomes, and moresomes? All the time! I'm the sexual adventurer." Those things can be great if you really do want them. But if you are telling yourself to want things because it keeps a standard in place every time you get to tell your fantastic stories about your escapades, you have to be honest and ask yourself why you are making those choices, and come back to making your choices from a place of agency and authenticity.

Cultural Expectations

Other stories maintain certain stereotypes, or gender or cultural role expectations. "Well, I have sex when my husband wants to, not really because I like it." That's a common story women who have "duty sex" tell. They are continuing the behavior and tell the story because they want to be a dutiful wife and please their partner. The good wife. Is that the story you want to have? Is that the sex you want to have? I've met a lot of men who are committed to being "good guys" and respecting women. They will often subjugate their own needs and not acknowledge parts of their sexual desire so that they can uphold that image. Can you hold a story of being a good guy or a good girl and allow yourself to have desires that are really yours even if they seem incongruent with the stereotypes you've learned?

The stories have a way of keeping the behaviors that go with them in place. What if you want to do something new or different? How do you deal with the dissonance when it challenges who you think you need to be?

Proving Yourself or Posturing

Another way people use their stories is to make them a "fuck you" of sorts. "I fucked someone I'm not supposed to be fucking. So there. Take that!" It's common for adolescents to do this, but many adults never outgrow these immature patterns that keep distance between them and others. And usually there is a need to be superior in the "fuck you" stories, which actually indicates tremendous insecurity. If you are secure in who you are, you don't need to use a story as a "fuck you." Time to stop posturing and figure out who you really are and what your true underlying need is.

IF IT DOESN'T SET YOU FREE, IT'S NOT TRUE

One of my mentors, David Neagle, often says that when determining our own truth we must ask ourselves, "Does it set me free?" If it doesn't, then it's not true. I find this perspective so helpful in allowing people to parse through what is really going on with them and figure out what needs to be let go of and what to keep. You can get lost in your stories of who you are or why your sexuality is the way it is.

I highly recommend "The Work" by Byron Katie in order to question your thoughts and the stories you create out of them. She has developed a simple yet profound process to help people stop suffering by questioning their thoughts and asking, "Is it true? How do I know it's true?" And then, "Who would I be without this thought?" The answer to this question can be so revealing. If you keep retelling yourself stories that don't set you free, you've got to find ways to interrupt these thoughts and tell yourself more empowering stories. You are not meant to be in constant pain over the stories you tell yourself. We've all had some, many of which relate to places of shame and trauma and are stories that need to be told, witnessed, and then released (more on that in the next chapter).

UNLOCKING THE SILENT VOICE

Many women choke, like I did, when they need to speak up about sex, or in sex. It's common for women to feel muted sexually for a lot of reasons. We aren't socialized to speak up for ourselves, we don't know what we want so we don't know what to ask for, we feel uncomfortable saying "no," we feel we might be judged for saying "yes," we are afraid we'll be rejected, we don't want to seem like we don't know what we are doing sexually, we just don't like any confrontation, and we've never had great sexual communication modeled for us.

Most people like a sexual partner who speaks up for herself and says what she wants or doesn't want because most people want to respect your wants and needs. If they don't, they aren't worth your time anyway. If you don't say what you are a "yes" for, you won't get it. If you don't say what is a "no" for you, you forsake yourself. Neither scenario is favorable.

As far as feeling sexually inexperienced or not knowing what you want . . . it can be so freeing to just say that. I often hear from women that they don't know what to say. They get the words all stuck in their throat and can't get anything out. Here are some openers that can cue your partner to help and engage:

"I feel confused right now and I'm just not sure what to say."

"There's something I want to say, but I'm having a hard time getting the words out."

"There's something I want to say, but I'm afraid of what you will think."

"I don't have a lot of experience with _____, but I'm interested to learn more and see if it's something I might be into trying."

"I like kissing you. I'm unsure what else would feel good."

"I like you, but I feel shy about it."

"I'm not sure what I desire right now. Would you help me explore it so I can figure it out?"

"I need some help figuring out what to do/what I want."

"I like what you are doing with your hand there. Can you make an adjustment in pressure/speed/position . . . ?"

There is an invitation, if not an outright request, in each of these openers. Invitation and request will go a long way in breaking the ice. You have to start somewhere, even if it's just acknowledging how awkward you feel but that you want to talk about sex. Most people feel awkward, so just putting that out there can help disarm your partner or date and open up communication. We think we are supposed to have it all together and be perfect when it comes to sex. Sex is not perfect. You don't have to be perfect. There are so many unknowns. It's okay. It's vulnerable to admit you don't know everything about sex, and sharing that vulnerability is actually what will bring you closer to your partner, because they probably feel vulnerable too.

If at all possible, get yourself into a situation where you can learn and practice talking about sex. Taking a class or being in a program that is designed to help you explore it does more to get the frog out of the throat than nearly anything. Maybe you host a women's night in which you come up with sex questions and you talk about them. Everyone will be relieved to have an outlet for the conversation! Having people in your life who are skilled and comfortable talking about sex is immensely helpful.

After overcoming my initial shock in SOC152, I was desensitized by both Professor Baldwins' ability to nonchalantly discuss the formerly unspeakable. The mute girl smashed on the couch under her boyfriend recovered. I learned to really talk about sex. My growing outspoken passion spurred me toward a deep desire to do something meaningful for others, and that opened the door to a rather unconventional path. It changed my story. I have no regrets for any of my experiences now and I fully embrace them for how they formed me.

Unlock your silence, unleash your voice, and rewrite the stories that keep you small and from stepping into the sexual being you want to be. Sex will be better, life will be better, and it might lead to something totally unexpected.

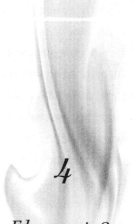

4

Element 2:
RELEASE

MAKE SPACE FOR THE SEXUAL SELF YOU'VE BEEN WAITING FOR

In this chapter, we are going to make room. We have all taken things on in our sexual lives that have not served us or no longer do. Release is about letting go of the guilt, shame, patterns, and trauma that have you stuck, afraid, sad, and disenfranchised from your own body and sexuality. It's about letting go of beliefs about yourself or about sexuality that keep you stuck.

There is so much we have to release about sex. Sex itself can be an enormous release, yet so many of our feelings, thoughts, beliefs, and experiences about sex are small and tight. They need to go so we can fully enjoy sex and our sexuality now and from this day forward. Let's get spacious about sex.

When we are young, we all take things on that

ultimately do not fit who we are as we grow into our adult selves. We get them from peers, parents, boyfriends, girlfriends, and other people who influence us. We get them from religious doctrine, media, and other cultural frameworks. It is a developmental rite of passage to release the values, beliefs, and feelings we were taught and do not feel aligned with, so we can find out who we really are and live by the belief system that is right for us as adults, as independent agents of our own lives. What do you need to release in order to be the sexual person you want to be? What ideas, beliefs, habits, and approaches need to go? What healing needs to happen so you can make space for what you want to bring in?

NAOMI'S STORY, PART 1

When Naomi came to participate in my Women's Sexually Empowered Life Program in her early twenties, she was a brilliant, talented entrepreneur who was beginning to create the life she wanted. I had known her peripherally since her teen years, and I was impressed by her intelligence, savvy, and thoughtful feminism. She was only twenty-two, but was well on her way to standing fully in her own power. I am always delighted when young women show up. Many are not ready for this work in their twenties, but Naomi certainly was. She was not only ready, she was excited to take on the world as she stepped into her own sexual power and grace, which required her coming into her sexual identity and shedding the shame she had carried about it for much of her life.

I knew from a very young age that I was attracted to other girls, but I grew up in a really heteronormative place and I had a lot of fear about it. I confessed to my mom, and while she didn't explicitly say it was bad, she urged me to keep it a secret and not tell anyone else. I could not hear the loving concern in her voice, only the fear and the whispered conversations she had with my dad where he once sarcastically said, "Oh great, now we have to move." I felt that there was something wrong with me on a core level . . . something bad, different from other people, that was troublesome and a burden for those close to me. I had to disguise and pretend to be normal. Being my true self was dangerous for me and bad for the people who loved me.

I had my first kiss with my best friend when I was eleven years old—a sweet, innocent moment in my room one summer evening while a thunderstorm rolled in. She was my confidante, and I loved her fiercely. Her family, however, was strongly Catholic and did not like me. Before too long, they decided that we could no longer be friends and we weren't allowed to speak anymore; my former BFF went along with it while I was left heartbroken.

The next year at school, she was passing notes in class with her new best friend and described the kiss, saying that I had "made her do it." Someone picked up the note and read it aloud to the class while the teacher was out of the room, and before long all the kids in my grade came up to me and taunted me for being a lesbian.

I was so deeply humiliated that I didn't tell anyone—not even my mom, because I already believed that she considered this part of me a burden. We did not talk about my confessions of queer desire for many years because I had so much shame. I managed to get through the rest of the school year until the rumors died down and slowly found a group of friends who were more open-minded. I dated girls in college but didn't want to come out to my parents and felt confused about my sexual identity/orientation—"bisexual" didn't fit and I felt unworthy of calling myself "queer." Since I had mostly been with men, I was scared of being told by a "real queer person" that I was "not queer enough."

Naomi was carrying a lot of shame about who she was as a sexual person and it was holding her back from stepping into her true sexual self, her desires, and being who she really was. Her process of healing that shame and releasing the beliefs she had taken on from her peers and her family made it possible for everything to change.

WHAT ARE YOU MAKING ROOM FOR?

As you consider what you will need to release, start by thinking about what that release will make room for. What do you want to bring in? Do you want to feel more pleasure and sexual freedom? Do you want to learn how to have unencumbered orgasms? Do you want to feel comfortable being beautiful, sexy, and confident? Do you want to claim your true identity? Do you want to bring a lover into your life with whom you can explore sexual ecstasy to the depths? Do you want to bring in full-out enjoyment of your body? Do you want to feel whole and free? What does that look like? How do you want to feel in your sexuality? How do you want to feel in sex?

Part of this process is having some idea for where you are going.

SEXUAL VISIONING

1. What Do You Want to Bring In?
Take a few minutes to freewrite about what you want to bring into your life around your sexuality, sex life, relationships, and personal power. Who do you want to be as a sexual person? What do you want to experience? How do you want to feel?

2. What Will You Need to Release?
Then write about what you know you will have to give up or release in order to make space for this vision. What beliefs, values, patterns, relationships, or emotional states will you need to let go of?

As you reach toward being something bigger and more expansive than you have ever been, you will have to release the things and people that keep you small and no longer serve your journey and who you are becoming. Sometimes that feels hard, but it's necessary. In order to be something new, you have to make room. You have to give something up. It's the quantum physics of personal growth.

Voids always get filled with something. As you release and make more space inside of yourself and in your life, you will fill it. So get clear now on what you want to fill it with. Even if it's just how you want to feel. Do this with great intention. Leave it up to chance and you might find yourself on another circuitous journey when you really want to go right for the gold.

THAT BIG MOMENT OF SEXUAL SHAME

I had that place of sexual shame: the one where a woman is terrified to touch her own body and doesn't know how to have an orgasm. I was one of the millions of women who carry an insidious shame because they never taught me about my own pleasure, my own body, never named my clitoris, and kept subtly instructing me to strive to have vaginal orgasms.

For me, it had a clear beginning when I was shamed as a little girl who took great pleasure in her discovery of the unique smell of the magical kingdom between her legs. When I was about seven or eight years old, I started a ritual that was very satisfying for me. I noticed that my genitals smelled very different from any other part of my body. Having a normal curiosity, I would touch them through my clothes and I would smell the scent of my own body on my fingers. I found it fascinating. I liked it. I enjoyed the scent of my own sex, even at that little age.

One day, I was following my mother outside at Rosicrucian Temple and probably without even thinking about it, did my little genital touch-and-smell ritual. I thought I was being stealth, but my mother whipped her head around, glared down at me, and said in a stern whisper, "Stop *touching* yourself and *smelling* yourself!" She really emphasized "smelling."

I was stunned. I knew enough to know not to do this totally in bird's-eye view, but her reaction was so dramatic that I thought, "This must be *really* bad." Already, my body, my senses, and (though I didn't have a word for it at the time) my sexuality were all suspect.

Her unintended shaming was highly effective: I didn't touch myself again for *ten years*, not even when my high school boyfriend and first love, who tried tirelessly to help me orgasm, moved my hand to my vulva during sex in an attempt to help me help myself. Trained at age eight, I instinctually yanked it away. I had internalized that it was bad to touch my sexual body parts so deeply in that brief, three-second exchange that it prevented me from touching my own genitals except to clean them until I entered adulthood.

I had been taught not to ever touch myself in order to feel pleasure. I felt additional shame that I couldn't orgasm. I had no idea how to figure it out and just thought that if my boyfriend kept trying hard enough, eventually we'd figure it out and it would happen. But I had to release the idea that someone else would do it. I had to do it myself. I had to learn the mechanics of my own body, and that required releasing my shame around self-pleasuring and masturbation and the idea that someone else was responsible for my pleasure.

It was not until I went to college and my sexuality instructors gave me permission, an assignment in fact, to go home and touch my genitals that I actually did so without reservation. Me and my yoni were reunited. It took a little while, but the orgasms that eventually came washed away the shame that had kept me alien in my own body and from my own capacity for pleasure. I could see truth because finally, I figured out how to have an orgasm! There was no way this was "bad." And then I had an orgasm with a partner for the first time! It was indeed possible! Finally, I understood how my body worked and what felt good. Finally, I felt in control of my pleasure and I took full responsibility for it. Finally, I could show my lover how I liked to be approached and touched.

My story is hardly unusual. We all can conjure a moment when someone shamed us about sexuality, our body, our gender, our desire, our pleasure, how we love, or how we do sex. We all have stories of squashed curiosity or sexual ignorance. My mother had hers. What does that shame do? It keeps us disconnected from truth, desire, and joy.

Those moments were what they were, and they might have been painful. Yet we have to love ourselves enough to heal and move beyond them into the truth of our own wholeness. To heal sexual shame is to embrace something new about sexuality. Education and new experiences are balms for healing our shame and growing as sexual people. Ultimately, we each have to free ourselves and let go of the shame and other feelings that keep us stuck and dissatisfied.

NAOMI'S STORY, PART 2

Those shaming moments have tremendous long-standing impact, as in Naomi's experience of homophobic teasing. She says:

When I participated in the sexual empowerment program, thirteen years after my shaming experience at school, I had a flash of understanding that almost tore me in two. I suddenly saw the ways in which I still carried this shame about my sexual self, and how it had prevented me from feeling whole, from believing I was worthy of the relationships and community I really wanted. It was like a huge weight came off me all at once. Very soon after that I moved to a new place, found a welcoming queer community, and was able to tell my family about my experiences as a young girl. My mom was upset to hear about everything that had happened without her knowing. I now realize that if I had told her what was going on at the time, she would have supported me. My shame had prevented me from reaching out for help, which just deepened my feelings of isolation and unworthiness.

In retrospect, it is incredible to see how quickly things changed for me and how much opened up in my life from this one realization. I was able to look dispassionately at the past and recognize that there was nothing wrong *with me the whole time—I just had had a bad experience and had been in shame about it. Once I let it go, things changed almost overnight. People whom I hadn't seen in a few months would do a double take and ask, "Wow, what have you been doing?" because my energy was so much more open, warm, and inviting. I noticed that I was able to laugh more and be more spontaneous in different areas of my life because I was no longer repressing a huge part of who I am. And very quickly, I met an incredible woman with whom I am now deeply in love. My family loves her and our relationship is celebrated by our community. So this realization about my queer shame, and releasing the story I carried about how being queer made me a burden, has been a profound part of my liberation as a sexual being and a whole person.*

RELEASE AND MAKE ROOM

Let's examine some of the key things you might want to release in order to be sexually powerful, whole, and at home, as Naomi did.

False Beliefs about Self, Sexuality, and Others

As you begin to identify who you want to be and how you want to experience your sexuality, notice what beliefs you have held about who you are and about sexuality that seem out of alignment. They may be things you just accepted because they were a norm in your community, like "Sex before marriage is bad," or some version of "Good girls don't have that kind of sex/fantasy." They may be beliefs that were ingrained in you or in your family because of religious values. Allowing yourself to develop a new set of beliefs and to stand confidently in them is making room for the people and beliefs that really feel right for you.

Who You Think You Need to Be as a Sexual Person

Many people are limited by who they think they should be sexually. You internalize messages about who to be sexually based on your gender, your age, your size, your body, your attractiveness, your identities or perceived identities, your race, your social status, and your family roles, among other things. Naomi thought she had to be (or play) heterosexual. You might think you have to be a sexual initiator, aggressor, or submissive, or play some other role. There is a constant pressure to conform to certain standards, whether you are in Christian Sunday school, the military officers' wives club, or an LGBTQ (lesbian, gay, bisexual, transgender, and queer) community. How have you learned to pressure yourself to be sexually? What have you told yourself is not okay? What are your predetermined ideas about how you should behave as a sexual person?

No community is impervious to this pressure around sexual expression. Even in sex-positive communities sometimes there can be an unacknowledged pressure to be sexually active in particular ways because, you know, we all *love* sex so much. That's not okay either— and pressuring people about sex in any way is not sex-positive. How you want to be, how much or what kind of sex you want to have, and what territory you want to explore or set boundaries around is all up to you. There is no "right" way to be a sexual person.

Culturally, women learn that our sexuality is worth something, that our body is worth something, that our sex is worth something. For many women, self-worth becomes very tied up with how sexually desirable we are—so we work hard to be desirable. Many women act out sexually, sometimes having sex with many partners, not because they really want to have sex, but because they want to feel loved and they want to feel worthy. They don't want to feel alone. The intimacy of someone's body and sexuality is a way to feel close, to feel they are being loved, even if it is merely a physical act. Ulterior needs keep many women giving sex when they don't want to. That kind of giving is actually coming from a place of shame rather than empowerment.

It's helpful to have some like-minded people along the way with whom you can share and talk about sexuality openly. You get to be you. Don't let others tell you who to be, sexually or otherwise. When you let go of what you think you "should" be, you get to grow into who you really are. And if that means having many sexual partners or some other abundant sexual expression, fantastic. Go for it.

Shame

As experienced by both me and Naomi, shame can deeply impact us sexually. Shame is a belief that we are somehow bad or unlovable, and it is often connected to an underlying fear of being left alone. It's likely that most of us will experience shame at some point, and it can work its way into your psyche and make it hard to be fully sexually expressed or free. Shame tends to feel heavy, and it thrives as the person who feels it isolates and doesn't tell anyone about it like Naomi did. She was alone in her shame, and that made her shame grow. It's when we tell others and receive compassion for our stories that we dissipate our feelings of shame.

Author and shame researcher Brené Brown talks about healing shame and what is required of us: "Shame cannot survive being spoken. It cannot survive empathy." In fact, "shame depends on me buying into the belief that I am alone."

Speak about it in the right contexts where you can receive empathy and compassion and feel the shame fall away. This happens constantly in my weekend programs. Women speak the unspeakable stories, they talk about the things they never talk about, and at last get to lay down their shame and stories that have held them back for years. Witnessing this process is one of the most gratifying parts of my work.

Guilt

Sexual guilt is pervasive. Many people feel very guilty about their sexual feelings, fantasies, and thoughts. Much of a person's sexual guilt in this regard comes from learned religious or cultural beliefs. What kind of sex you should want. What fantasies are not allowed, or are not right in the eyes of God. How you should feel about sex. Who you should be attracted to. Well, what if you like something else? Maybe your fantasies would be unpopular—but they are yours. If you have guilt about something you desire sexually and you decide to let the sexual fantasy come alive, you would probably question it because you had been told all your life it was wrong.

Clarify the voice that told you your desires or fantasies are wrong. Was it a voice from your peers, religious community, media, or parents? You could make a choice to not feel guilty about your own desire or fantasy. This is not easy for people who have been heavily programmed by guilt, but you've got to start deprogramming yourself, and it begins by finding your own voice and separating your desires from the desires other people have for you. If you have not upheld your own boundaries about other people's projections about sex, it might be time to actively work on communicating them.

The place where guilt can be useful—provided we do not get stuck there—is that guilt can sound an alert about a place where we are acting out of alignment. If we are feeling guilty about something we have done or not done that truly didn't feel right to us, then we know that our actions are not matching our beliefs, our identity, or our values for how we wish to live our lives and engage in relationships. Identifying your guilt can help you course-correct and do it differently the next time. But you really have to take a hard look at the origins of guilt and see whether it's based on ideas you want to respond to or whether it's about someone else's expectations of you or issues that have nothing to do with you.

INQUIRY ABOUT GUILT

When you feel guilt coming up, ask yourself: "Is this something I need to examine or learn from, or is this useless guilt?" To determine which it is, think about whether the activity is harmful or limiting to you or another person. Does it violate your rights or your sense of freedom? Does it violate someone else's rights or their sense of freedom? If it does not, then it's useless guilt and a waste of energy. Let the guilty feelings go and get support if you need it to work through what is coming up for you.

Trauma

Trauma harms our sexuality and is almost always disempowering. Many people experience some kind of sexual trauma in their lives. All trauma demands healing. When people experience childhood sexual abuse, where adults or older kids did not respect their bodies or boundaries from a young age, their ability to set boundaries is typically impeded. Poor boundary-setting abilities can impact how people approach sex (or avoid it) for the rest of their lives. Some children are severely hurt physically, emotionally, mentally, and spiritually by childhood sexual abuse. They may have had injuries to their sexual body; they may have been lied to and manipulated; they may have been taught to be quiet and keep secrets about their sexuality;

they may have been coerced into sexual relationships they had no emotional skills to manage or understand.

Many people who experience sexual trauma when they are young feel grief about not getting to have an innocent exploration of sex as a young person or feel like they missed out on an important sexual development process. Many ideas about who they are, their sense of self-worth, and the meaning of their sexuality as it relates to the abuse are tucked away into their subconscious, driving how they presently behave in relationships and sex. This scenario is especially profound if the trauma happened before the age of seven, when their conscious reasoning mind did not have the ability to question what it was being taught. When the trauma occurs to a child who does not have the ability to refute and fully understand it for what it is, their mind and spirit will tend to normalize it in order to make sense of it, including whatever they thought it meant about them. If they are supported enough or empowered enough to work on healing and deprogramming all those early messages, they can step into their own true empowerment. It takes self-determination, and it can take years, but no one is broken and everyone can heal.

For some people this is a deep wound, and they spend a big chunk of their life working on their sexual healing. It is common that people who have experienced sexual assault or abuse will also experience post-traumatic stress disorder (PTSD). Working with a PTSD specialist can be really important.

The deep shame that can follow a sexual assault cuts to a person's core. Having their most vulnerable, personal part of themselves harmed, violated, and controlled can leave a person feeling unsafe, unloved, or unseen. Many times our culture and people who love us don't believe us, or blame us for our own sexual trauma because they don't know how to handle the pain and level of shame in that experience. The shaming message that is often internalized is "I have no value" or "I did something to deserve this."

"TRIGGERS" DURING SEX

You can get activated or triggered when you get touched a certain way, spoken to a certain way, are in a sexual position that takes you back psychologically to an abusive experience, or have some kind of flashback that takes you out of your present experience and into past trauma. You can also be activated about your health status, a disability, body image, or another important aspect of your sexuality that you have struggled with. The response to an activating experience can often be to end sex altogether. Sometimes that's what you need to do. Yet sometimes it's possible to move past it, or to stop to process something, change positions, or make some other kind of adjustment and keep going. If you feel like you don't really like sex at all, the cycle of feeling triggered can intensify. The more you avoid something that feels unpleasant, the more unpleasant feelings can grow.

A new way to approach triggering moments has four parts:

1. **EXPERIENCE THE FEELING/TRIGGER:** Notice the feeling coming up in you without judging it.

2. **BRING AWARENESS:** Recognize it as a trigger or an old program or identity. If you can, tell your partner it's happening so they can support you in the moment. Sometimes a partner might feel defensive or think it's about them. Let them know it's a tender place and that it's not personal. If they have a hard time understanding, decide whether you want to continue, make adjustments, or need to get more support. Not everyone will understand or be able to get it during an intimate sexual moment. Take time to develop strategies that work for you.

3. **MAKE A REQUEST AND USE TOOLS:** Whether you can discuss it or not, you can shift positions, let yourself

cry, make an adjustment, or start to do something different. Make clear requests and allow yourself to move through in the way that's right for you. Taking care of yourself is vitally important, so do what you need to do for self-care. You will be able to more fully show up in sex when you take care of you.

4. **REPLACE WITH A NEW SCRIPT:** Thoughts are powerful. Remind yourself this is different—this is not your abuser, this is your partner or lover and they want you to enjoy sex, or you want to enjoy sex and not superimpose an old script or wound. Changing how you think about this situation or about sex will shift how you feel, and that awareness can ultimately change your patterns so the activation happens less.

If you don't want to have sex, don't. That never feels good for you, or for your partner if they are a conscious, caring human being. If you want to but you are having a hard time, know that triggers don't have to halt everything, and you don't have to stop and relive it every time. That's often unproductive. You can choose a different kind of sex or intimate act and learn to move past it more quickly or with less emotional expenditure. Shift the energy and come back to the present. Know that persistent triggers may require more support from a professional therapist and are often not easily overcome. Be patient with yourself, acknowledge your needs, and allow yourself the support and time you require to heal.

Sexual trauma can make it nearly impossible to trust others and often shuts down a person's sexuality entirely. If your association with sexual energy and activity is that negative, you can completely disconnect from your sexuality and be unable to see anything positive in it. Until you take the step to get help, you might put your sexuality on hold or behave in sexually inauthentic or even harmful ways. I believe we can fully heal and inhabit our sexuality even after great trauma. Humans are so resilient. We can choose to have a new relationship to trauma and other experiences. Sometimes it means releasing an intense identification with the victim part of our self (more on that in the next chapter) and reframing the experience. For instance, rather than viewing yourself as a "victim of sexual assault," see yourself as "someone who has experienced sexual assault."

PATSY'S STORY, PART 1

When Patsy contacted me, she was the youngest private client I had ever had. At twenty-three, she was ready to heal from the sexual abuse history that had impacted her life in more ways than she could even see. She wanted to become sexually empowered and to improve her relationship with her partner, whom she cared about deeply. She signed on to work with me for a year right out of the gate, in a commitment to deep growth and expansion, and I was often impressed by her thoughtfulness, maturity, and depth.

> *My father sexually abused me from the age of three to nine years old, at which point he confessed and went to prison. Over the years, I have experienced so many different emotions about this. Grief, shame, confusion, rage. My mother collapsed emotionally and spent the next decade of my life trying, with limited success, to heal. It was just the two of us, so as she battled with depression, anxiety, and a soul-crushing guilt, my emotional needs often went unmet. I*

tried to take care of her so she could take care of me—I learned to censor myself, to never say anything that could possibly be hurtful, to do nice things in order to make amends when I, inevitably, couldn't make her happy.

When I began having romantic and then sexual relationships, these patterns played out again and again. I had no idea how to ask for what I wanted, how to speak up when I was unhappy, how to be with someone else's unhappiness instead of running for the hills. I experienced a lot of anxiety around consent and boundary setting—my attempts at both were confusing and fragile. And, for the most part, these challenges were reinforced by cultural norms. Most of us are not taught how to handle conflict in healthy ways. Most of us are not taught how to communicate our sexual needs—or, for women, even value that we have *sexual needs. I was under the impression that my partner should know what I wanted and give it to me—and when they turned out to be incapable of reading my mind, I felt incapable of reaching out. I actually broke up with my first boyfriend by simply refusing to speak for hours until he gave up and left!*

I did a lot of work exploring my history and the ways it plays out in my present. I needed to identify patterns before I could release them. Possibly the biggest breakthrough for me was learning to honor my behavior as it was. So many of my worst habits came from a desire to be good—ways of not upsetting anyone, of making others happy, of getting my needs met however I could. When I honored that I am and always have been doing the best that I can, instead of beating myself up for not being perfect, I found I had some space to relax. In that space, I began to love myself.

A False Sexual Bar

Sometimes you don't like sex the way everyone around you seems to, and trying to make yourself or convince yourself to like it is a losing game. If you don't like what people are telling you to like, don't pretend to.

I want to say something people don't often say in our culture: it's okay not to like sex. What is hard is when you are in a relationship with a partner who likes and wants sex and you don't. You might not be the best match, or you might need to create an arrangement where your partner can get their sexual needs met in another way. Nothing is wrong with either one of you; you have different needs. You want to make your partner happy, you want your partner to be able to have a sexual life, but you don't want one—at least not the way they do.

If you find a partner who shares your dislike for sex, then that could work for you. Sometimes that's the best match, and it does happen, but more often one person ends up forsaking themselves: either the person who dislikes sex has sex they don't want to have, or their partner denies themself a sex life (with others at least) because they want to be with their partner who does not want sex. That's not a great situation for either person.

DISSOCIATION

Sometimes people dissociate from their bodies entirely during sex, during medical exams, or in other vulnerable situations. Dissociation is a process where the mind temporarily distances itself from the body or the present experience because it is too much for the psyche to process. This loss of connection may affect you psychologically and might affect your sexual functioning. It can be hard to stay present during sex for a person who dissociates. If you are having sex you really do not want, a common response (especially with a trauma background) is to dissociate. Cognitive behavioral therapy, meditation, touch therapy, and mindfulness practices can be really helpful in changing patterns around dissociation.

If you want to heal this so that you don't dislike sex—if you really want to want and like sex—then that's different. It requires some diligence to change the wiring so that you can feel excited about sex and enjoy it. It requires giving yourself permission to take it slow and to figure out what you really do like. Sometimes women think they don't like sex, but it's because they've just never had great sex and their bar is so low, they don't know what "good sex" is. You and your partner will have to be patient as you discover what a sexual life could look like without false expectations or a particular form of sexual conduct you think you *should* have. There is no true "should" that is right for everyone. Find your true north in sex.

Insecurity and Fear

Walking around focused on your insecurity as a sexual being and being afraid of sex or your desires keeps you fragmented and unable to embrace the sexual life you could have. As Patsy let go of her anxiety, she was able to show up in her sexual relationship in a way she never had. Even if her fear came up, she learned to speak it anyway and build a connection rather than the distance and disconnection she had unwittingly become adept at creating.

When you are in a close relationship with a lover or friend, one way to deal with insecurity and fear is just to name it when it comes up, and that can open the door to dialogue that otherwise feels hard. "I'm feeling insecure right now, but I'd like to be closer to you." "I'm feeling fear and anxiety about having sex tonight. Can we discuss what we are up for?" It's so simple, and it works. If the person you say it to is caring, they will help bridge the gap and come closer to you. Let go of the insecurity and fear, or see the fear, acknowledge it, and move forward anyway. Fear is an indicator that there is a piece of learning for you to gain. See it as a gift and a guidepost for what you might need to move through or beyond so you can heal and grow.

Letting Go of Attachments

The more you can let go of your preconceived ideas about how love, sex, and relationships have to look, the more you can create the relationships you really want. The co-creation that can happen in a loving relationship of any type is beautiful when we can show up as our full selves, ready to do the work and be present. Let go of attachments that relate to needing to control or have things your way.

You might have other things you are attached to because they are a real boundary for you. You have limits. You draw that line in the sand and you don't go beyond it because that's what is right for you. We all need boundaries in relationships. Boundaries are healthy. They are how you teach people to treat you. So ask yourself, "Is this a healthy boundary? Or is it an attachment to a particular way of being or outcome?"

Identities That No Longer Fit

Identities are an important way we assert who we are in the world. Sexually, they often help us connect the dots about our behavior or inclinations. As I've discussed, sometimes we are carrying old identities that no longer serve us or just are not an accurate depiction of who we are anymore, and they keep us small. Stop identifying with the things that don't light you up. Your entire life is a creation, so keep creating yourself. Avoid getting stuck being someone or something you really are not or don't want to be anymore. Letting go of an identity can mean losing a community or special relationships, yet we always fill a void and maybe you'll find a new community that is more aligned with who you are today. Don't get stuck being an old you because you are afraid of loss. Ask yourself what you might gain if you stepped into something new and more authentic.

Relationships

Relationships are the place where we play out our previously learned behaviors, where our subconscious needs rise to the surface, and where our insecurities become evident. They are a repository for all of the experiences that have brought us to where we are today. Relationships are the place where we face great betrayals and deep healing.

The majority of people treat relationships as either an achievement or a given. Few people do conscious work on how to be their best selves in their relationships and work on healing the damaging emotional patterns they bring into them. As we get into "committed" relationships, they are generally assumed to be mutually monogamous but frequently are *not*. We begin to build a life or a social environment with a lover, and as our lives get more entwined, it's more difficult to question and change the roles each person plays and the dynamics we create together.

Personal expansion doesn't always mean staying in a relationship. In fact, it often means having to leave a relationship that is not serving you, that you have outgrown, or that is actually harmful. This might fly in the face of the commitment you made, so you may tend to choose the commitment rather than choose yourself and look at why you made this commitment in the first place.

Sometimes we have dysfunctional desires that need to be examined. If you desire something or someone that impedes your ability to live your life, or if you desire something that puts you directly in harm's way, like an abusive relationship, it has to go. If you enjoy a desire and have fun with it and no one gets hurt, it's coming from a healthy place. If you desire something that would hurt someone else or yourself, that's a dysfunctional desire. You have to look at it honestly and stop the hurtful behavior.

I recently spoke to a woman who very much wanted to work with me as a coach, who had some big questions about her sexuality and places that needed attention. After we spoke, she told her partner about it and he got very angry. He told her she did not need someone's help and thought it was ridiculous to work with a coach to improve her sexual life. The implication was that he was "enough" and that she shouldn't need help around sex. By association, if she needed help, it might indicate that he also needed help, and that was just too much for him. She chose to listen to him and not move forward in the work, although I know it would have been a huge game changer for her—and it probably would have meant she would have had to leave him eventually. I don't think she was ready for that possibility.

Sadly, many people choose to be in a limited relationship that doesn't serve them rather than be alone and work on fully growing and expanding. If you stay, you've got to do the work together that is required for each partner to grow and expand within the relationship, and that includes sex.

If you do not have the makings of a fully realized relationship that includes caring, communication, growth, and mutual benefit, then walk away. One of the most common examples is going back to an abuser over and over and convincing yourself to stay because you love them. Love is not enough. You will never change an abuser. They will keep you in the cycle of lies and abuse that keeps you coming back so they can do it again. And it tends to escalate over time. Love yourself enough to walk away. An abuser is incapable of fully loving. Their wires are crossed and they've got serious work to do. You can't do the work for them and you can't save them. But you— and only you—can save yourself. Whether you are in an abusive relationship or one that is unfulfilling, your choice is to stay and actively work on it or get out and work on you.

Time alone is an important way to do your healing and get clear about who you are and where you are going. This is often very hard to do from the vantage point of a relationship, where another person's needs, expectations, and demands may obscure your true desires. Sometimes we have to let go of relationships that just are not aligned anymore. It could be a fairly healthy relationship yet it's holding you back. Maybe you are not compatible sexually. Maybe you want different things. Maybe it has run its course. Don't be afraid to let it go if that act will free you both to have what you really want in life. That is real love. Sometimes our paths diverge and the most loving thing is to let go, release the person, and build something new. It allows room for someone you are really compatible with to come in. Love yourself enough to know when it's time to move on. Release the relationships that aren't right for you.

WHAT MAKES IT HARD
TO RELEASE?

It's hard to release the things we know we need to let go of for several reasons. First is that you've become accustomed to the beliefs, feelings, relationships, and behaviors that need to be released. You've created identities and relationships around the old dynamics. If you release them, you have to find a new anchor, a new belief system, new relationships, or new habits—and that can feel scary. When you are accustomed to the old way, change is hard. Yet change is necessary and it will come, whether you direct it consciously or life directs it for you. It's so much better to be in the driver's seat making choices about what you want to happen in your life.

It might be hard to release the old and unhealthy ways of being because you don't think you can have more or deserve more. This belief can be buried deep in your subconscious self and you keep sabotaging change so you can keep proving to yourself that better or more will forever elude you. When you don't have a strong sense of your own self-worth, you might not make decisions that are good for you because you don't believe you deserve good treatment or that what you want matters. This might mean you put yourself in risky sexual situations or that you don't ask for what you want and need sexually. If you are not used to your pleasure being important, you won't pursue it. Many people just do not advocate for themselves because they do not believe they deserve more or can have more. They have unhealthy relationships or end up in abusive situations that maintain their low self-worth.

Everyone who has self-esteem wounds has to tackle them. Getting to the core of that wound is about truly learning to love yourself no matter what, and to learn to put your own needs above others'. It's likely that with low self-esteem you will engage in people-pleasing, and in sex, that means doing what you think your partner wants without regard for what you want and not asking for what you need. This makes you vulnerable to retraumatizing experiences because you won't speak up or set boundaries. Learning sexual assertiveness, communication, boundary-setting, and request-making is essential. Loving yourself enough to know that you deserve good, healthy, fulfilling, consensual sex is the core of your work.

Finally, you might have a hard time releasing because you just don't know how to do it. No one ever modeled anything different for you, and you need role models, education, information, and support for a new way of being.

PATSY'S STORY, PART 2

I started this work on my sexuality because I was miserable about sex, both doing it and thinking about it. As the work progressed, I realized that all the upsetting emotions, all the negative patterns I had in sex also played out in the rest of my life. It all really came down to not valuing myself—not asking for what I wanted, not bringing up what upset me, not feeling like I could say no. These things all played out subtly in all of my relationships—from my partner, to friends, to professional relationships. Sex was where they boiled over because sex was the one place where I didn't feel like I could turn to anyone else for support or advice.

To change my emotional patterns around sex (and everything else), I had to admit how much of my power I gave away. It was so easy to feel like a victim—it was much easier to blame others for not meeting my needs than it was to acknowledge that I was actually preventing myself and others from meeting them. Stepping into my own power has been uncomfortable. My fear has fought me every step of the way, crying out that I am asking too much, that I will be hated, abandoned, alone. Yet every step has proven this false. That fear still exists in me, and I still have more power to reclaim, but the work I've done so far has drastically improved my quality of life. I can easily give voice to things that would have eaten me alive in silence a few years ago, all because I have faith that my needs are worth meeting.

After a lot of time and energy put into releasing my old ways of being, I feel more like my true self than ever. It's like shedding old layers of skin, getting closer and closer to being my deep core self at all times. And that self is wonderful. I truly believe that each of us is self-actualized, deep, deep down. That shining, brilliant, true self is buried under old scars and open wounds, under pollution and muck and other people's old junk, under layers of protection we feel we need, under masks and costumes and elaborate charades. Doing the work to clean all that up and come into my own power started by realizing that I was capable of making my life a safe space to be my whole self. And from there it's been about putting one foot in front of the other, day after day, and being kind to myself when I pause to rest.

TECHNIQUES FOR RELEASE AND MAKING MORE SPACE

There are many techniques you can use to release what holds you back and make more space within your being for what you are bringing in.

ECSTATIC BREATHWORK

There are hundreds of ways to breathe. This is one to try. Ecstatic breathwork can be expansive and exhilarating. When you do deep-breathing techniques, sometimes the body gets so overwhelmed with new oxygen that you will feel dizzy. Your body isn't used to you breathing so deeply. If you get dizzy, just adjust your breathing or your position so you don't faint, and know that it's normal. You might also feel a tingling sensation or a temporary paralysis in your fingers, hands, or feet. This contraction of your muscles is called tetany, and it's normal. It is temporary and will last only a few minutes. It's a sign your body is really taking in the breath.

1. Sit cross-legged or stand with feet slightly wider than shoulder-width, knees bent, back erect.

2. Set a timer for 3 minutes. As you get practiced, do it for 5 minutes or more.

3. Begin to count your inhale and exhale at 5 counts. Inhale for 5 seconds, then exhale for 5 seconds. Try to make them even, so you are receiving and releasing breath equally. On your inhale, fill your lungs as fully as you can, and release every bit of breath you can when you exhale.

Breathwork

When you are out of sorts, off, in a pattern of sabotage or telling yourself unhelpful stories, bring it back to your breath. Breath is the way we make space internally and it's the thing we give ourselves every moment of every day. Breath is life force. Doing some deep

4. As you get comfortable in your breath, start to speed it up. Count it off at 4, then 3, then down to a 2 and even a 1 count. Breathe rhythmically. In. Out. In. Out. Say it to yourself. Receive. Give. Receive. Give. Inhale. Exhale.

5. Keep going and don't stop until your timer goes off. All of your focus is on your breath filling your body, touching every cell in your body with fresh life force.

6. You might feel fatigued and want to stop. Keep going! Pushing over the hump is where the juice is. If you stop with breathwork, you probably also stop with sex. There is that place in sex where you could keep going and have an orgasm, but many women stop. Don't stop until it's time.

7. When the timer dings, slow down your breath easefully until you get back to a normal in-and-out breath.

Notice what happens in your body. Notice the space you create. Notice if your mind feels more relaxed or quiet. Don't be surprised if you feel tingly or even orgasmic. This is why it's called "ecstatic." This is a wonderful practice to do when you feel stuck in any way. Play with your breath and enjoy the ride. You can even do this with lovers or friends.

breathing or ecstatic breathwork is a way to energize our bodies, get out of our heads, and create more spaciousness. Breath helps us to release what we are holding in our bodies and to clear the muddle in our minds. I can't underline enough how important and powerful breathwork can be. Breath is the fastest way back to your body.

Voice

If you have a need to release old stuff, it might be stuck in your throat chakra. When you are in a safe place like your home where no one will bother you, you can give yourself space to use your voice, express what feels stuck, and let it out. Let yourself make sound. Use your voice to play, sing, emote, or say a blessing. Sing to the mountains. Dance and play with sound. Play with vowels. Cry. Wail. Release pent-up anger. Say the things aloud that you never let yourself say. Make extra noise when you self-pleasure. Enjoy the playground of sound.

Movement

Movement in the body is a great release. We have stuck points in our bodies, and just moving and allowing something new to emerge can be freeing. Dancing, running, yoga, acrobatics, exercise, or other kinds of movement gets you into your body and helps it let go of what is weighing you down. Movement is always a good go-to when you feel stuck because it is the opposite of stuck and unmoving.

Time in Nature—Give It Back to the Earth

Spending time in nature is a great way to release what ails you. Lie in the grass and breathe into the earth. Cry into the earth. Release. Hug trees and feel the energy passing between you and this great living thing. Swim in the ocean, a lake, or a river and let the waters wash over you. I love to get knocked around by the waves in the ocean because I can feel the healing salt water literally take away the tension in my body and ease the achy parts. Nature is the greatest healer. The earth can hold the things you are ready to let go of. Give it back, ground it, and release.

Sexual Support Team: Bring Sex-Positive Influences into Your Life

Bring new influences into your life and remove negative influences that keep you stuck. This book is one such influence. There might also be people you can bring in: friends, teachers, healers, and communities who will support your healing process. Bring in new voices and experiences that will allow you to let go of your old ways of being and step into the new ones. We all need this. Think of it as a sexual support team. Who is on your team? Bring them in and assemble the right team of people to help you move to a new place as a sexual person. Stack your bookshelves with new ideas and beliefs.

As you question and purge what does not serve you, bring in what does. Release is essential so you can have the sexual life and be the sexual person you really want to be. Now let out a great big breath.

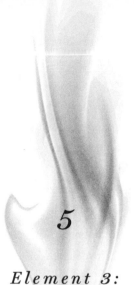

5

Element 3:
EMOTION

SHOW UP AS EMOTIONALLY POWERFUL

To be a woman on fire, you've got to accept emotional responsibility. It's a part of growing up. To some degree, every one of us learns harmful emotional patterns that do not serve our relationships. You can't skip this part of your development. It's the self-knowing eyeglass, the locus of skilled self-expression that separates the women who are unstoppable in their relationships, in sex, in their work, and in the world, from those women who will keep staying stuck replaying old emotional patterns that don't allow them to be who they deeply want to be.

Some of the hardest work you will ever do in your life lies in Element 3. In order to have powerful and authentic intimate relationships, you must eliminate your destructive emotional patterns—both internally and in relationships. You have harmed yourself and others with these patterns, and they have kept you in a place of immaturity, smallness, pettiness, unrealistic expectation, and insincerity, and that keeps you from rising to a more exalted level in your relationships. Your emotional development requires attention, yet most people do not put real investment into being emotionally potent.

I hear from women often that they want deeper intimacy in their relationships. They really want a partner who can show up fully and meet them in a place of power. To be emotionally powerful requires skills. You have to develop your emotional skills in order to have more deeply intimate relationships. Skills are something you learn to do well by education and practice. This chapter is about those emotional skills.

This requires tremendous honesty and self-reflection. Most of us have enormous blind spots around our emotional patterns. Typically we are forced to deal with our emotional demons when something big happens: a death, a divorce or breakup, an accident, a health or family crisis. Life tests us, and we have to find out what we are capable of as we face things that can either take us down or make us love ourselves so fiercely that we'll never forsake our own true love again in an unhealthy, toxic relationship dynamic with someone else.

Many people carry an attitude that relationships are just what they are, and fail to see that this important part of life requires conscious effort. It's similar to the idea that we don't have to learn sex. The refrain "It's just the way it is" is thrown around frequently, and yet *nothing* is "just the way it is." There is a cause and effect in everything. You are the cause: your relationship patterns, your dramas, your upsets, your life circumstances are the effects. If they aren't what you want, then you've got to look at how you are causing yourself pain and turmoil. You have to look at your part, for it's the only part you can change.

EVERYONE HAS LIMITATIONS

We all have limitations. Limitations are things we are not capable of doing, awareness we do not have, expectations we can't live up to. You have emotional limitations, and identifying them is the best way to work with them so they stop getting in the way so much. For instance, in my early twenties, I was still in a raw place, healing from my own sexual assault history, and I was speaking the word *rape* in describing my own experience for the first time. I applied to be a hotline worker at a rape crisis hotline. When the director of the program interviewed me and asked me questions, I broke down in tears when my own tender history came up, making it clear I was too vulnerable around this issue and that I was not ready to do the work. I was not invited to volunteer because I was not strong enough to be there for someone else at that time. I needed to tend to my vulnerability and healing first.

Much of the emotional pain and turmoil in relationships relates to wanting things from someone else that they simply are not capable of providing, and taking it personally when they don't. It's not about you—it's about their limitations. It doesn't mean they don't *want* to give to you—it means their awareness or capability is not in a place that would *allow* them to do so. Identifying the limitations in a person you are emotionally close to can help you to stop expecting things they cannot deliver, which prevents you from experiencing so much pain. If you cannot accept their limitations, move on.

WHERE YOU LEARN EMOTIONAL PATTERNS

You develop your emotional patterns while growing up as your parents transmit daily lessons via their behavior and expectations. You get your patterns from roles you play in your family and how they play out. You get them from the culture of your family, the way the women of your family behave, and from the rules of these relationships performed each day. Most of this information gets taken into your subconscious, where you store it until you begin to have your independent relationships outside of the family, and bam! There are your patterns.

You practiced these patterns with your family and you learned them well. You discovered that you must defend yourself in some way. You worked hard not to be the thing everyone is convinced you are (pretty-but-stupid, the clown, the fuck-up, the perfect child, the responsible one, the slut, the insecure one) or you go right into proving everyone right because they all think it anyway. You are clever with your self-sabotage either way.

Everyone is emotionally vulnerable, whether you recognize it or not. Yet most people try to hide their vulnerability—either from other people or from themselves. Learning what your emotional vulnerabilities are is a key part of your being able to protect yourself in the right places, make cogent decisions, and show up as an emotionally present person who can have a deep experience with sexuality and intimacy.

There are parts of yourself you protect and that you learned to defend. I was the oldest child in a family of three siblings, raised by my dad as a single parent. I got blamed for things all the time because I was the oldest and "should" be responsible, "should know better." So in feeling blamed, I learned to put up my dukes and defend myself. I'd spent my life feeling like I had to explain myself by defending my actions and proving that I was not all I was being accused of. I had to realize that these habits and patterns were not useful to me in my adult relationships. I was creating a defensive energy that was not helpful in being closer to the people I loved and who loved me. Instead I created walls in my intimate relationships, which kept me from getting my needs met.

Your vulnerabilities stem from both your past experiences and your current abilities and skills. If you experienced abuse as a child, you probably have some vulnerabilities related to that abuse. If you were sexualized, you might have sexual vulnerabilities. If you were abandoned, you might have a vulnerability around fear of abandonment. If you were bullied and picked on, there could be vulnerabilities around teasing or power dynamics that might engage bullying. People—especially young people—are resilient and can handle a lot more that we often give them credit for, but that doesn't mean that a vulnerability didn't develop. And people can heal and sometimes move beyond it entirely.

When you have a vulnerability, part of yourself is at risk of being emotionally triggered. This will happen in your relationships, which is why your emotional health is so intertwined with your relationships (social health). Without awareness, you will make decisions about relationships based on those triggers and your responses. Learning about your own vulnerabilities is a way of identifying the things that might trigger you before they happen, so that you can prepare yourself for ways to respond and get support when you find yourself feeling vulnerable.

Your sexual patterns will show up in repeatedly similar ways: being defensive about your sexual skills/experiences/abilities/likes, shutting down and withdrawing when sex is wonky, not asking for what you need, or feeling unwanted and therefore unattractive or sexually inadequate.

Ironically, subconciously we think these patterns help us by protecting us, but they actually keep us from getting the things we most want. It's hard to see what you are doing when you are in the midst of it. Usually someone else will point it out or it will create conflicts. If you continue to defend yourself, you'll keep creating the same dynamics. We all have to learn to be less defensive or self-protective if we want to be close to other people.

What I've seen many women do is this: she starts with a story she tells herself and it upsets her, makes her angry, afraid, or sad, and she spirals out of control with the story, becoming obsessed, and then she projects all the meanings she's created about that story onto others. She goes deep into defending the sad story where she feels smaller and her view becomes more myopic. She can't see any other possibility for what's really true outside of this story she's made up. The deeper she goes, the harder it is to get out, and the bigger the lesson becomes. We could call this an emotional spiral.

When I teach classes on communication I ask people to raise their hand if they grew up in a family where there was healthy, respectful communication, and almost invariably no one raises their hand. So how do we learn something we never had modeled for us? We were all taught disempowerment. Claim this work of empowering yourself into a new way of being so you can show up powerfully in your relationships and have the clarity and happiness you really want. Realize you have different choices for how you want to be in your relationships. You can choose to develop an understanding of your own defenses and vulnerabilities and change your defensive behaviors because you can handle yourself in a different way.

RECOGNIZING YOUR
DEFENSE MECHANISMS

We defend ourselves in an array of ways. Any defense mechanism you have emotionally will also show up sexually. Let's look at some common defense mechanisms and some examples of how they might show up specifically around sexuality. Ask yourself if you engage in these defenses either often, sometimes, or never. Be honest in your answers, and don't be surprised if you find that you engage in many defensive patterns. Most people do.

DENIAL: Ignore or pretend things are not really happening so you do not have to deal with them

Examples: *"Our sex life is amazing! I couldn't be happier"* (inside you are really unhappy) or *"My partner would* never *cheat on me."*

REPRESSION: Bury painful experiences or even "forget them" because they are so painful

Examples: Forgetting that you were sexually abused or raped. Drinking or other behaviors that can keep you from remembering painful events.

PASSIVE-AGGRESSION: Rather than ask directly for what you need, you slam doors, get sarcastic, or expect people to figure out what you want; use the silent treatment when you are upset with someone

Examples: Huff and roll over dissatisfied after sex, but tell your lover everything was great. Get up and shower after sex without a word. Storm around when you feel sexually rejected. Be cruel sexually (verbally or physically) to act out your aggression. Manipulate someone else sexually.

DISPLACEMENT: Having a difficult feeling about one thing and then "taking it out" on someone else

Example: You have a hard "mom" day, and when your partner comes home and wants to be close to you, you pick a fight and get angry with them. (This can also be passive-aggressive.)

PROJECTION: Attach your feelings, experiences, or stories onto others (who do not have that experience or feeling), as if to convince yourself they are not yours so you do not have to feel them

Example: *"You just don't want to have sex with me, do you?"* (When *you* don't want to have sex.)

RATIONALIZATION: You make excuses and logical arguments to avoid taking responsibility for inexcusable actions

Example: *"I'm just not feeling very attractive, so when I slept with that other person it was because I needed to feel sexy, not because I wanted to hurt you."*

SUBSTITUTION: Things get difficult, so you replace a goal or a person with a new one so as to avoid dealing with the original situation

Example: *"He just wasn't meeting my needs, so I broke up with him and now I have a new boyfriend."* (Same pattern ensues.)

WITHDRAWAL: Disconnect from people when you feel challenged or overwhelmed

Example: You pull away affectionately, sexually, and/or emotionally from your partner, shut them out, and quietly deal with your emotions.

WITHHOLDING: Withhold love, attention, sex, or resources from those you love as punishment when you feel hurt

Example: After a fight or when your partner doesn't do what you want, you refuse to have sex, maybe pretend things are fine, but internally you are still upset and unwilling to give.

CONTROLLING BEHAVIOR: Try to control everything and everybody by telling them how to do/not to do things and impose your way (and likely get frustrated when it doesn't work)

Examples: Decide when, how, what position to have sex. Complain about how your partner got something wrong that they did for you out of love.

COMPLAINING: Complain about things instead of addressing them in a constructive way—you probably like the attention that complaining gets you (see Controlling Behavior) and yet it always takes you away from the present experience and from being able to receive

Examples: Complain about your body, about your pleasure, about sex, about the attention you get or do not get, about how your partner does it, about their inadequacies, and then wonder why they are avoiding being sexual with you.

DISSOCIATION: Check out mentally during an experience, or parts of the experience become inaccessible emotionally, usually due to past trauma (this is a common reaction to sexual assault/abuse)

Example: During consensual sex your partner touches you in a particular way (or during a pelvic exam something happens) and triggers a painful memory, so you "leave your body" mentally and are only present in a physical sense.

UNDOING: Attempt to make amends by doing something to try to undo the harm you caused so as to smooth it over and not to actually grow or change the situation in the future

Example: You scream and act out in an emotionally aggressive way with your lover, and then you offer sex, a massage, or to make them dinner to help them feel better, yet the next time you get upset you react the same way.

SUBLIMATION: Channel unacceptable impulses, thoughts, and emotions into more acceptable ones; use suppressed (erotic) energy somewhere else

Example: You aren't having as much sex as you really want, so you busy yourself with a creative or work project or physical workouts and funnel the energy there.

HUMOR: Make inappropriate jokes as a response to a tense or difficult situation (humor can be a useful stress reducer when appropriate); humor can be a form of sublimation

Example: You feel uncomfortable with or even angry about a friend's choice to have an abortion and you make jokes about how much easier it will be to not have that stinky crybaby to take care of.

FANTASY: Use imagination to escape problems without addressing them; channel unacceptable feelings or unattainable desires into imagination

Examples: You are dissatisfied with your sexual life and are constantly preoccupied with your fantasy life instead, maybe to the point where you begin to have unrealistic expectations of your partner based on your perfect fantasy. You watch porn compulsively while avoiding addressing sexual issues in your relationship.

IDENTIFICATION: Take on someone else's characteristics in order to avoid something difficult

Example: Your partner is controlling, maybe even violent, so you eat what they like, have the sex they like, or mimic their behaviors to keep the peace.

INTELLECTUALIZATION: Overuse of thinking, reasoning, and critical analysis to distance yourself emotionally from an unpleasant experience

Example: Overanalyze the mechanics of your sex life rather than being intimate or having sex, and push through whatever is blocking you. It's easier to think about/talk about sex than to do it or feel something about it.

COMPENSATION: You feel insecure or anxious about some part of yourself, so you build up another part in order to avoid feeling that insecurity

Example: You don't feel sexually desirable, so you work hard at being smart and competent in the hope that you will still be attractive.

We tend to feel like "I'm the only one. No one else does this." But it's not true. Everyone learns to defend, overcompensate, or behave in ways that can be manipulative, controlling, withdrawing, or passive-aggressive because most of us simply do not grow up in families where people are direct, speak up for themselves in ways that make them powerful, and communicate respectfully. We don't learn healthy ways to ask for what we want. That leaves us mimicking poor behaviors to get our wants and needs met. And because sexuality tends to stay largely in the closet, we can be doubly unskilled with how we show up here because of our anxiety and inexperience.

All this said, our defensive behaviors are not always unproductive. Sometimes they are necessary. Because we might be dealing with emotionally unskilled people or people who we cannot trust with our vulnerabilities, we sometimes need our defenses to be up

OVERCOMING EMOTIONAL DEFENSES

1. Choose one or two emotionally defensive patterns you want to change. Start by tracking your pattern for at least two to four weeks. For each instance, note for yourself when it shows up, what happens, what you were feeling inside, and what you could have done differently.

2. Then look at your data and look for patterns in your overall experiences. Are there certain people who trigger you most? Certain types of situations? What are they?

3. Once you identify some of your patterns, ask yourself, "How can I react differently in these situations? What can I do to experience this differently?" Make a list of alternate ways of dealing with these situations when they come up.

4. Begin to practice the new ways of being. The more you choose something new, the easier it will be to not react but rather to choose your response.

   There is a downloadable worksheet for tracking your defensive behaviors in the *Woman on Fire* online portal.

---

for our own protection. The key is to learn when they are needed and to make conscious choices not to allow ourselves to be run by unconscious defensiveness.

NEURAL PATTERNING

Part of why our patterns and defenses became vulnerabilities or limitations is because of the neural patterning that accompanies these developments. Much research has been done on the way we develop neural pathways in our brains based on our habitual behaviors. The more we engage a particular reaction or thought pattern, the more that neural pathway becomes defined in our brain. You have a particular emotional reaction and the neural pathway forms. Each time you have that reaction, the neural pathway is strengthened. Each time a similar situation occurs, you are already programmed to react in that particular way by the neural pathway. Eventually the reaction becomes automatic. This is part of why it's so hard to learn to react differently and where the term "knee-jerk" reaction comes from. Knock on a knee and it always kicks.

It requires effort to consciously choose a new response or action. But the good news is that as you choose something new, a new neural pathway is created for that new behavior or way of thinking. It doesn't feel natural because it's new, and the pathway is not nearly as strong, so it will require real effort to choose the new way. But each time you do, you strengthen that new pathway and the possibility of this new response becomes much greater. And even more encouraging: as you develop the new neural pathway, the old one weakens. So it becomes easier and easier to choose the new way and release the old knee-jerk response until it's no longer a habit.

ARE YOU RUNNING YOUR EMOTIONS? OR ARE THEY RUNNING YOU?

I don't want to be at the mercy of my emotions. I want to use them, to enjoy them, and to dominate them.
—OSCAR WILDE

Emotions and how we react to them are not uncontrollable, but you would think so in the ways many people are often controlled by them. Think about the times when your emotions have felt the biggest and most all-encompassing. How did they become that way? It's likely you were in a situation that was so counter to what you needed that you became overwhelmed by your emotional misalignment. Becoming a powerful emotional woman involves learning to use your emotions as a guide for where you are and to identify your needs and wants so you can move through difficult emotions more gracefully and rapidly.

When you are sad, depressed, jealous, angry, in a rage, or resentful, your emotions are telling you to reconnect to your source or center and get clear. You can move your emotional state gradually to a better place by consciously choosing it. You can also stay right where you are, attached to feeling bad by feeding the negative thought patterns, and therefore the emotions that keep you feeling bad.

Thoughts impact and sometimes create feelings that we then experience in the body as emotions. So a big part of the work in shifting out of harmful emotional places that lack personal power and agency is to work on what you are thinking and the perspective you are coming from with your experiences. Emotional patterns can look like this:

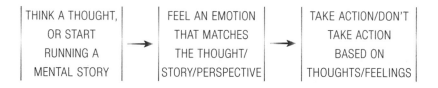

| THINK A THOUGHT, OR START RUNNING A MENTAL STORY | → | FEEL AN EMOTION THAT MATCHES THE THOUGHT/ STORY/PERSPECTIVE | → | TAKE ACTION/DON'T TAKE ACTION BASED ON THOUGHTS/FEELINGS |

As you work on shifting your perceptions and ways of thinking about your sexuality, pleasure, and your body, it can be gratifying because it frees you from your habitual reactions that keep you replaying the same story over and over, that keep you in the same unhealthy relationships, the same conversations, and dating the same type of person. Sometimes you must remind yourself that your lover is not your father or mother and that they do not have the same motivations. You can choose not to create the same old dynamic by playing a different role.

Within our patterns are our life lessons. Once you understand the lesson and you cease to think the old story, feel the old feelings, and behave in your old habitual ways, you release the pattern. You got it. Move on to the next piece of growth. There is always more to learn.

EMOTIONAL IMPACT ON SEX

Many people experience very strong emotions related to sex, for a variety of reasons. Emotion is experienced in the body, and because sex involves the body in often intense ways, there can be a strong feedback loop between sex, the body, and our emotions. Sex is powerful—it makes us feel extremely vulnerable. It's a place where we open up to another human being on a physical, emotional, and spiritual level, and we often allow ourselves to be raw. If you are letting go of control and really allowing yourself to experience true full-body pleasure, it is extremely vulnerable. The bliss and release that can happen is rarely experienced in any other way. Allowing someone else to see you in a sexually vulnerable place feels risky for a lot of people.

Protective barriers can quickly come up after letting your guard down in this sexual vulnerability. What if they don't like me anymore? Or as much as they thought they did? What if they reject me? What if they don't want to be as close to me after this? What if they use my vulnerability against me? Such underlying fears might have you feeling agitated, nervous, scared, or angry after a sexual encounter.

Sharing sexual experiences with another person also creates a unique connection to them, and emotions can run deep. Strong attachments can form, and attachments can lead to overwhelming emotional states. Tracking your own emotions related to sex and the partners you are with is important so that you make sure you are having sex with people you want to be sexually vulnerable with and that you are managing your expectations and, possibly, theirs.

When your emotions about someone get intense, you can engulf the person if you don't manage your emotions well. You can avoid displacing potent emotions or emotional expectations that are unrealistic or inappropriate on your lover. People have different ways of thinking about sex and different needs around it. If for you it's about creating a deep, lasting connection with someone and taking the relationship to a more committed place, and for them it's about having fun or releasing tension, that's a setup for disappointment and hurt if you aren't clear about the different needs sex is meeting for each of you.

PEOPLE-PLEASING AND EMOTIONAL INAUTHENTICITY

Emotional inauthenticity is a huge barrier for many people when it comes to sex. In my work with women, by far the most common emotional pattern that prevents them from having what they really want is people-pleasing. It is astonishing how prevalent this behavior is among women. People who are codependent, or overly preoccupied with what others are doing, as people-pleasers are, will tend to have low self-worth and feel chronically insecure. They tend to be reactive caretakers and spend a lot of time in anger, anxiety, and fear because they care-take everyone but themselves and that is aggravating. Because a people-pleaser seeks outside approval from others and is overly determined by the moods, thoughts, opinions, and actions of others, they tend to lack control over themselves and their own feelings.

Sexually, this is a recipe for not being able to be present or enjoy pleasure because the focus is always on what the other person is thinking or feeling, how much they are enjoying it or liking you, what they want and need, or being afraid of losing control. As a people-pleaser, sex will rarely be about you and your enjoyment, and you will never be fully present to the experience.

If you are someone who people-pleases, you are going to be emotionally inauthentic in sex if you don't look at how your people-pleasing shows up. People-pleasing sexually might look like:

... Having sex when you don't want to

... Telling your lover you like what they are doing sexually when you don't

... Agreeing to sex when you really want affection or something else

... Agreeing to sexual acts you don't want to do

... Resenting your partner for desiring sex

... Not asking for what you really need sexually

... Pretending to like sex when you don't

... Having duty sex or receptacle sex (you feel obligated and you only do it for your partner)

... Faking an orgasm

Ultimately your people-pleasing puts you at risk of emotional inauthenticity as you pretend to be okay about situations which you are not, and it can also lead to some deep-seated resentment that will not serve you or your relationship. It will feel like self-betrayal—and it is. That self-betrayal keeps you in a place of emotional self-estrangement and poor self-care. That doesn't feel good.

ANGER, FRUSTRATION, AND RESENTMENT

We plant our emotions in our bodies, and sex can tap into those energies and stir them up. Vaginal or anal penetration can tap into

"FUCK YOU JOURNAL"

When I went through my divorce I started a "Fuck You Journal." When I was angry or at risk of spiraling down with my story, I would write everything I was feeling and thinking in the journal and get it out on the page. I'd write in big bold letters if I wanted, almost screaming at the page. The page could hold that for me and I got to get it out. I'd feel the release and move on. I kept it throughout my recovery and healing, and after it was over and I no longer needed it, I never looked at it again. It was an outlet for me and I didn't mean half of what I wrote, but I was angry and needed to say it all, unhinged and uncensored, which was incredibly cathartic.

If you are going through something that is bringing up a lot of anger, resentment, or strong emotion—or if you've never really gotten in touch with your anger, start a "Fuck You Journal" and let yourself have that receptacle for your worst feelings, acknowledging that feelings are temporary. It's an opportunity to recognize what your feelings are and express them. You can then choose to take some productive action with the energy it brings up in you if that feels like a next step.

emotions we don't even realize we are holding inside. There is some real credence to the term "anally retentive," which usually means someone is wound up a bit tight or is controlling. We hold tension and can hold anger in our anuses, at our root. Sometimes a penetrative experience in either the vagina or anus can unleash a lot of emotion, which is one reason there can often be tears, laughter, or even rage during or after sex. If you don't address your anger, you will take it out on yourself, your partner, your body, or the relationship. Left untended long enough, the frustration and resentment will build, leaving you angrier.

In general, women need way more permission to be angry and need more tools to express anger in a healthy way. There is a lot to be angry about. Sexual inequality is a major issue that affects us all: the many ways women are subjugated to men; the inequity of sexual pleasure and enjoyment between men and women; women's invisibility and men's privilege; racism and the way women of color are impacted, to name a few.

We all need healthy emotional outlets. When was the last time you went into the woods and just screamed? Or stacked the pillows on your bed and beat your fists into them? In the day-to-day, working out or other physical activities can release anger. Many people use their art and creativity as a place to express it. Baths and swimming can help. Anger needs to be released in some way or it will implode on you or explode on someone else in careless ways.

The four basic emotions are anger, fear, grief, and joy. There is nothing wrong with anger. It is the energy that moves you toward action. Like all emotions, it is trying to tell you something. Nothing would get accomplished in the world without some healthy anger propelling it forward. If you stop judging your anger as bad and begin to see it as an energy, you can choose to use it productively and become more adept with it. You might have a lot of anger built up around sex. Let it out. Give it a healthy outlet and pleasure will have more space to exist.

MY STORY OF RELATION TRANSFORMATION

When my nine-year relationship started to unravel, so began the most profound shift of my life, one that forever changed me. I became aware of my walls and of her limitations, and we went to work. As someone who was helping people with sex and relationships for a living, I still had plenty of my own blind spots. Anyone with an abandonment wound will tend to stay too long in unhealthy relationships and give too many passes for bad behavior. I gave myself and my partner those passes.

We worked with two different therapists until the ultimate demise of our partnership. The point of our therapy was not to "save" the relationship. What was important was the process of that work and what it taught me about myself, what it taught her about herself, and realizing what we'd each accepted in this relationship that was unacceptable and in some ways even unwittingly cruel. Our codependent patterns exacerbated the core problems in our ability to relate. Her withholding and my control were the perfect match.

The pain of our breakup was immense, bigger than any pain I'd ever experienced because the betrayal was so complex and multilayered. I sank into a deep place of grief in my recovery from that breakup. I cried every day for a year. A friend would simply ask, "How are you doing?" and my eyes would well up. I felt so much loss, not so much in the relationship changing, because that possibility had been on the table for some time, but for the painful way it changed. For our inability to stand with each other in our own power to say what was true. But ultimately I accepted that we needed to experience the breakup just as we did in order to learn what we each needed to learn, to be able to grow. It was perfect as it was, and we were each freed.

To free myself, I had to change my story. I had to stop telling people what happened in the breakup. Every time I'd see a friend who didn't know what had happened and started asking questions, I'd feel compelled to retell the story until I finally realized I was just rewounding myself over and over. So I stopped telling it. And eventually the story changed.

I remember clearly the day I got to what felt like the bottom of my grief. I was home alone and I cried and screamed for hours in my room. I let it rip. The pain was so big. I had not only lost my partner, I'd lost my best friend, my travel companion, my favorite playmate, and the woman I'd made a life with for nine years. I wanted to call her so she could feel how big my grief was. I wanted her to feel it too. I even dialed her number, but I hung up. I couldn't leave a message. I knew it was not about her. It was about me.

This grieving day was catalyzed by an old close friend who had written me a letter that was hard to read—but it was the most real and deeply loving thing anyone had said yet. He'd watched me be in pain and he knew that place himself. He also knew I needed to grow, let go, pack it up, and leave the pity party. He gave me a compassionate kick in the ass that propelled me to move forward. He cared, and he demonstrated it by showing up honestly in his letter. I knew the power of his words. They cut in wisely and sharp.

I read the letter a few times and let it sink in, burned sage to clear the air, lay before my altar, and wept like a baby. The grief was intricately connected to my mother leaving when I was seven years old. I'd done years of therapy about that, but I knew that original wound was the anchor to the deepest part of my pain. Everything about that early abandonment was triggered. There was a profound connection to the betrayal patterns in my family in my breakup.

Then something almost magical happened.

In that deep, seemingly rock-bottom part of my grief, I opened up. I felt profoundly connected to the world. My face was swollen and numb, my body heaving and exhausted, yet my yoni was tingling and alive. I know that anytime my genitals pulse like that, there is something I am supposed to pay attention to. I felt a deep place of oneness with humanity, with every person who had ever experienced a loss—every mother who lost a child, every lonely person who lost their love. It was comforting, for what experience is more human than grief and loss—besides love? I'd experienced the deepest love I'd ever known with this person, so naturally the other side of that incredible love was this deep loss and huge well of grief.

Out of all of that came incredible lessons about who I had been, who I had allowed myself to be in the relationship, and what was no longer acceptable to me moving forward. I stopped crying on a dime or feeling so much anger at the painful flashbacks and memories that would pop into my mind.

As I healed and I saw how my friends and loved ones were able to show up for me (or not), I also learned on a soul level what I needed from those relationships and I was able to set boundaries—either just for myself or ones I communicated to those I loved. I learned who could hold me in that tender place and who could not. People tend to siphon themselves out quickly when you have a big emotional need as I did at that time. I didn't judge them for not being able to be there when they couldn't. In a mature move, I honored their inability or limitation without holding it against anyone and I honored my own needs by focusing on the people who *could* be there.

A few months after our breakup, before her final move out of our home, my former sacred companion and I did a powerful and very loving ritual to honor what we called "Relation Transformation." It was beautiful. It was the most intentional way I have ever shown up in relationship. We cooked one last meal together in our shared home, and as we moved from room to room, we told stories and laughed as we shared memories of each part of that house that was the setting for our love and shared life. We expressed our hopes and fears for our future as individuals and our transforming relationship. We marked each other's bodies with blessings for what was to come. That ritual of dissolution allowed us to reflect on what a gift our relationship had been, to acknowledge how much we appreciated each other, how deeply we'd learned and grown with each other, and to move forward and reorganize our relationship so that it could be healthy again, accounting for the new circumstances that would impact it. It was a new start that took several years to fully integrate.

If we approached breakups as the breakthroughs they always are and ritualized them as we do marriages, people would be so much healthier. We ritualize death and birth. Why not ritualize both the commencement and demise of a union? Sometimes there is too big a fissure to allow for such a loving communion. I felt blessed to have the space with my ex to honor the nine years we had chosen to share with each other and to transform the relationship with intention. I also did ritual alone with myself to release my own grief. We spoke of doing a ritual with the people in our lives as witnesses—those who had been impacted by our love—and they were many. You can do a relationship transformation ritual in many ways. Intention and ritual is so much better than the big angry leavings, the betrayals and rage, the stalking of the ex, and the dark resentment. Change the way you leave and change the way you live.

CHOOSING TO GROW

After my divorce, I was beginning to build and create relationships with more awareness than I ever had before. I spent several years being consciously single, focusing on building meaningful friendships and reorienting myself to my inner core—undisturbed and undetermined by a partner who wanted things from me or from whom I wanted something. What a freedom to not have that. I'd spent my whole adult life in relationships, and to be in a place of not having to navigate someone else's needs at all was incredibly liberating. Each day was about me, who I wanted to be in the world, what I wanted to do, and how I wanted to live my life, rather than about how I needed to negotiate with someone else.

I took time to do the work and love myself through it. Unfortunately, for most people, it takes a big rupture to wake us up and help us see the work we need to do in order to get what we want. It tends to be when big breakups, divorces, or betrayals occur in our closest relationships. What a gorgeous opportunity to turn your life around, to do your work so that you are ready to receive the love you truly want to experience. At their root, all of these relationships end up being about how much you will love yourself.

Some people stay together and do the work. It's wonderful when that can happen—but it can't always. Relationships are necessary structures to allow us to look at our patterns because our patterns show up clearly in close relationships. If you are in a relationship with someone who is even slightly interested in doing the seriously challenging emotional work with you, then it can be done. My experience is that in most relationships, one person tends to catalyze more of that work or desires it more, while the other person isn't really aware of it or interested in participating. They would rather go on, oblivious that there are things that require attention and growth. The defense mechanisms of denial and avoidance are a powerful demon that keeps many people from living fully.

Because most of my clients are women, I tend to see many heterosexual women who want more in their relationships but are partnered with men who "don't get it." Sometimes their male partners do not even see why they should support the work their lover is doing, and struggles can ensue about the investment of time, energy, and money. But really the fear is "Will she outgrow me?" And the truth is, she might. Sometimes loving yourself means letting go of someone you are close to.

At some point, there is a choice to make. Do I stay in a relationship with someone who is not on a path of self-transformation but perhaps meets many other needs of mine, or do I leave in search of someone new who can meet me at the evolutionary edges, someone who wants to grow *with* me? Do I leave in favor of myself and my truest desires? Sometimes the choice ultimately boils down to whether you will choose yourself over someone else. It's not always an easy choice to make, but if you are forsaking yourself in order to be in the relationship, why are you there? Why are you settling for less than you really want and deserve? I have witnessed so many people settling for years and years, unsatisfied for huge chunks of their lives. If they are aware that they are settling and are rationalizing it, they are usually pretty sad about it.

It's hard to face the question of who you choose when you are in a long-term committed relationship, especially if you've made a vow that is "for life." So ask yourself, "Am I living fully in this relationship?" No matter what, live full-out. And know that you must be willing to give things up and be uncomfortable if you want to grow. It's an ongoing process. There is never a point when you say, "Oh, okay, awesome, I've arrived! I can just kick back and be happy now!" There is always more to discover as you grow. The challenge is to find your joy along the way.

SHOULD I STAY OR SHOULD I GO?

In building your emotional empowerment, you show up differently in all relationships. Sometimes it's hard to know if you should stay in a relationship and work on the issues it's bringing up or walk away. If you have a pattern of walking away or abandoning ship when things get hard, you might look at that before you do it yet again. If you have an attachment wound and you tend to stay in situations too long, to the point of them being unhealthy for you, then you might need to go sooner this time in order to grow.

YOU NEED SOME CRITERIA FOR DECIDING HOW LONG TO MAINTAIN RELATIONSHIPS. ASK YOURSELF:

"Am I becoming a better person because of this relationship?"
"Is this relationship supporting me and the other person to grow both as individuals and together?"
"Do I like who I am in this relationship?"
"Am I often unhappy, angry, resentful, or in pain?"
"Is it psychologically, physically, sexually, or spiritually abusive?"

You've got to be honest with yourself about what is going on and how it's impacting you. Sometimes you have to walk away and preserve yourself. Sometimes it's not only worth staying to work on things; it's the only way through what blocks you from becoming your best self.

JACQUELINE'S STORY

Jacqueline had married young and her husband was the first sexual relationship she'd ever had. She came to me just as she was turning forty, in the midst of rearranging her life post-divorce. She had two children and she needed to redefine her life and her livelihood and to open up to the relationship she wanted but had never had. We immediately began to look at the unproductive patterns she had in many of her relationships, at the ways she made herself small, put her needs last, and her inability to really go for what she wanted.

When I started my journey I was in the midst of a painful divorce that had left me bereft of my life as I knew it, but curiously free to explore myself anew. I had begun to excavate and examine myself and my life from a new perspective, and I wanted change. I wanted to grow and transform. I had a vision of the kind of woman I wanted to be—a woman who was wise, warm, a bit wanton, sexually free, joyful, and beloved. I wanted to be a woman with resonance in every part of my being! My examination revealed how discontent and unfulfilled I had been in my marriage sexually, emotionally, spiritually, and energetically.

I desired a fulfilled experience of my sexuality and of myself when I started. I was frustrated and felt like I was missing out on a vital part of life that other women experienced; a part of what it was to be a woman; a part of me that was joyful, creative, and divine but also wild and carefree. I was afraid and shy about asking for my needs to be met, especially my sexual needs. I didn't even know what my needs were. I had no defined sense of what I needed, what I wanted, or how to create it in family, relationships, professionally, and socially. I would say I was completely unfulfilled within and without. I was timid around sex and tended to avoid it or feel like I was bad at it or didn't know how to do it in the "right way."

This work blew up the idea of playing it small, hiding, feeling lack, or a sense of being denied something. It forced me to peel away my layers and get to the core of who I was and the life I had created and take responsibility for the ways I had settled for less than I wanted, deserved, or was worthy of. At the core, I had to look at how I did not feel worthy and did not love myself and as a result had accepted and created relationships in my life that supported that same kind of consciousness—friends/family/lovers who did not acknowledge my worth, did not love and honor me, and did not acknowledge the love I was giving. I remember clearly the day that Amy Jo said to me that I have to give myself all the love I want to receive if I really want to have love in my life, and that was the one thing I had never done for myself. The mirror was held up for me to really see that all the relationships in my life were reflective of how I had treated myself, and wow, was that a wakeup call!

I have become deliberate and conscious about how I want to be seen and received and how I use my sexual energy. I am deliberate and conscious about the kind of life I want to live, the kind of work I want to do, the kind of man and relationship I want to have, the quality of friendships I need to sustain me, and, more important, I have and continue to create the new world that allows me to have it all. I am more aware of how people view me and what my gifts are. I have put boundaries up that didn't exist in the places and spaces I needed them, and I have opened doors and torn down walls that were denying me the fullest and most joyful experience of myself. As I became more sexually empowered I noticed that relationships that no longer supported my highest good fell away and new relationships with all kinds of exciting people have blossomed as a result.

I would say my journey around sexual empowerment has been a

journey around really understanding myself, trusting myself, learn-
ing how to be authentic, and recognizing the power I have within. I
have embraced my curves and softened my edges. I have laid down
my sword and I am a softer, gentler, wiser version of myself. I have
stepped into the fullness of myself and my power.

Jacqueline experienced an emotional ripening that not only allowed her to show up differently in her relationships; it opened up doors in her life. She did the emotional excavation that was required so that she could truly open to being a more public figure and a powerful businesswoman.

PEOPLE SHOW YOU WHO THEY ARE

We have many convenient perceptions about people. We decide someone is a certain way and often we fight against who they are. People are who they are and where they are in terms of their limitations, and it's important to pay attention to that when creating a relationship so you avoid forming expectations they cannot meet. Total setup. This is one of the biggest mistakes people make in relationships. Trying to make someone be a person they are not never works. It only causes distress.

Maya Angelou said, "When people show you who they are, believe them."

Believe them! They tell you from the get-go who they are. They are showing you where they say yes and where they say no. They show you how they handle boundaries and how they communicate. They show you what they are capable of emotionally. They show you their clarity or lack thereof, their boundaries, and their need for control. They show you how much they are willing to be walked all over or how they stand up for themselves. They show you their patterns around anger. They show you what they will do in the name of joy and pleasure.

You can see who they are if you allow yourself to. Little things count. Don't discount the "minor" things. In the long run, those minor things add up to be major things, so it had better be what you want or, at least, what you can accept.

I was surprised at the way my partner ended our nine-year relationship, and I sat in stunned disbelief and sadness in our therapist's office. She said, "Really? Are you surprised? It makes perfect sense to me. I'm not surprised at all."

Our therapist could see it clearly, but I had gotten so used to the parts of my partner that led her to end our relationship in the avoidant way she did that I had ceased to see them and how much of a setup they would be for us both. But she was being consistent. She was a withdrawer and didn't handle most situations directly. I was controlling and sometimes too direct. Perfect imperfect match, as is often the case.

I have a ritual I really like to do when I start something with someone else, like an artistic collaboration, a project, or moving in and creating a household together. We each write down our hopes and our fears for the project or whatever it is we are creating. Then we share them and talk about them. A year after my divorce, I found the sheet of "hopes and fears" I had written with my former partner when I first moved in with her ten years prior. We had started with this ritual. We each sat and wrote our hopes and fears for living together and sharing space and then we shared them with each other. There it was, right there on my list of fears: "I'm afraid she won't speak up when something is wrong."

My stomach dropped when I saw it. I knew from the very start what was so obvious to our therapist. Of course she avoided saying what needed to be said, and her avoidance hurt me and ended up feeling like a betrayal. I had betrayed myself. But one does not think about what it will "look like in the end" when you are beginning to love and adore someone. When we were deep in our therapeutic process and teetering on the brink of survival, I remember our therapist telling me that if it was going to work I had to accept her. Ultimately I could not. I needed more. Emotional skills that include direct communication now hold top spot on my list of necessary qualities in a partner. Never underestimate how important those skills are and seek people who care about developing emotional skills.

People show you who they are all the time. Listen and check in with yourself. Is this what I want? Will this person meet my needs for this relationship, friendship, or partnership? Can I accept them now as they are?

START BY FORGIVING YOURSELF

It can be quite painful to realize how you have expressed strong emotions in ways that have hurt people you loved. As important, if not more so, is how you have hurt yourself. It's painful to dive down into your isolated hole and separate yourself from the true you that craves connection and authenticity.

An essential component in healing your harmful emotional patterns is forgiveness. You cannot continue to punish yourself for how you have behaved. You have, probably unknowingly, punished yourself and others with your unskilled emotional responses. It's time to end the cycle of punishment that keeps someone (mostly you) always having to pay for whatever it was that made you sad, angry, disconnected, and deprived.

Serious release work, letting go, and forgiveness of yourself and others are absolutely essential in order to move on and create a new way of expressing yourself emotionally and sexually. Guilt for what you've done and have not done will *not* free you from your anxiety. Shame about your behaviors will bind you even more to your pain. It is a process to shift your damaging emotional patterns. Today is a new day. You get to start fresh. You get to love yourself in a new way. You get to release the past and choose to be all of who you are in the present. You get to choose emotional craft and skill over powerlessness.

It can be hard to do this alone. You may want the assistance of a healer, coach, therapist, or women's circle to work on your forgiveness process. However it happens, I suggest you ritualize it and do it fully and wholeheartedly so that you can clear out what holds you down and set yourself on a path to develop your future relationships consciously. If you decide to ignore this part or pretend you don't need it, it will pop up again. An acknowledgment process that allows you to see where you went off track and to understand how you contributed to unhealthy emotional situations, see the lessons in them, and move wisely forward will ultimately free you.

PERSONAL FORGIVENESS PROCESS

1. Write yourself a letter of forgiveness detailing the behaviors you are sorry for: the ways you have abandoned yourself, not been true to what you really wanted, beat yourself up, your emotional inauthenticity, your defensive patterns—whatever is getting in the way of you being who you really want to be. Say everything that needs to be said and how you want to do it differently in the future.

2. You can bury the letter or burn it. You can put the letter in an envelope and send it to yourself or have a friend send it in a month or three, or some other agreed-upon time. Do whatever feels right. And then let the letter and its contents go.

3. If you've really hurt someone else with your patterns, write them a letter in the same spirit. You can give it to them, read it to them, or choose to keep it to yourself, but at least write the letter. It's the first step in taking responsibility for the parts of you that need to change. This is emotional empowerment.

CHOOSING EMOTIONAL
RESPONSIBILITY

To know you do certain unhealthy things is one thing. The question is, will you take the next step and work to change them? Few people will choose to earnestly do this work and actively behave in new ways in their relationships. It requires humility, honesty, and a laying down of arms, which means being vulnerable.

Learning to see vulnerability as a strength is a momentous perspective shift that allows us to be far more powerful in our relationships. Brené Brown says it so beautifully: "Vulnerability is the birthplace of everything we hunger for." Indeed, vulnerability is the cornerstone of both sexual confidence and deep intimacy. As we take the risk to be an open-hearted person, we can be confident because of our presence and honesty. That allows us to be more of our true selves and find the people who love and accept us for who we really are. That means we can develop deeper intimacies.

What feelings are your thoughts creating? We often feel justified in feelings of resentment, anger, vengeance, and getting even. As we justify it, our anger grows and can even turn into rage if we feed it enough. Then what? Keep feeling anger, resentment, or rage, which might seem powerful because we go into a place of superiority as we engage the story about why we are angry. But it's not powerful—it's disempowering, unconstructive, and if it's bad enough, even debilitating. If we're seeing red, it prevents us from functioning well. Reaction reinforces unproductive patterns.

In order to take emotional responsibility, make a conscious action that will allow you to work the feelings into a more productive state. You can choose different thoughts as you question the ones you are having. Oftentimes you've made up your mind in your own internal dialogue, so you leave yourself no room to expand your thoughts or be open to a totally different interpretation. As we discussed in Element 1, ask yourself, "Is this true?" You could take empowering action with those you love or whomever is a part of the situation you are upset about. If you find yourself saying, "You make me so mad," or "You made me jealous," or other similar things, question it. It places you in a victim space where someone else is responsible for your feelings. No one "makes you feel" anything. Each of us is responsible for our own feelings. We can never be fully empowered until we accept that responsibility.

PLAYING THE VICTIM

You cannot be fully empowered and be a victim at the same time. They are antithetical. We all have a victim self. That victim self believes that things happen to it that it cannot control, and it does not like to take responsibility for things. Your victim self will put responsibility on others and then complain or want pity when unwanted things happen. People create a victim state in many ways, and it prevents them from taking full responsibility for their life, emotions, and circumstances. It keeps them from overcoming adversity. Most people deny their victim self and have a hard time seeing it.

In order to become fully empowered, it's essential to stop feeding and placating your victim. It's also important not to feed the victim in other people because it really doesn't help them. You can be compassionate for things that are difficult without fueling the fire in the victim self with messages of "poor you" or by taking pity on a person. That never empowers them to change what is happening and to step up.

Examine how your victim self shows up emotionally, sexually, financially, and in other parts of your life. Where your victim is running the show, you've not stepped into your power, and there are things to unpack. Until you overcome your victim, you'll stay stuck.

LEARNING TO LOVE *YOU*

I believe the most fundamental human developmental task is to learn to love oneself fully and deeply. We often have blind spots about how much we love or don't love ourselves. We show our self-love in how we treat ourselves.

Are you kind and compassionate to yourself?

Do you forgive yourself?

Do you lovingly correct your negative behaviors and work on doing it better the next time?

Do you beat yourself up or can you let things go?

Do you plague yourself with shame and guilty feelings or do you love yourself even when you are not at your best?

Do you have a sexual relationship with yourself?

Do you engage in healthy self-care practices?

How do you show up for *you*, especially when you feel vulnerable?

If you don't express self-love, you can't possibly express it to others. A great way to identify your own blind spots is to notice your complaints about how other people treat you. These complaints give you a clue. Take a look at those same emotional patterns in yourself. You are bound to see connections. Do you complain that other people aren't there for you and yet you put others first over and over again, failing to be there for yourself? Do you complain that others don't follow through on what they said they would do for or with you and yet you don't follow through on your own commitments? These things bother you because you are actually not doing them for yourself.

If you have codependent patterns, it's important to spend some time with you, focused on loving you and practicing your own self-care. Love is active—there are many actions you can take to show yourself how much you love yourself. Can you be with yourself? Can you be alone? Can you shut off the gadgets, television, and noise, and just be with you and love you in whatever emotional space you are in? Can you be totally present with yourself? That is where true self-love spreads its wings. When you are totally happy with you, you show up as that self-fulfilled person in relationships, and it makes you an amazing person to be with.

SHOW UP AS EMOTIONALLY POWERFUL

How do we show up as emotionally powerful? Here are some ways to step it up.

Be Clean and Direct

Learn how to directly ask for what you need and desire without attachment to what the person will say. Practice asking for what you want and accepting "no" as an answer. If someone says "no" to you, a great response is one taught at Cuddle Party events: "Thank you for taking care of yourself." Removing your defensive patterns from your communication will help you to be clear and clean in your communication by stating what you want without expectation, guilt-tripping, or other kinds of manipulation. If you are not used to getting your needs met and have felt deprived in your relationships, it may be hard to remember that someone is not actually trying to deprive you. Train yourself to believe they are taking care of themselves in saying what they can or cannot do. Trust that they want to be giving to you and that when they do give, it's genuine.

Be Giving

Are you being giving in your relationships emotionally? Do you expect things from others without giving of yourself? Do you show up emotionally for people? Do you listen attentively without being out to lunch or checking your phone? Do you respond when they make requests? Do you ask what they need when they are having a hard time? Do you show up when you say you will? How do you show up? Being giving emotionally means being emotionally present and willing to go the little extra mile for the people you care about when they need support. It also includes being giving to yourself and to them by saying "no" when you need to. Your "no" honors yourself. You can still be giving by saying what things you *can* do, even if the thing they asked for is a "no" for now.

Learn to Accept Rejection

Dealing with rejection is part of life. Internalize the idea that someone's "no" indicates they are taking care of themselves, which is about *them*—not *you*. Stop seeing a "no" as a hurtful rejection and start seeing it as emotional honesty, which is far healthier than an empty or inauthentic "yes." The sooner you get over your fear of someone saying "no" to you the sooner you'll start going for the things you most want in life. It's not about you. Say, "Thank you for taking care of yourself" and move on.

Don't Go Spiraling

When a small feeling about something gets bigger, and still bigger, and turns into overwhelming emotion that overtakes you, your emotions start to run you and you can quickly spiral emotionally. You start to criticize everything. You think nothing is right. You become reactive. It's an unproductive spiral. It's dark and dank and you don't want to stay there. Learn your triggers and patterns and work earnestly on them so you can stop an emotional pattern that is a disservice to you and your relationships. Don't let yourself spiral down into an emotionally obsessive, unhealthy place that's difficult to emerge from.

Handle Your Jealousy

People often have a lot of shame around their jealousy. Yet jealousy is a common emotion. Jealousy is a sign there is something you are insecure about, oftentimes nothing more. If you begin to feel jealous, you are either insecure in yourself or insecure in the relationship. Identify which one it is so you can address your jealousy appropriately.

If you are insecure in the relationship, there may be a need to do some work to feel better in the relationship. You can make reasonable requests of the other person to compliment or validate you, to connect with you in a particular way, to show love, or to remind you of the importance of the relationship. Often just having a reconnect with the person is all that's required to let jealousy go. However, if there is a real reason for you to be jealous because the relationship is, in fact, insecure, then thank your jealousy for alerting you to address something deeper that's getting in the way of your intimacy and tackle it in a healthy way.

Handle Your Insecurity

If you are insecure in yourself, that's another story. When you feel insecure, you might need to reconnect to yourself, your own innate greatness, and your ability to create powerful intimacy. You could also ask for support or validation from your partner, friends, or family if you are having an insecure day or week, or focus on reminding yourself how much you do have in your relationships. I've witnessed people own their vulnerability in this arena on social media or by e-mail and ask for what they need. Sometimes you need to call your BFF so she can remind you of your total awesomeness.

If you are jealous of someone else, remind yourself that their existence and good qualities do not take anything away from yours. Be inspired rather than threatened by the beauty in others. No one's light needs to dim yours. It is there to uphold goodness and elevate you, not take you down. There is room and a need for all of our lights. When it comes to your own insecurities, you have choices: you can make up stories about yourself and all you are incapable of, you can decide to work on what you want to improve, or you can accept that some things are just not your strengths. But everyone has strengths and positive qualities that add value to our world. Focus on your value and strengths to get out of an insecure spiral. Feeling insecure just makes you feel bad. It does nothing to improve a situation. Recognize the stories you tell yourself based on your insecurities and ask who you would be without the story.

The Three Rs: Remind, Replace, Release

There is a simple three *R* process to help you to emotionally evolve when you are in an unhealthy emotional state. 1) *Remind* yourself to choose a different response. I say remind because, with any experience, you know what's better for you, even when you are in the thicket of emotion having a hard time seeing out. 2) *Replace* the old behavior/reaction with a new one. 3) As you try something different, you *release* the old way of being in action, thought, and feeling state.

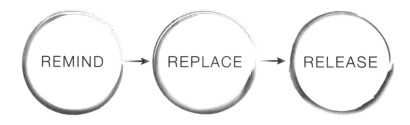

REMIND → REPLACE → RELEASE

Choosing an empowered and intentional emotional response will guide you toward a much more joyful and fulfilling emotional life. It's worth retraining yourself so you can show up as the emotionally powerful woman you are meant to be.

LIVE IN JOY, PRESENCE, AND PLEASURE

When you are fully present in yourself, you can be present with others. When you are in your pleasure, you tap into your deep joy. A woman who is on fire is in her joy and full expression—she emanates her light in the world and showers it on those around her. People are drawn to her because she is magnetic, warm, and alight. Fuel the right emotional states. Cease to give energy to the emotions that make you feel bad. Each day ask yourself, "What will bring me the most joy today?" and act on that question. Energy reproduces itself, so your joy and love can multiply. Depending where you are in your emotional development, this may feel like an enormous shift, but even little steps make a big difference. You are fully capable of taking total responsibility for your emotions. Transform your destructive patterns and become the most powerful emotional being you can be.

6

Element 4:
BODY

KNOW AND RADICALLY ACCEPT YOUR BODY

In my Women's Sexually Empowered Life Program, we spend an entire weekend on the body. I ask the women questions about how they feel about and experience their bodies, and they line up in the room along a spectrum in the place that identifies what they think and feel. Ask yourself where you currently place yourself on this spectrum:

AGREE > > > DISAGREE:

1. I like my own body.

2. I often give my body negative energy.

3. I intentionally hide parts of my body in the clothes I wear.

4. I spend a lot of time on organizing, primping, and fixing my appearance.

5. I have made decisions about relationships because of my body or my feelings about my body.

6. I have made decisions about sex because of my body or my feelings about my body.

7. My feelings about my body have restricted my choices.

8. My treatment of my body has put me in risky sexual situations.

9. It's hard to let go of how I feel about my body when I am having sex or being physically intimate with someone.

10. If I felt differently about my body, my sex life would be different.

11. If I felt differently about my body, my relationship(s) would be different.

12. A partner has said things about my body that have made me feel bad about it or have hurt my feelings.

13. Family members have said things about my body that have made me feel bad about it or have hurt my feelings.

14. If I could, I would trade in my body for a different one.

15. I am working on loving my body more.

16. I accept my body just as it is.

I remember in 2013 asking a group of women whether they agreed with those statements. As the women discussed their feelings about them, I was struck by the vast amount of energy they spent disliking, critiquing, trying to improve, or beating up on their bodies. I listened intently and took in the mass negative energy they had toward the temples in which they lived, how betrayed they felt, how dissatisfied and distraught some of them were about their magical bodies. In that moment, I realized that this is perhaps the single most effective and pervasive reason women are denied their full personal power. As I witnessed how these women—women who actually want to work on themselves—waste so much time and energy in negativity and even turmoil over their bodies, I could only imagine how much precious wasted energy women spend on this body self-hate worldwide.

PILAR'S STORY, PART 1

Pilar found me online and called me because she was about to turn forty and felt she really wanted to break through with her sexuality. She was a well-educated producer from the Caribbean who had grown up with different norms about sexuality, and she had been fortunate to work with many teachers and healers and had done a lot of personal growth work. Yet she didn't understand the full nature of her sexuality or of her body's capacity for pleasure. She had not had a lot of experience being partnered—instead she had focused on her career, being a businesswoman, and building her life in other ways. It was time to address her sexuality, and she was ready. A core part of our work was on her owning her own body, pleasure, and sexual confidence. Here's how she described it.

> *What made it hard to accept my body is that it's not the body I think I would like to have. I struggled with self-abusive thoughts about my body, thinking I was too fat, cellulite, big thighs. I had convinced myself that no one would want to be with me because I didn't have the "perfect" body. I felt a lot of shame around the fact that I didn't have the type of shape that I admired on other women. It never stopped me from having sex or being able to orgasm, but I was so abusive in my self-talk that it was destructive and punitive.*
>
> *I am normal sized, toned enough, healthy, fit, active, sexy, and attractive—but it's "not good enough" because I hate my thighs. Most of my challenges came from comparing myself to other people and wishing for something other than what I had. Logically I knew that was rubbish because I knew that I possessed my own unique*

gifts that, to be perfectly honest, I value far more than the mere
physical. But emotionally it was always a different story. It was
like I was blocked—maybe because it was something that I felt I
could not control or change—but it was a constant recurring mental
block that made me feel much shame. In fact, it is still something I
battle with every day. It's hard to let go of self-loathing because it
can bring a perverse kind of pleasure.

ACCEPTING YOUR BODY

Indeed, one of the biggest blocks holding people back from having the sexual empowerment they really desire is that they do not love or accept their body. We walk around with these critical tapes running in our minds about our bodies, putting energy into hiding our bodies, feeling desperate to improve what we cannot accept, and we hold ourselves back from living. Many women spend their lives hiding, avoiding being too close, fearing their sexuality, because they are so deeply uncomfortable and unhappy with their bodies. It is a jolting realization to think of how much of our potential we waste on things we cannot change or simply do not fully understand and how much this holds women back from our true wholeness and having the fulfilling sexual experiences we so desperately want.

What would it mean for you to break your patterns of body abuse and learn to radically accept the body you've been given with grace and gratitude so you can begin to enjoy your body in ways you didn't know (or forgot) you could? Part of radical and whole acceptance of your body, no matter your body type, age, ability, or hang-ups, is learning about how it functions so you can enjoy it and take more pleasure in it. As you take greater pleasure in your body, you build your confidence and sexual self-esteem as you discover, accept, and love the body you've been given.

It's ludicrous that body types go in and out of style like fashion.

Our bodies are our bodies. How you dress yourself up might change, but the body you have is the only one you get. You don't get to trade it in for a different one like a new car. The process of learning to love your body wholeheartedly will empower you as a sexual being. This doesn't mean it isn't fun to change and adorn our bodies. We do so in many ways. We pierce our ears and other parts, get tattoos, wear makeup, color our hair, change its style, paint nails, and build muscles because it's part of our self-expression and how we want to look. Yet it's important to make distinctions about why we do things to our bodies. Are you coloring your hair because you love the color or because you are terrified of gray hair and what it means? Do you wear makeup because you enjoy dress-up and glitter or do you refuse to leave the house bare because you are afraid of being seen without it? Are you losing weight because it makes you feel better and more healthy or because you feel ashamed? Are you obsessed with having an unattainable ideal body weight or type, or are you finding the weight and fitness level that's right for you? Ask yourself questions about why you do what you do and whether your reasons support you loving and accepting your body and your aging, or whether they contribute to more self-hatred. It's impossible not to feel pressures around our looks, but you can change your relationship to those pressures and how you respond to them.

RADICAL ACCEPTANCE VS. FIGHTING WHAT IS

The body has been made so problematic for women that it has often seemed easier to shrug it off and travel as a disembodied spirit.
—ADRIENNE RICH

Why spend your life fighting what is? You were given a beautiful body in which to live, and spending your hours, days, weeks, years directing negativity at it does not improve anything and, in fact, it can make you sick. Literally. People make themselves anorexic, develop chronic illnesses, or have recurring issues with their sexual and reproductive organs because of their body shame and hate. Direct enough negative, angry energy at your body and you will affect its cellular structure—it will respond. Not all bodies have the same capacity or ability, yet we can all learn to accept what we do have and are able to do with our bodies.

Tara Brach, author of *Radical Acceptance*, says: "Radical acceptance has two elements: It is an honest acknowledgment of what is going on inside you and a courageous willingness to be with life in the present moment, just as it is. I sometimes simplify it to 'recognizing' and 'allowing.'" To apply radical acceptance to your body means to acknowledge your feelings about your body and to be with and in your body as it is, ceasing to need it to be something else.

There are so many aspects about your body you cannot control and there are many that you can. What are the things you can actually change and what are the things you cannot change? People spend so much of their lives being angry and upset about what they cannot change. This fixation robs you of your joy.

PILAR'S STORY, PART 2

One day, Amy Jo said to me that if I knew what I was doing, could see myself doing it, and knew that it wasn't true, then why was I doing it? "That's a choice," she said, "so just stop doing it—no explanations or stories—just don't do it!" That was one hell of an aha moment for me, because I realized I was addicted to the self-abuse in some way, so I did what she said—I decided to just stop negative or abusive self-talk about my body or legs. And I also removed myself from any and all environments that encouraged or stimulated com-

parison in me. So I stopped exercising with certain friends who were very competitive, things like that. It was a liberation.

I still struggle with it, but I accept and love and embrace my body. It's curvy and sexy, and as one male friend said to me, "We need something to hold on to." So I just decided to let that old negative story go. But I also realized that in order to feel good I had to stay well with myself by being active and eating a certain way—once I'm doing that (skinny or not), then my body image is balanced and positive. So I committed a hundred percent to only doing things that I felt nurtured my body instead of punishing it and trying to force it into submission as I had done in the past—for me that means exercise and food that feels good and right to me. And it works.

Learning about my body and pleasure has impacted my sexuality as a whole. I experience much more sexual pleasure—better orgasms, more confidence, a feeling of liberation and freedom from something that had me bound in the past. I am much more open and willing to explore with partners. I am much more confident in my sexiness and am aware of how I am perceived by men—I am more willing to show my body as well.

Dissatisfaction leads to so much pain. Let's refute a few of the lies that keep us striving for an unattainable ideal and hurling negativity at our bodies, and then let's fill in some of the blanks most women have about their bodies with new knowledge.

BODY LIES THE MEDIA TELL

Many people and corporations are conspiring to make you hate your body so that you will buy their skin-care products, get yourself a tummy tuck or the latest fad surgery, and spend lots of money trying to attain the unrealistic ideal they have conjured for you. The mainstream media tells a very specific story about the bodies and sexuality of women. We should be thin. We should not have cellulite or wrinkles. We should have vaginal orgasms. We should have small, symmetrical labia. We should have shapely, round, symmetrical breasts. We should gasp and look beautiful when we orgasm (and simultaneously with our partners). We should be pretty and sexy all the time, at any cost. We should be young forever.

Let's briefly look at the story we consume and break out some real bona fide truth with these five facts.

FACT #1: NO ONE LOOKS LIKE THE WOMEN IN THE MAGAZINES, NOT EVEN THE MODELS THEMSELVES. Every woman is primped before photography to an unnatural degree, and after the photos are taken, every image is airbrushed to "flawless" perfection. No blemishes, no dimples, no cellulite, no tan lines, no wrinkles, no pores. Photos are made to look like china dolls. Women are continuously made into flat, two-dimensional beings devoid of variation. When there is variation—like a woman who is more round or curvy, more masculine, or when a photo runs in a tabloid of a real woman in a bikini with no airbrushing—she is critiqued online and by the media in cruel, disgusting ways. Her entire credibility is questioned because she is not a "perfect," flawless image of a twenty-first-century manufactured, thinly bodied, skin-perfect, feminine woman.

FACT #2: WE ARE ALL IMPACTED BY PERVASIVE MEDIA IMAGES. MEDIA LITERACY IS A REQUIREMENT. If a woman watches television programs and takes in print and online advertisements every day, how could she *not* begin to believe something is wrong with her? None of us are impervious to the influence of these redundant media images. I keep myself on a pretty strict media diet, and I think this is helpful to avoid internalizing harmful, damaging media messages. For the most part, I do not watch mainstream television, read mainstream magazines, or listen to mainstream radio. I'm sure I'd have many more hang-ups if I consumed more mainstream media. Cutting these sources of harmful messaging about *real* women out of my life assists me in keeping a more realistic view of women's bodies, aging, sexuality, possibility, diversity, and beauty. It helps me to feel good and have love for my body in all of its imperfections, not to mention the bodies of my female lovers.

I was traveling for work last year. In my hotel room I flipped through channels to see what was on. Because I do not have cable at home and rarely watch TV, I'm sort of fascinated when I do watch it. All the morning programs were on—which are ostensibly primarily viewed by women. I could not believe how many ads came on for plastic surgery, cosmetic enhancements, and products designed to help us "fix" our looks. The ads were long with testimonials from women who had done said augmentation, talking about how happy they were or how it had changed their lives. No doubt the sponsors paid premium price for that ad space.

We cannot afford to be passive recipients of our media, nor can we make the media go away. What we *can* do is choose to be critical

OBSERVING THE SELF: SPECTATORING

We are media-saturated and often the framework for our image of sex is visual media. This has impacted us so much that people often behave like they're in a movie and they adjust themselves for the best camera angles in a gross level of self-consciousness that fakes them out of the actual experience they are having. Spectatoring is watching yourself have sex rather than being fully present in the experience. You become voyeuristic in a self-critical way that restrains your pleasure, your voice, your orgasms, and your body. If you have a pattern of spectatoring, you are living sexually outside of yourself. It's time to come home and get present so you can more fully enjoy sex.

about it so we keep a realistic view of the diversity of our bodies, of aging processes, of pregnancy changes, and a more honest reality of the images and messages we are consuming. We must actively engage with our media and critique its unreal, harmful standards. And we must teach this skill to our children for their well-being. This is not negotiable. Make decisions about your own media diet. Refuse to watch programs that make you feel bad. Refuse to be a participant in this machine as much as you humanly can. Let people close to you know you are on a media diet just as you might let them know about other health or behavior changes you are working on. Ask them for support. Get the TV out of your bedroom. Throw out the old magazines. Subscribe to more empowering ones that show real women. There are many now. You will have people in your life who buy into the media madness. Set the best boundaries you can with them and refuse to participate in body hate.

FACT #3: AGING CHANGES YOUR BODY, YOUR SKIN, AND HOW YOU LOOK, NO MATTER WHAT. It's crazy that we still live in a world where we think we can avoid aging, that we can be the one who wasn't changed or impacted by age. Look in the mirror. Do you look like you looked ten years ago? Twenty? Thirty? No. Your body changes as you age. Your skin wrinkles to show how much you've laughed and frowned. Your skin relaxes and with less elasticity, you have looser skin and more cellulite. Gravity has an impact after all those upright homo sapien years. Your hands will look different. Your skin will have more freckles to show how much fun in the sun you had. And frankly, I think most women become more beautiful with age because they become wiser and more secure and at home in themselves. That is sexy. Forever young is not a reality any of us will achieve. Ever.

FACT #4: PERFECT DOES NOT EXIST. In fact, perfect is boring. Different bodies are attractive to different people. And a variety of bodies keeps our world diverse and interesting. If we all looked the same, it would be boring, and the body that was different would be the interesting one. There is no universally perfect body. Part of the irony is that it is oftentimes the things that make a woman's body womanly that we are taught to abhor or that women want to change. We have hips and curves, yet we are taught to emulate models who are too thin to have hips and curves. At its core, this is a terribly misogynist idea: get rid of what makes you womanly. Why do we call petite women a "zero"? Strive for zero? We want you to literally waste away into nothing. We are taught a dreary refrain to be smaller and more contained, yet sexuality is so big and we are meant to have huge ecstatic experiences regardless of actual body size. If you want to work toward a goal, strive to make your sexual and bodily experience as expansive as possible with every body or life phase.

FACT #5: MAINSTREAM PORNOGRAPHY DOES NOT DEPICT REAL SEX OR BODIES. There is no perfect body and there is no "standard" vulva. We all have the same genital parts and, like our faces, they vary widely in their size, shape, position, color, and composition. Because so many porn stars have had labiaplasty and other surgical augmentations of their genitals, and because they are all shaved, women have begun to believe there is a standard way their vulva should look. Mainstream porn has promoted a set of sexual norms around appearance as well as performance. The norms it sets about sexual functioning are typically that clitoral stimulation and cunnilingus are brief lead-ins to jackhammering and that women should have vaginal orgasms that are explosive. Mainstream porn has contributed to thousands of women feeling bad for needing clitoral stimulation, using vibrators, and for the way their genitals look. It's important to point out the contribution of mainstream pornography because it is ubiquitous and so many people have no other window into how other people have sex and what it actually looks like. Thankfully many women and queer people are now making feminist porn featuring real women who are paid well and depicting real orgasms. Shifts are happening.

HEALING GENITAL SHAME

All vulvas look different. The only "normal" to compare your genitals to is *your* normal. You should know what's typical for you and how yours looks, so if something is off or looks or smells different, you know to get it checked out in terms of your health. Otherwise, embracing the normal variation of genitals is essential. Women are now spending thousands of dollars to have surgeries on their genitals—cutting their labia because they think they are too big (imagine men wanting to cut down the size of their genitals!), tight-

Educate yourself about real female genitals! This is the fastest way to bust through any shame you might feel and to embrace your unique genitals.

HERE ARE SOME RECOMMENDATIONS:

… Check out Betty Dodson's vulva drawings, all drawn from real women's vulvas, at: http://dodsonandross.com /blogs/carlin/2010/05/bettys-vulva-illustrations. This whole series of drawings is also published in her classic book *Sex for One*.

… Betty Dodson's genital art gallery with photos of real people: http://dodsonandross.com/gallery/genital-art

… The book *Femalia* by Joani Blank is a collection of beautiful full-color photographs of vulvas done by various photographers.

… *Cunt Coloring Book* by Tee Corinne is also a fun way to enjoy the variety of beautiful vulva shapes in the world.

… Visit the Georgia O'Keeffe Museum in Santa Fe, New Mexico, or look at her work. Heck, just look at nature: there are vulvas everywhere.

ening the vagina to produce "more pleasure" (For whom? For male partners, not us), bleaching around the anus, and hair removal. This is madness. And it is largely because there is no knowledge of the genital diversity that is normal. I am fortunate that between my work and my personal sex life, I have seen a lot of "real" women's genitals and I am privy to this diversity. Every time I teach about female anatomy, I show images of real vulvas in order to debunk the staid ideas about what a "normal" vulva looks like. Hint: It looks like you.

CULTURAL STANDARDS

I know the cultural tide does not support what I am saying. It's like swimming upstream in a huge river into a powerful downstream current. Every time you make a little headway and start to like and enjoy your body a bit, more water is rushing at you. You grab for a root or branch to hang on to, but the rush of unrealistic expectation and pressure keeps coming.

We are deeply impacted by messages we get about our bodies from our family, community members, peers, and partners. I have heard many women talk about harmful comments from family and partners about their bodies and how that affected their sexual self-concept. For example, being told they were too thin or boyish and therefore unwomanly and unattractive, or that they were too curvaceous, big-breasted, and fat and therefore slutty. It's important to remember that your mothers, grandmothers, sisters, and aunties took in the cultural messaging too, and they often will spit it back at you without realizing how damaging it is. Notice how body talk was modeled for you in your family and with your friends. How did your close female role models relate to their bodies? What self-criticism did you hear in the women you were close to? This body talk can be toxic, and you will likely reproduce those patterns until someone

FULL-BODY LOVE RITUAL

Here is a ritual you can do in order to release some of the body negativity you have and bring in more acceptance and love.

... What body lament are you ready to end? Ask yourself what messages or expectations you are ready to let go of about your body. What would it mean to really accept your body as is? To step into that place of radical acceptance?

... Write down the messages that you have taken in about your body and how it should look, feel, perform, or function that are no longer helpful to you. Write down every thought about your body that you have internalized, every harmful message you are ready to let go of. Get it all out. Scrawl across the page.

... Read it over and acknowledge the painful ideas you've been carrying and believing. Decide to let these messages go. When you are ready, ritually burn the paper and verbally state that you are

---

breaks the cycle. Let it be you. Let it stop right here so you don't indoctrinate your own daughters and nieces into feeling distraught about their bodies. Be a healthy role model.

I believe one of the most healing actions a woman can do to love her body more is to be exposed to the true diversity of beautiful female bodies in the world. I highly recommend you give yourself the experience of being in women's spaces at some point in your life. It can be as simple as the gym or you could go to a women's festival or event. Seeing other naked bodies and the whole array of body types

releasing these ideas about your body. Watch them go up in flames.

... Then take a ritual bath or shower to rinse those ideas away. If you choose, you can prepare some mud or create a mixture of milk, honey, and flowers to anoint your body with. As you spread it onto your body, enjoy the process with great intention. Take time to anoint and then rinse. Appreciate running your hands over each part of your body in the water, and give gratitude and blessings to each part as you do. Include the scars, the stretch marks, the rolls, the blemishes. What do you appreciate or embrace about each part of your body? How will you treat it from now forward?

... Finally, when you find yourself lamenting again in the future, what will you do to snap out of it? Make a list of five to ten tools you can use to help yourself feel better and not get stuck feeling bad about your magical temple. Keep that list in a place you can easily access when you need the reminder.

that exist in reality instead of the *one* body ideal we are taught to believe is real is so healing. It is so rare that we get this opportunity to see beyond the unattainable stereotype and into what really exists in the world. There is so much gorgeous diversity, and when you actually see it and take it in, you bring different body images and expectations into your psyche. You are reminded that there is absolutely nothing wrong with you.

I'm not going to spend more time breaking down the problematic nature of the cultural push to be young, thin, waifish, light-skinned, and all of the unrealistic beauty standards. You know this intellectually. I want to focus on the empowered action you will take to create a relationship to your own body that supports your feeling good in it and making choices that are right for you. That begins with understanding your sexual body.

SELF-EXAM: TAKE A LOOK!

Women can't just see their genitals by looking down the way men can. If you have never looked closely at your own genitals or have never seen your cervix, it's a must. Get acquainted with your own body and build your understanding of it.

YOU WILL NEED: A stand-up mirror, a good desk lamp or powerful flashlight, and (optional) a speculum and some lubricant.

INSTRUCTIONS: Lean back on propped-up pillows with knees out and place the mirror where you can see your genitals. Shine the light and explore your parts. Appreciate the shapes and textures. Taste your juices. If you have a speculum and want to look inside, you'll need to lubricate the speculum bills and insert it with the handle up in order to open it. It can sometimes be challenging to find your cervix with a speculum if you've never done it before. Attending a workshop where you can do this or working with a coach who can guide you can be a powerful experience. This is one of my favorite things to teach.

RESOURCE: If you feel ready to try this, you'll find a link in the *Woman on Fire* portal for full instructions on how to do a gynecological speculum self-exam.

BONUS: Offer verbal affirmation to your sexual body parts. Thank them for all they do for you, or make a new commitment to honor or explore them.

UNDERSTANDING YOUR
SEXUAL BODY IS ESSENTIAL

"Do you want to see your own cervix?" asked the midwife. I was on the table with my feet in mitten-covered stirrups. "Really? I can see it? Yes, I want to see!"

The nurse-midwife handed me a small mirror and shined the light into my vagina. I reached between my splayed knees with the mirror in my hand and there in the reflection was my glorious, previously unfamiliar cervix. It was right there, and I could see it clearly with my own eyes. No longer a myth I believed because I was told it was there, I had proof. I was seeing it myself. It would no longer be a mysterious yet important part of my body. I would get to know it and understand it intimately for the first time. No more trips to the GYN because I "lost" a condom in my vagina. I would know my vagina inside and out.

I remember how happy I was leaving that GYN appointment, displaying the pride of a twenty-five-year-old woman who knew the inner workings of her own body, of a woman no longer in the dark—and a cervix reserved not for the viewing of doctors and other "authorities of the body," but one whose owner had reclaimed her sovereign agency over her body. It was a huge moment in my own sexual empowerment, where the mysteries of my vagina lost their power over me, and I relocated that power inside with my newfound knowledge. That midwife did me the biggest service by offering me that mirror, so I could feel empowered as the wise owner of the body that was being examined.

However you learn about your body, it's some of the most critical and awe-inspiring information you will ever take in. Your sexual parts are an amazing nexus of shapes, structures, fluids, nerves, neural pathways, chemicals, hormones, muscles, and organs. To discuss it all is beyond the scope of this book, but I want to share some of the most important aspects of your sexual body, and I encourage you to forge your own expedition to really know and fully appreciate your sexual body and its capabilities.

SANDY'S STORY, PART 1

In her early forties, Sandy came to me in a lot of pain around her sexuality. She had struggled with her history of childhood sexual abuse her whole life. She experienced pain with penetrative sex and, on top of that, had recurring health issues that made it hard to have a fulfilling sex life and maintain a long-term relationship. She could orgasm without penetration but regularly experienced pain after orgasm through half of each month. She avoided sex because of the physical and emotional pain it brought her. She really wanted to heal and break through around sex and her body, and she feared that she was sexually broken and somehow unfixable. She very much wanted to have a lover with whom she could feel pleasure, insisting that it would help her feel "normal."

*I had no sexual voice. Because **incest was my introduction to sex**, I never learned where I ended and another began. Intercourse was painful. I had seen over twenty gynecologists and they couldn't figure out what was wrong. I was never taught that I had my own personal map of pleasure to explore that had nothing to do with pleasing another. Porn has done such an incredible disservice to women. I can't be banged like what I see in porn. And I had no other ideas of what sex was like, because women's erotica made sex—with waves and waves of orgasm, taking someone deeper and deeper into a woman's body—pretty puzzling too.*

I thought that somehow I would find someone who loved me enough that I would just change, even as I worked so hard to change to feel "normal." I wasn't "desperate for a man." I was desperate for guideposts of normalcy: that I could be loved and "keep" a loving relationship like those all around me seemed to have. I treated any potential boyfriend as the last possible chance for a relationship; the Last Man on Earth. This put enormous pressure on me to perform, in and out of the bedroom. In fact, I was usually much happier alone. It was a break from trying to get "it" right.

Here I was, an accomplished woman, with years of therapy under my belt, never having been shown or told that my shame was pervasive and that no one could change that but myself. It felt like Amy Jo kept downplaying my trauma history. It took a while for me to see that to really be the full sexual being I wanted to be, I couldn't hold on to my protective label of incest survivor. Amy Jo deftly led me to what was on the other side of shame, to see and feel myself beyond the painful sexual experiences that had handicapped me. That, no matter the story, it's still just a story, one that I can write as I moved forward. Without additional sexual referencing or ever trying anything new, there would have been no new story to write without Amy Jo's tutelage. I could continue to hide under my label of childhood sexual abuse survivor and protect myself in fear or face the fears of intimacy that all others have to face too.

One of the biggest fears I carried was to be a terrible lover because I so often experienced pain through penetration. Even once I got my pelvic problems in order and understood what aroused me, I was still entrenched in a need to please a lover.

I will never forget the day I got an ecstatic e-mail from Sandy telling me she'd had a coital orgasm. She felt like she was in on the secret that had been kept from her her whole life. She hadn't thought it would ever happen for her, and when it did, her agency over her body shifted and her belief that she could heal and that she could actually enjoy sex grew. She learned how to have sex that wasn't painful, and she slowly continued to explore with her new lover what worked and what didn't work for her body.

DEMYSTIFYING
FEMALE SEX ORGANS

There has been a long debate about the importance of the vagina vs. the clitoris in women's pleasure and which organ is the center of our pleasureverse. Let's assume they both win and treat them both as important. Most women derive pleasure from both in varying degrees and cocktails of effects. Your vagina is the actual canal, the orifice, the opening into your body at the core of your labia. Your clitoris is a series of erectile structures that sit above and to the sides of the vagina, framing the vulva, if you will. Most people know it as that little button that can peer out from beneath its hood that when touched just right makes women go wild. The clitoris is far more complex than this reductive myth and so is the pleasure-inducing activity that will make you feel so good.

Most of us get limited education about our sexual anatomy in school. I sure did. I'm now an anatomy geek, so let's discuss the many pleasure-providing structures that are a part of your sexual organs.

Your Vulva

Your vulva refers to the collection of structures that make up your external genitalia. You have inner labia, which are hairless, and outer labia where hair grows. Often called labia minora and majora (minor and major lips), this is a misnomer because many women's "minor" labia are more major than their "major" labia. Any part of the body without hair is a more sensitive part, so the inner labia can be particularly sensitive. Some women are insecure about having large inner labia, yet this is an important sexual structure. Imagine men feeling self-conscious because of an extra-large penis. That would seem crazy. This gender double standard is mind-numbing. If you have larger inner labia, they are part of your version of "normal" and they are highly sensitive, so enjoy them!

Your Vulva

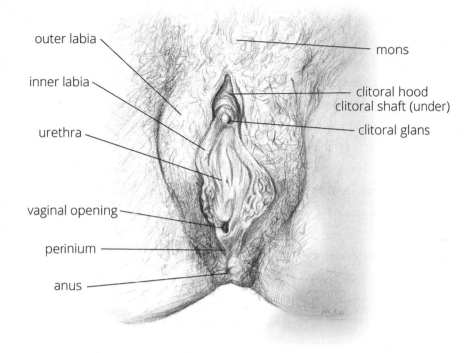

outer labia

mons

inner labia

clitoral hood
clitoral shaft (under)

urethra

clitoral glans

vaginal opening

perinium

anus

Your labia enclose like petals or wings around the opening to the urethra (where you urinate from) and the opening of your vagina. They can be many shades of pink, red, purple, or brown, and their shapes and thickness vary greatly. Some are paper-thin and some are quite plump. Asymmetry in the labia is common. At the top of the labia is the clitoral glans and shaft and its other structures are inside and unseen.

Sometimes just stroking and massaging the outside of the vulva is a good way to bring blood flow into the genitals and build arousal. There are two vestibular bulbs underneath the outer labia, which are plump spongy tissue and part of your erectile structures. When stimulated, they will fill with blood, plumping up the labia and the whole vulva. You can explore different kinds of massage and touch and see what feels good for you. Play with pressure. Pressure against the vulva stimulates the organs within and under it. And be sure to look in the mirror before, during, and after arousal so you can learn how your genitals change with arousal.

Your Clitoris

With somewhere between six and eight thousand nerve endings, the clitoris is clearly an important and central part of your pleasure. In fact, it's the only organ with a sole purpose of pleasure in the male or female body. Your clitoris has many parts: the head or glans, which is the part you see, connects to the shaft that runs vertically above it, and there are two crura, or legs, that flank both sides of your vulva. All of these structures are erectile tissue, which means that when you are aroused, they fill with blood and become erect, in the same way a penis becomes erect. You don't see your erection in quite the same way, as it is more subtle and internal.

Your Erectile Tissue

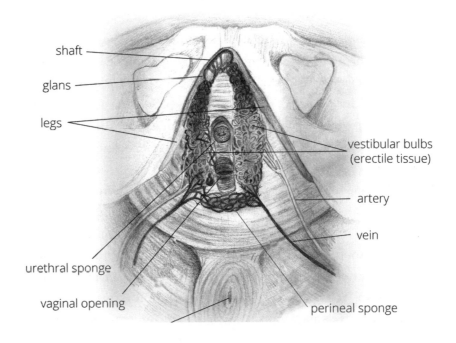

shaft

glans

legs

vestibular bulbs (erectile tissue)

artery

vein

urethral sponge

vaginal opening

perineal sponge

What you will notice is that your vulva gets plumper and it will become richer in color (deeper reds, purples, and browns) as you get an erection. Your clitoral glans will pull back farther underneath its hood and won't be as visible when you are erect, unlike the penis, which becomes more pronounced.

There are many ways to explore your clitoris. You can apply pressure directly to the glans, above it on the shaft, or more indirectly via the inner labia, which are attached to the glans or hood at their upper tips. Some women need to be aroused a bit before the clitoris is directly touched or touched with much pressure because it's so sensitive. Some like light, feathery touch, some like more firm touch. Sometimes using fingertips will be satisfying, sometimes larger surface area of flats of fingers or palm works better. Play with speed and hand position. Many women use vibrators because of their consistent stimulation, and oral sex is a great way for many women to experience pleasure on their clitoris. We generally need consistent motion and technique to get to a heightened state of arousal. Some women feel pressure about how much time they take to become aroused or to climax. There is no need to feel bad about taking time—it's perfectly normal, and it takes as long as it takes. Letting go of the "I take too long" story will free you tremendously so you can have more pleasure and be more present sexually.

Your Vagina

There has been much debate about whether the vagina has many nerve endings and how much of a sexual organ it is because the idea of the "vaginal orgasm" was touted as superior to "clitoral orgasms" by Freud. We know the clitoris is deftly important to women's pleasure because it is a tremendous pleasure center and there is a concentration of thousands of nerves there. Many feminists have framed it as superior to the vagina in order to express its importance in the power of pleasure and to shift women's pleasure away from being in service to male sexuality and pleasure. Yet there is no doubt that the vagina is also important and is a pleasure epicenter for many women.

The opening to the vagina can be sensitive and looks different on every woman. It sometimes resembles a mouth or a flower with petals, or it can have a variety of shapes in the tissue. The vagina is muscular and is lined with sensitive mucous membranes that are soft to the touch. The vaginal walls provide some fluid for lubrication and will engorge during arousal. The opening tends to be tighter, and the inside of the vagina can change and open dramatically when a woman is aroused to accommodate penetration by fingers, a penis, a toy, or a hand.

Many women love the feeling of being penetrated, of a thrusting motion inside of them, or of being filled. There is an emotional vulnerability in being penetrated that a person knows intimately if they've had the experience. You are inviting someone else into your body, and that is more significant than most people acknowledge. And so many women have had it "taken" from them that they feel intensely vulnerable to a point where it's hard to surrender to the pleasure of penetration.

In exploring what works for you, consider how much you want inside of you (from just a finger to a large penis or hand), the depth that feels good, the angle, and the pressure. Some women really like pressure against their cervix internally and others do not like it. Some like pressure toward the upper wall (where the G-spot is) and some don't. Some like the friction of a lot of in-and-out movement and some like smaller motion that results in less friction. The intensely hard thrusting that is so common in porn is one way some people like intercourse, but it is not a standard for women's pleasure. There isn't a right or wrong way to have intercourse. The erectile tissue of the vestibular bulbs and the clitoral legs that flank the vagina are part of what make the in-and-out motion of penetration feel so good, because they plump up as they get erect, become more sensitive, and are stimulated by the movement.

If you've never penetrated yourself, try it. If other people are going to be invited there, why not have the experience yourself? The inside of a vagina feels amazing to the touch: it is a lush "rubyfruit jungle" that deserves appreciation and exploration. Fingers can be particularly good because they are adept and can crook to varying angles and can grow in size by just adding another. You might like different things on different days. There is not one way to enjoy it.

Your Muscles

You've got a tremendous muscular system in your pelvis that makes everything work better and feel better. Most people have heard that they should exercise their PC muscle or do their "Kegels." But what

Your Muscles

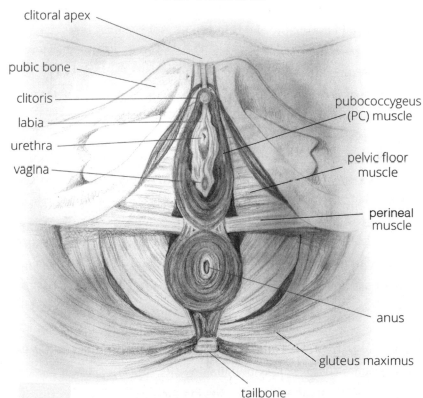

clitoral apex

pubic bone

clitoris

labia

urethra

vagina

pubococcygeus (PC) muscle

pelvic floor muscle

perineal muscle

anus

gluteus maximus

tailbone

are we really talking about? Underneath the exterior genitals are layers of muscle. How else would women be able to push babies out of their vaginas? The PC, or pubococcygeus muscle, attaches at the pubic bone near the clitoral apex and runs underneath the labia around the urethra and vagina, around the anus, and attaches at the coccyx (tailbone) in the back. It's like a sling that holds the whole pelvic bowl in place. There is a muscle that runs straight across the perineum at the base of the vagina separating it from the anus. And underneath all of that is the entire pelvic floor muscle, which forms the foundation.

Strengthening these muscles impacts your pleasure. The stronger they are, the more they do for you. You can do this by tightening them like you would to hold in urine and then releasing. Do at least twenty repetitions a day—anytime, anywhere—and it will have a positive effect on your experience of pleasure; it will also make birth easier if you have a child and help you to avoid urinary incontinence as you age. You can also practice isolating parts of the muscles (a more advanced trick).

Because these muscles line the vagina on both sides, playing with contracting them and releasing them when you are engaged in intercourse or other penetration can improve your pleasure, and your partner might also enjoy it during intercourse. When you insert a finger in your vagina, play with contracting your muscles and see how it feels around your finger. Many women's experience of orgasm and pleasure extends to the muscles in their legs and feet. When having an orgasm some women need to have their thighs tight and clenched or like to push against something because the pelvic and leg muscles are connected.

The "Me-Spot"

A few years ago I was talking with the participants in my women's sexual empowerment program about the G-spot—which was named after the guy who was the first physician to discover and describe it:

Mr. Gräfenberg. (I'm sure many women before him had discovered it themselves.) I told them I thought it should have a new name, because it's not about some guy's discovery—it's an integral part of a woman's body. They came up with a new name we all liked: "The Me-Spot."

The Me-Spot is not actually a spot at all—it's a structure. There is an spongy, erectile tissue that surrounds the urethra. It protects the sensitive urethra from too much pressure and, as with all of your erectile tissue, it also engorges with blood when you are aroused, which can provide a lot of pleasure. The urethra is parallel to the front wall of the vagina, so you can feel it through the wall if you insert a finger and crook it toward the front of your body. Stimulating this part of the vagina can often lead to ejaculation or "squirting" because there are fluid-filled glands within the urethral sponge that, if stimulated enough, will result in a gush of fluid for many women. This is normal, and if you squirt, just use extra towels or get waterproof sheets so you can enjoy yourself without feeling embarrassed and making yourself hold back. We rarely hear of men holding back ejaculate for fear of embarrassment. Why should women?

Ejaculation

Studies have been done in order to figure out just what this "female ejaculate" is made of. A recent pop science headline stated a myth that even the research didn't state: "Study Concludes That Women Who Squirt During Sex Are Actually Peeing." Nope. The research actually says urine is "indicated," along with prostatic fluid. Yep, female bodies make that too.

Sex educator and nurse-midwife Sheri Winston proposes that female ejaculation is antimicrobial and designed to keep potential infection-producing agents out of the urethra. Given that women often get UTIs (urinary tract infections) from sex, it makes a whole lot of sense that our bodies would have a function to prevent infections that can cause potentially dangerous kidney and full-body infections. Where's the research on that? It's a really good research question. Our bodies have amazing ways of building immunity. Women have been reporting ejaculation, and indeed it has been documented for millennia in old Chinese texts, the *Kama Sutra*, and by Aristotle. It's not new and it's not a myth. Ask any woman who experiences it. Yet some folks avidly try to discredit ejaculate among women.

Regardless of the content of the fluid, which does contain prostatic fluid from the paraurethral or Skene's glands, it results from a sexual event. Calling it "bed-wetting" or attempting to shame women because it contains urine is totally dismissive of the arousal that creates it. Amy Luna Manderino of the Sex Evolution proposes we call it an "orgasmic flush." This highlights the fact that sexual arousal produces the fluid. And since urine is primarily water, of course our bodies would use that to flush out what it doesn't want. It is likely that ejaculation has a function, as Winston purports.

If it feels good, let loose and enjoy your orgasm. I know that my orgasms that include ejaculation tend to be pretty powerful. I would not want you to miss that because of unnecessary embarrassment. And if you don't ejaculate, there is nothing wrong with you. Not everyone does, and you can still have incredible orgasmic capacity sans squirting.

Your Fluids

People are often confused about where all the fluid comes from. Women emit it from three different places. Much of our lubrication comes from the vaginal walls—sometimes called "vaginal sweating" in textbooks. Not a very sexy way of describing it. The vulvovaginal (Bartholin's) glands produce some of this fluid. Second is the ejaculatory fluid I just discussed, which comes from the paraurethral glands in the urethra sponge and the urethra itself, often via stimulation of the Me-Spot. And third, we get some of our fluid from the cervix—often called "cervical mucus" (so not sexy). That's the fluid you often see in your underwear.

The cervix releases fluid that differs at varying points in the menstrual cycle for women who are premenopausal. It goes from menstrual blood to a more slick, clear fluid that becomes sticky and gooey during ovulation to a more milky fluid toward the end of the cycle. As women age, there will be less copious fluids and this can be distressing for some women. Knowing what is normal for you by paying attention to your body is important in each phase of life so that you'll notice when or if something smells or looks different or is out of whack. You are the best gauge for that because women have different amounts of fluid—some are juicy all the time, some less so. Your fluids have natural smells that tend toward musky, and that scent is part of your sexuality—it's your sexual scent. It's part of what your lovers are attracted to and what draws you to people you find attractive.

Using your fluid as a measure of your excitement and arousal is not an accurate gauge. You might be really juicy but not turned on or ready for any kind of penetration—yet women's partners will often take it as such. Or you might feel fairly dry and yet be super-charged-up. Only you know when you are willing and wanting. You've got to communicate that to your partners. And even with a copious amount of natural fluids, most women will need a bottle of lube at the ready to make clitoral stimulation and vaginal penetration comfortable. All lubes are different: some are stickier, some taste better than others, some dry up faster. Explore a variety of lubricants, and when you find a brand you like, buy a large bottle of it. Essential!

Your Anus

Your anus is a part of your sexual organs. It is connected to all of that intricate spongy and erectile tissue, and it is highly innervated.

You have a perineal sponge that can be found between the vagina and the anus that gets plump like the other spongy tissues, and the PC muscle wraps around the anus, so it is all connected. The anal opening is particularly sensitive and often provides a lot of pleasure during oral stimulation (analingus) or manual stimulation. Many people of all genders like anal penetration from a finger or something larger that creates a full feeling, because the anus is supersensitive. Some women like to have both vagina and anus penetrated simultaneously in order to experience the most heightened pleasure.

Many people have issues with playing with the anus because they get anxiety about fecal matter. You can use latex or nonlatex gloves (I like the sexy black ones) or finger condoms if that is a concern. Some people use enemas prior to anal play to clean out the rectum. You always want to wash up and be careful not to get fecal matter under the nails and then introduce it into the vagina or other parts of the anatomy that will react to it. You could get a bacterial yeast infection (itchy!). The other thing to be aware of is that the anus is not as stretchy as the vagina and the sensitive tissue can tear more easily. Two words: use lube.

Exploring the anus can open up whole new levels of vulnerability, pleasure, and orgasmic capacity for people of all genders. I recommend you include your anus in your self-exam and/or self-pleasure sessions.

Your Uterus and Cervix

Your uterus and cervix both play active parts in your sexual arousal and pleasure. Often treated as passive organs that wait to be probed by active egg-seeking sperm, they play an integral role in helping sperm and in "natural selection."

The uterus is a muscular organ that swells with blood when you are aroused. The cervix is the lower opening into the uterus—the part that comes down into the vagina. When aroused, the uterus and cervix pull up and back to allow more space in the vagina. This has been called vaginal tenting or ballooning. The vaginal walls are rugae tissue (wrinkly or ridged), which can expand and elongate during arousal to accommodate more. The uterus and cervix assist that elongation. They also change with the menstrual cycle, moving farther back in the body during ovulation and then dropping down low during menstruation.

Many people joke about the stereotype of sex being more connected to love for women and yet the physical body aligns with this idea energetically. The uterus is partially held into place by two major round ligaments, which attach the uterus right into the muscle fascia under the labia. There are also two major arteries and nerves that attach from the top of the uterus right up to the heart. So the heart, uterus, and genitals are all directly connected.

Many women feel the uterus contract and move in the body during orgasm and there is no doubt the uterus plays a role in pleasure. Yet medical authorities often act as if it is a useless organ if a female patient won't be having any (or any more) children and will often routinely recommend a hysterectomy even in cases where other interventions could work. Ask questions of your health care providers. Don't take their word at face value, get more than one opinion, and do your research. Women have had many disempowering experiences with doctors who are not thinking about repercussions on sexual pleasure because medicine has never been very concerned with female sexual functioning and pleasure, except to make money. You will have to make it important—don't rely on your medical providers to do so.

Your Nervous System

Sex educators often joke about how important the brain is for arousal, and it is indeed a critical part of sexual excitement, pleasure, and orgasm. The brain is directly connected to the genitals through the autonomic nervous system and two major nerve networks: the pudendal nerve and the pelvic nerve.

You have a unique, wildly intricate network of nerves that attach to the brain and spine and connect to the genitals and reproductive organs. Each person has her own unique combination of nerves, and there are nerve bundles in the clitoris, vagina, cervix, perineum, and anus. Some people might have more active nerve networks in some parts than in others, which is why our preferred erotic sensations vary so much. One woman might love action on her cervix, while another barely feels her cervix. Some women will orgasm from vaginal penetration, while others won't. Some will really respond to anal or clitoral stimulation and others will respond less. The depth of the nerves also plays a role. For some women, the nerves are deeper in the body tissue, and for others, the nerves are closer to the surface and easier to access. Different parts of the brain are activated when different structures are stimulated, which means pleasure sensations and orgasm can vary widely.

There is a feedback loop between the vagina and the brain. The autonomic system activates respiration, lubrication, and heart rate, which can cause engorgement, muscular contraction, and orgasm. Many chemicals are firing in the brain and are involved in this whole feedback loop. When your conscious mind quiets, you can experience more of the juicy expression that this system produces, including heightened pleasure.

SANDY'S STORY, PART 2

As Sandy saw that she could enjoy sex, could orgasm more easily, and that she was not the "hopeless" case she had feared, I worked with her to take it slow and to experiment and discover what she actually wanted and to ask for it.

Things started to change over twenty-five years in, when I finally learned that sexuality is whatever I want it to be. I say, never give up on sex. I got answers to my multiple pelvic problems. The other mystery uncovered was that I still rushed my experiences! Amy Jo reminded me of one of the most important sexual basics: be very aroused before penetration. Doctors and books would say the same, but she led me to discover for myself what "ready arousal" actually felt like. The original pain caused anticipation of pain—bracing myself for penetration—and I was a mess of shame as a "sexually dysfunctional" woman because I only understood arousal from movies where the female antagonist rips off her clothes and mounts or gets mounted in the next breath.

My current lover and I explore and take our time. I may or may not desire penetration, and I've learned my body, so I know when I'm actually ready. A part of my partner's excitement is never knowing what's on our menu. I think a lot of heterosexual women have avoidance patterns like I had because they don't always want to go to intercourse and can't fully articulate to themselves and their partners that they have other desires.

Expressing my voice through sex opened a world to the wholeness I was seeking. One thing I learned is to touch my lover for my pleasure. That was a big game changer. I had the basic sexual skills in knowing anatomically the best spots and moves for men. But I was an automaton, concerned with getting him off, cutting off myself from the experience. Now I explore a body for my own enjoyment. If he wants to make requests (since I now know I'm not ever doing something "incorrectly"), he can, and I'll give it a go. Every single body is different, and it's now fun for me, rather than pressure-filled, to discover who likes what and how. Concerning ourselves with the other's pleasure rather than discovering it for ourselves is the buzz-kill. By having fun exploring another's body, I finally understood how amazing my aroused body is to a lover. My confidence soared after this discovery. Whereas before, I often felt used and broken because I didn't connect to the arousal that was happening between us since I was only concerned with getting another off and staving off my pain. I still experience pain after orgasm in my menstrual cycle (and know when to avoid orgasm), but look at all of what my body can experience!

Once I really took charge of choosing what I wanted, I now could "go further" than I had imagined. I finally feel safe and excited now that my sexual model has penetration as a side dish rather than the main course. If I have a partner who can't expand his view of sex beyond penetration or orgasm through penetration as the sole goal, he likely won't be my partner for long. I still have to remind myself not to push for anything, like orgasm, because then I get caught in my head and short-circuit and nothing happens. I like to concentrate on pleasure in my body and connecting to another, and if "more" happens, great. But no goals.

I was healed of much of my physical pain, but my true empowerment came when I took the reins and voiced first to myself, and then aloud, what I wanted to experience. It was a powerful barrier that hid me from my true self, but once broken was freeing for all other aspects of myself.

THE ELUSIVE FEMALE ORGASM

An alarming number of women still do not know how to have orgasms. As my mentor Betty Dodson likes to say, it's not that they are "inorgasmic," it's that they are "pre-orgasmic"—they just haven't learned how *yet*. Our bodies are widely different, have a huge range of potential, and there are numerous reasons why someone might have a hard time climaxing. One of the biggest is the lack of comprehensive information that is still so pervasive about female sexuality and pleasure.

For a woman who has never had an orgasm, to finally bust through the barriers and experience that level of pleasure can change her entire outlook about sex and her sexuality. It is not a small thing. When women experience pleasure and bliss on a regular basis and gain the confidence that comes from knowing their own bodies and how to have orgasms, they become empowered in every other part of their life. The world looks a little brighter and more possibility opens up. They become more at home in their bodies, or "embodied," and that body presence is part of how they walk, talk, and interact with the world. No longer feeling like there is some secret being kept from them, women tend to feel a sense of internal agency and power that shines with self sexual knowledge. Few talk about that because we tend not to talk about such things, but that doesn't diminish how profound it is. Women of all sizes and shapes who walk with confidence are sexy. Your body type doesn't matter when you exude confidence and pleasure in your temple.

If you are ready to experience more pleasure, you have to learn how your body works and what makes you come to orgasm. Many women wait, thinking their partners will figure it out or be able to "give" them an orgasm. Let there be no more waiting. It's about you figuring out what the orgasm is about for you, what needs to happen, how you like to be touched, and how much time you take. It takes as long as it takes, and the way you like it and the way you are wired for it will be as individual as you are. You've got to crack the code and then translate it to your lovers. That's where the communication skills are going to come into full effect so you can really get what you want.

For lots of tips on how to explore your body, I suggest you read my first book, *Lesbian Sex Secrets for Men*, coauthored by Kurt Brungardt (originally written under my nickname "Jamie"). We just published the second edition.

EXPLORE, EXPLORE, EXPLORE

Your discovery of your body is an ongoing expedition. Enjoy this journey. As you learn more and more about what is pleasurable, what your parts look like, feel like, taste like, and do, you become expertly acquainted with your own capacity for pleasure and the magic of your body. Feeling adept gives you confidence, and confidence helps you enjoy your body and sex more. As you age and your body changes, you want to build your relationship with your body and continue to be curious about it like you would a lover. Discovery can be endless, and it enriches your enjoyment of life.

It is essential for your own sexual empowerment that you absolutely learn to love and accept your body. Your body is the temple you live in every day; it holds your spirit and allows you to experience unbelievable things. Why would you abuse your own temple? Your body is a miraculous system capable of feeling and experiencing immense pleasure. Getting rid of all negativity about your body, remembering to breathe, eating good food, exercising, living in pleasure, and enjoying moving and loving your body every day are keys to becoming more embodied and healthy in your body love. Stand in front of the mirror and appreciate your body. Touch the parts you've been meanest to and apologize—embrace those parts in their seeming imperfections. The reprogramming might be an ongoing activity. Do whatever it takes, for you need this body to feel alive and vibrant. When was the last time you thanked it for all it does for you? It gives you so much every day.

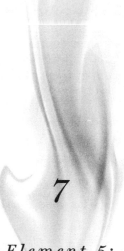

7

Element 5:
DESIRE

ACTIVATE DESIRE AND CREATE
A SEXUAL PRACTICE

Desire is a fundamental part of sexuality, and of life itself. You wouldn't get out of bed each morning without a desire moving inside you. Your desire propels you toward your life, toward living, toward relating, toward creating. Your desire guides you and drives you to grow. It calls you toward action with the promise of being bigger, having more, and experiencing life more fully. Sex can be shockingly transformational when you fully move into desire and see your desire all the way through. That momentous shift is life-altering, as the exchange of life energy is enormous and abundant, whether it is with another person or between you and life itself.

Some spiritual traditions teach that a state of non-desire is what we should strive for, that detaching from earthly desire is what is most spiritual, most elevated, most desirable. People tend to have a lot of guilt and baggage about desire. *"Should I really want this?" "I don't deserve that." "If I desire things in this physical world, I must not be spiritual enough." "Having sexual desire is bad."*

Depending on your upbringing, you may have been taught that certain kinds of desires are wrong. Your family, religion, parochial schools, caretakers, doctors, therapists, or other authority figures may have taught you many rules about how to feel sexually, how to express your sexuality, and who to be as a sexual person. Your peers also may have had strong beliefs, misconceptions, or even myths that they spoke as hard truths that you believed, causing you to feel shamed, isolated, or bad about yourself or your desires.

I believe that if we are going anywhere in our lives, we must be in a natural state of human desire. There is nothing undivine in desire. Just the opposite. Desire is challenging when we are never satisfied with anything we get and we're constantly off searching for the next greatest thing. Feeling desire does not have to mean unhappiness with where you are or what you already have. So the question may be "Can you simultaneously experience desire and gratitude for all you have?"

If you are striving to do something with your life, to create something, to feel good, to improve your relationships, to grow, to be happy, or to connect to your higher self, you are in a state of desire. You are here to create something. You were born to be creative. There is a natural state of desire in your wanting to create. Sexually, desire reminds us of our ability to feel, to connect. Desire fuels flirtation, seduction, and good sex. Desire moves us to engage in good conversation and other forms of friendly intercourse.

Desire is divine. Desire is rich. Desire—if it comes from a healthy place—guides you toward the wholeness you seek. You are already whole; your desire just reawakens the dormant parts that you think are missing but may just be asleep. You would not have desire without being capable of fulfilling it.

WHEN DESIRE BECOMES CATASTROPHIC

I delivered my first TEDx Talk, "Owning Your Sexual Power," in Napa Valley in 2014. On the break, I had lively conversations with people about how they would parent their kids differently and how my talk gave them a new perspective on sexuality and its importance. One woman wanted to engage me in the idea of desire after hearing me talk about how I want to live in a world where we are each guided by our own internal desires.

She got really stuck on the idea of unfettered desire. She said, "I agree with what you said—but that desire part, I don't know about. How can you say that desire is good? If we encourage people to follow their desires, what about pedophiles? You didn't talk enough about that. I needed to hear more about that. I just can't accept desire as blanketly good."

I responded, "What you're talking about is a dysfunctional desire. If you desire something that will harm another person, harm yourself, or take away someone's freedom, it's dysfunctional. I'm talking about people connecting to their authentic, healthy desires—allowing themselves to follow those desires and not judge them as bad. I'm talking about healthy desire that will create more life for you and for others, desire that connects you to your creative sexual self."

Should I have not mentioned desire at all? No. Desire was important to mention regardless of the discomfort it inevitably brings up in some people. So why did she go to the worst-case scenario about desire? The question wasn't "What if I desire someone who isn't my husband?" or "What if the thing that I want makes someone else uncomfortable?" but literally the worst thing imaginable for most people. Catastrophic desire.

Just bringing up the idea of desire at all puts fear in many people. To really give people permission to identify their desire and to follow it brings up so many "what ifs?" that people will abandon the idea altogether and stay right where they are with desire: not feeling it, not acknowledging it, not going for it, denying it, judging it as not okay, suppressing it, or being frustrated by it. There is a built-in fear that people just won't be able to handle desire.

In my experience, people are in a lot of pain about desire—especially women. Many people believe deep down that they'll never have their true desires, so they avoid going for their desires at all. They avert the inevitable disappointment of an unrequited desire, and so they stay in "not enough." That's not the way to really live passionately, full-out, all-in. Many women do not know what they desire sexually, and this confusion causes them distress.

MICHELLE'S STORY, PART 1

When Michelle, a thirty-three-year-old designer and entrepreneur from Ohio, first came to me, she knew she had some sexual trauma to work through and that there was something about her sexuality that was holding her back, but she didn't quite understand what it was. She was frustrated in her sexuality and in her marriage. When she talks about where she was then, she says

I was afraid of the power and themes in my sexual voice. I thought I needed to control all that in order to be a professional and to sort out past traumas. I found out that I was just suppressing my desire. I told myself that sex was bad, and that exploring sexuality was

bad, I felt really conflicted in my story and couldn't understand what to do with my desire.

Michelle worked with me as a private client over the course of six months and attended one of my weekend workshops, where she had some profound shifts. I could feel the tightness she felt around sexuality, and yet she was committed and open to doing this radical work on herself so she could free herself in her marriage as well as in her business and the greater whole of her life. She had squashed any desire she ever might have felt.

I needed to release control. I was mitigating my whole life. I did not know how to handle my desires or how to integrate them into my life. They seemed incongruent with where I was in my reality. I needed to go to Al-Anon and to see how the alcoholic patterns around me were contributing to the way I was stuffing my desires away and controlling my life. I needed to release all the ways that I was giving my power away and not making decisions for myself. I felt really insecure and ashamed of who I was and how I was being, but I couldn't find a way out.

EMERGING DESIRE

Ideas like desire and sexual power scare people because we haven't done a great job of addressing them for the big, complex, and important things they are to us. When women are not tapped into their true desires or find it hard to allow those desires to emerge, it creates a blockage—not just sexually but in many areas of life.

For yourself, start by noticing whether you do the same thing as the woman at TEDx did, even in small ways. Does talking about desire make you uncomfortable? Do you sometimes repress the desires that well up in you? Do you go to the catastrophic worst-case scenario—thinking of all the ways your desire will be hurtful or shameful? Or can you see how desire opens up and expands your sexuality and your life?

I think many people have knee-jerk reactions because desire isn't safe. But neither is life. And it's not meant to be. If you spend your life trying to stay safe, you'll never take risks—and to live true desire means taking some risks. It's a built-in function of desire. To strive for more than you have ever had or have ever been, you've got to release who you were before. Are you willing to release that, truly and totally?

I believe that a world where people are guided by their own internal desires to be more, have more, and do something bigger and more expansive—sexually or otherwise—is a better world. It's so easy to go to the worst-case scenario. So let's not confuse it. It's healthy to strive for more. Life creates more life. Energy creates more energy. Ecstasy begets more ecstasy. Desire propels us to create what we are here to create.

A CONFLICT OF DESIRE

The most common issue women come to me wanting help with is their sexual desire. There are several key struggles women have with desire: they don't have any desire and never have; they don't know what they desire and feel confused; they used to have desire and it went away; aging or health issues have impacted their ability to feel desire; they have guilt about their desires, so they hold back; they have "too much" desire and judge themselves for it; or they have a different amount of sexual desire than their partner and that is causing discord in the relationship. Most women want to feel more desire and to understand their desire more deeply.

Sex and desire are culturally framed from a male perspective in ways most of us never perceive. They are also framed in a heterosexist way in which sex is assumed to center around penile-vaginal intercourse. This is slowly being questioned, but we have a long way to go. We have learned a very linear male, heterosexual model of sexual response:

DESIRE/EXCITEMENT → AROUSAL → ORGASM/PEAK → RESOLUTION

This does not reflect the experience of most women or people of other sexual orientations. In the recent past, research about sexual desire and arousal has been done entirely on men and on young people in their twenties and then extrapolated to the whole population. This is terribly problematic.

Desire has been identified as an issue for women that is centered in our brains, so big pharmaceuticals and researchers are avidly working to find drugs that can change women's brain response around desire. They see big dollars with the drugs they could sell, and already there are drugs that have *not* been approved by the FDA because the risks and side effects are too great. The disorders listed in the *DSM (Diagnostic and Statistical Manual of Mental Disorders)* have been called at various times hypoactive sexual desire disorder (HSDD), inhibited sexual desire (ISD), female sexual interest/ arousal disorder (SI/AD), sexual aversion disorder, female sexual arousal disorder (FSAD), and female orgasmic disorder (FOD).

It makes me dizzy. No wonder so many women think something is deeply wrong with them. Research has shown that nearly a third of premenopausal women and more than half of postmenopausal women fit the criteria for low sexual desire. Our sexuality has been so pathologized and medicalized, and the context of our lives has been so removed from all of the brain-focused research on our sexual experience, that most women end up with more questions and few answers. With all of these confusing messages about desire, no wonder people are left feeling like something is wrong with them if they have an unclear desire or lack desire. Problems with desire can lead to feeling like "I don't love right" or "I'm not desirable enough." None of us want to believe there is something fundamentally wrong with how we love or with our desirability.

We do know that sexual desire operates differently in women than it does in men based not only on biological factors but also in the cultural context of our lives. Sexual disorders in men have focused on the physical—boiling it down to making sure men can get and maintain erections. Men's sexuality also exists in a context, and this approach side-cuts looking at some of the underlying emotional and psychosocial issues for erectile dysfunction. Everyone gets shortchanged.

This picture is tremendously flawed because it doesn't take into account everything that can impact desire. There are a few things we need to seriously consider in order to address a lack of desire in women. The first is that many women do not know what they really desire sexually because they are following the sexuality of men—particularly those women who partner with men. We are taught this larger narrative about what sexual pleasure looks like and how to fulfill it, and many women just go along with this ubiquitous idea of sex: man feels aroused and wants sex, erection is present or imminent, there might be a little bit of what is often called "foreplay" to juice things up and try to get the woman in the mood, which leads to penis-in-vagina intercourse where the man climaxes and the woman, more than likely, does not. Game over. Not very satisfying, and yet millions of women have sex like this and never know anything else.

Lesbian, bisexual, and queer people tend to have a different orientation to sex. Because our roles are not pre-prescribed, there is more built-in freedom to explore, to broaden ideas of desire, and to ask the question: "What kind of sex do you like or want today?" There is also more communication because there *has* to be for same-sex couples to have sex. Heterosexual couples make assumptions about the type of sex they will have. There is an assumed penis-in-vagina approach to sex. For same-sex, gay, or queer couples, there is often an understanding that there are many kinds of sex that can be enjoyed and different roles to play. Open communication about sex helps people to figure it out and negotiate what they want, and having to negotiate helps to flesh out one's desire. You have to say it out loud.

If you removed the assumption that you would have this one particular kind of sex, what kind of sex would you want? Some women go blank when I pose this question because there aren't many models for other kinds of sexual experiences. It's difficult to remove the model from which you've approached sex your whole life. Yet you can have new and different kinds of sex and sexual play if you allow yourself to think about sex more broadly.

We also know that women are much less likely to have "spontaneous desire" that just erupts and leads to sexual play and pleasure. Many women think something is wrong with them because they don't spontaneously feel desire, yet many researchers have identified differences in male and female bodies that partially account for this. By and large, women have less testosterone than men do, although it varies. Because testosterone has a clear relationship to physical arousal, men can be more spontaneous or quicker to feel arousal and desire, whereas women can require more stimuli or time to get there.

A lot of women are having really unsatisfying sex with partners who are engaging in this unfulfilling aroused-to-orgasm, penis-in-vagina, done-quick model of sex and are not speaking up about it because they think this is what sex is supposed to be and that they should like it. Women are often a slower burn. We tend to need more buildup to feel sexy and fully aroused physically. If your male partner doesn't take the time to get you really aroused and just puts his penis in your vagina before you are good and ready and wanting it, it won't feel very good.

The term *foreplay* diminishes many of the sexual acts that actually arouse women and get us off. Calling it foreplay makes it seem ancillary to the main thing. Why are the things that actually bring women to orgasm, like manual stimulation or oral sex, not part of the "real" thing? They are indeed sex, and again, for women who partner with women, sometimes they are a much bigger part of sex. It's all sex. It's "all play."

As we talked about in the body chapter, you've got to know what turns you on and be able to teach your partner how to do it. That's not always easy. Some partners just don't have the touch you want. Some don't take enough time. Some men get so focused on utilizing their erection while they have it (afraid they'll lose it) that they skip all the things that will make intercourse actually feel good for you. Men have to learn to be better lovers, slow it down, develop more sexual skill beyond having an erection, and address you as a whole person. As you learn what your body likes and what your desires are, you have a responsibility to communicate it to your partners so they can meet your needs, or you will end up feeling perpetually unfulfilled.

Then there are the ways that life just gets in the way of desire and pleasure. Sex is not divorced from the life stress and emotional and mental states you experience. If you are not emotionally present, you won't be in your desire and pleasure. If you are thinking about the laundry and your long things-to-do list, you won't be there. If you are busy "spectatoring" (watching yourself have sex) rather than being *in* the sex, you won't be able to fully enjoy it. If you are focused on how your body looks or are feeling nervous about being seen, it takes you out of it. All of those mental and emotional states impact you. Desire exists within a context.

MICHELLE'S STORY, PART 2

Michelle did not come to me wanting to "fix" her desire. She came knowing there was this bigger picture, and it later turned out that her conflicts and suppression of her desire were at the epicenter of what held her back. After months of working on releasing her false ideas about sex and desire, embracing her erotic fantasies and her previously unspoken desires as well as her sexuality as a whole, Michelle had major breakthroughs in her relationship dynamics with her husband and started to make more money in her business.

Since I have started looking at bringing sexuality into my life as a holistic piece of who I am, I am noticing that my creativity is beginning to nourish me again. I also feel a natural power and authenticity that comes with that. People are more attracted to who I am, and I feel that I am attracting people who are also more aligned with themselves. I feel that I can agree more with my fantasies rather than be disgusted or embarrassed. It has been important to embrace my desire as it is. I realized that my sexual desires are not bad at all, and that I should be aware of them and allow them to be part of me.

Now I am happy about the desire arising within me and I know more ways to explore it, acknowledge it, and encourage it. In my marriage I'm more apt to say honestly when I don't feel like having sex, and it has helped my marriage come out of a toxic place. I feel empowered when I am allowing my real desire to emerge. When I see behaviors that I was using to give my power away around my career, money, and relationships, I see if there is something I can change about that to become empowered.

I've been experimenting with role-playing and how I might like my partner to treat me in bed. I realize that there are times when I might want to be controlled and have played with how to bring that in a little bit. I have given my partner clear instructions about that, as I never shared that before. I am starting to see other roles I might like to play and how I can go deeper with this.

I am beginning to notice the different moods that come up with my desire. I notice when sexual energy flares up and I ask myself what it was saying about a person or situation. I see if it might be directing me to something new. As I became more empowered, my desires shifted and they are more connected with my outer world now. They are fantasies that I can enjoy and play with rather than feel I want to put on the shelf and be ashamed of. I learned that desire is a good thing. Desire shows me things I might need to explore or try. And now I have the courage to try them. When I put things into practice I feel empowered and I learn more about myself. This empowerment carries over into how I show up as a whole. I now tell myself that sex is a part of who I am and it should be honored.

TENSION BUILDS DESIRE

One of the most common issues I hear from women is that their long-term relationship has lost its juice. They are frustrated by lack of sexual feelings and have lost sexual interest. The relationship might be very intimate and they feel a closeness to their partner—a companionate closeness, a feeling of being best friends—yet the sexual spark just isn't there. In some cases, it was once there and dwindled away, and in others, it was never really there to begin with. Some women judge themselves for making this component of their relationship important or for feeling dissatisfied with their partner because so many other things are so good. However, I think sex is really important in a relationship, and if it's not working, it *is* something worth fighting for. It can be a deal-breaker.

It's sort of a cruel joke that we have this cultural ideal of having a life partner with whom we share our daily living and experience, our bills, and mundane things, and we also expect to have a juicy, fantastic sexual life with this same person. I say cruel because, as relationship expert Esther Perel (author of *Mating in Captivity*) has discussed, it's really hard to maintain sexual tension with someone you are highly familiar with and from whom you spend little time away. Some couples even work together and almost never have time apart. Absence is part of what creates a more dynamic tension. Tension is what makes sex hot. There has to be a passion in the power dynamic, around missing each other and anticipating your reconnection, around roles and desires, around flirting, instigating, and receiving. When you are so familiar and comfortable with someone with whom you spend every day and night, it's hard to have a tension or passion that will spill into a sexy life. You have to work harder to create opportunities to actually miss each other. If you are in the rut of having the same sex all the time, you've got to change it up to keep it interesting. Rote does not sexy make.

Curiosity creates tension. Tension creates hotness. Absence creates wanting. Longing fuels passion. Whether or not you are in a serious partnership, tension builds desire. One of my mentors told me when she was in her sixties that the secret to her successful partnership of over twenty-five years was that she and her partner maintained their own apartments and had always kept their own spaces. That allowed them to have breathing room, to host each other and not take each other for granted or get used to the other being there like a piece of furniture you don't even notice half the time—until it gets moved or disappears. When I was in a long-term relationship in which we shared a home, my partner and I kept our own bedrooms and chose where we would sleep each night. This helped us to make fewer assumptions. It created space for each of us and intention about whether or if we spent our time together, slept together or alone, and was an important ingredient in our happiness. People who don't want to give their partner space and want to be on top of them all the time will eventually douse the passion like you would a flame without oxygen.

There is usually a strong tension when you first get together with someone. People in polyamorous communities call this "new relationship energy" (NRE). Most people will get a rush of NRE that fuels passion in the beginning of any sexy courtship. That energy simply cannot sustain itself. It doesn't mean there is something wrong with you or your relationship when it dwindles or disappears.

It just means you've moved into a new developmental stage of relationship that might be more about intimacy and companionship, and you have to approach sex in new ways to keep it juicy. Maintain healthy tension and that will do more for your desire than nearly anything else.

WHERE DESIRE LIVES

When I speak to women about their desire for desire, I ask them what it would do for them. I hear "I would feel more vibrant." "It will feel like I'm fully alive." "I would feel more freedom and wholeness." "I would experience life fully." "I would be more in my body."

Desire is that core for us. It is that engine that propels you to experience the world, to go for what you want, to live the life you really want to live, to connect to yourself, to lovers, to nature, to your creativity, to the divine. It is the pull to grow and have more of your life. It's that burning passion in you to do something special in your life, to be of service, to create something important. It's the invitation to expand.

The rich energetic center in your genitals, reproductive organs, and womb space is known as the sexual chakra and is the home of desire. Chakras are energetic centers in your body. Medical intuitives and many spiritual traditions outline seven chakras in the body (and some pledge there are several more outside of the body as well). The first chakra is your root, at the base of your body at your perineum and anus. That chakra is seen as the chakra of the self, supporting the second, which is the place of attraction and desire— for another or for something greater or outside of yourself. Desire is naturally about relationship and connection. The second chakra is also about emotion. It is the place of the self moving to connect with another and the place where we hold a lot of emotion. This chakra is considered the sexual and creative center of the body. It is the well of sexual-creative energy we all have to draw from in creating our lives, relationships, pleasure, creative projects, communities, art, sex. It is also the home of finances and money—the sex and money connection is so profound. I find that people run the same patterns around sex that they do around money. They are the two biggest ways we exchange energy, so it makes sense they would both be represented here in the body. They are also the two things people tend to desire most.

If we are blocked in these areas of our lives, it might show up physically as tightness, feeling locked up in the hips, or as ailments of the sexual or reproductive organs. I was speaking to a woman recently about her disconnect from her own desire, and she said one of her cousins told her, "You walk like you have a stick up your ass." She said she really felt like that, yet she was a bit surprised her cousin could see it. Sometimes when our energy is suppressed, it is visible in the way we move, in our stiffness, in the way we seem cut off from the waist down—or from the neck down (heady and disconnected from the body). There are common physical problems with the uterus and ovaries in particular: ovarian cysts, endometriosis, uterine fibroids, cancer. There is a lot of holding/retentive energy in each of these health concerns. Our bodies often reflect our emotions and the things we are plagued by. Emotion and energy will show up somewhere physically.

When you feel a desire, an urge to do something, or when you feel a sexual desire toward someone or something, where do you feel it? How does it show up? Your body talks to you, and if you train yourself to listen to it, you can learn a lot about yourself and allow it to guide you. Many women are not connected to their own feelings of desire because, again, we are taught to follow the desires of others for who to be, what to like, how to have sex, how to live our lives. If you've spent your life being told what to want, it would be difficult to know what you really desire. Recognizing this fact is a first step in tapping into what your true wants are, both sexually and in general. It can be a process to disentangle all of those external wants and pressures to tap into your own true desires. No pill will fix that.

Issues with knowing your own desire are usually directly correlated with people-pleasing tendencies. The more you are focused on others and giving them what they want, the more your own desires become obscured, until you can't see them at all anymore, almost as if they do not even exist. It's easy to feel deadened in your desire if you don't know what's even possible.

Building up your own emotional intelligence helps you to befriend your own desire. As you remove the unproductive stories, the people-pleasing behaviors, and the fog of undeserving-ness, you can uncover the desire inside of you that was there all along but went unacknowledged. You can break out of the assumed foreplay-to-intercourse model and see what else is there.

HOW TO BUILD AND ACTIVATE DESIRE

There are many ways to tap into your own desire and to build your second chakra energetically. When your second chakra is activated, desire is activated. When desire is active there is no sitting on the sidelines, no making yourself small. It means showing up and playing full-out. It means tapping into your core drive and essence that propels you to live your life's purpose and rich potential. There is a powerful way you connect in the world. Nurturing your desire supports you to do that.

Whenever your desire becomes deadened, some part of you is dull, repressed, depressed, not living up to its full potential. This is not a natural state and indicates something needs to change. You have to be courageous in stepping in and trusting that any change that needs to happen is what will create more life for you and those you share your life with. Many people come to a crossroads where they must choose their deep internal desire or choose someone or something else. At the end of the road, it's only you. If you keep forsaking yourself for others or for outside forces, all of it eventually falls away, and what will be left? You. If your spirit is feeling broken and afraid, how can you start to nurture it and stop betraying it?

WORKING THE SECOND CHAKRA

THE SECOND CHAKRA

... Home of pleasure, creativity, emotion, one-on-one relationships, power, money, control.

... Based in water: represents change, movement, flow.

... Where first chakra is the "self," the second is about the "other," communion, connecting to others one-on-one.

... Desire lives here. It is the instinctual pull to expand oneself, merge with another, move to another state of consciousness, a desire to grow.

Often when we are feeling stuck erotically, sensually, or sexually, it manifests in the part of our body that involves the hips, genitals, and reproductive organs. We can become conscious of how to use the energy of the second chakra to open ourselves to more pleasure and the experience of desire and connection.

CHANGE: In keeping with the quality of water that is alive in our second chakra, water where cells are moving and dividing, we learn to let our energy yield and flow, cleanse and change—like a river. How do you deal with change in your life? Are you the roller-coaster rider who holds on tight, trying not to let go? Or do you throw your arms into the air and scream with glee? Are you able to navigate change in ways that feel healthy and allow you to flow into the next phase of your life/relationship/work with ease? Examining how you deal with change will give you clues about your second chakra. It wants to flow. Being in flow is a state of being many of us strive for because we feel alive and rooted when we are in our flow.

CREATIVITY: Using your creativity—engaging in the act of making things—is a key way to activate your sexual energy. We were all born to create. Making art, playing music, writing, cooking a delicious meal, tending your garden, building community, or making love—all are acts of creation. And acts of creation activate your sexual energy. It's not solely about literally making babies, although that is a pretty phenomenal act of creation. (Seriously, we can take two cells and create an entire new human being. That's pretty damn creative! Take in the power of that.) So just think, your whole body is made of cells—all with the capacity to multiply and create something new. Our untapped creative power is so massive, we can hardly wrap our brains around what is possible.

We are meant to be creative beings. Where is your creativity stuck? How can you bring more acts of creation into your daily life? (Via art, thought, gardens, your home, communities, relationships, beauty, peace, kindness . . .) How is destruction operating in your life? All things are potential acts of creation or destruction. Your attitudes can foster acts of creation and open you up where you are shut down. Nothing lights people up consistently like fully expressed creativity.

UNION/COMMUNION: How do you honor others? What resentments are you carrying? How can you work to clear connections to others and create more unity in your life? Are you in the practice of clearing energy of others, especially those with whom you have difficulty? Where are people plugged into you and sapping your energy? How can you release those attachments? What umbilical cords need to be cut? Your core energy can become very depleted by your unhealthy attachments. What is weighing you down that you can let go of so that you can create more movement and ease in your life and in your body? Think about the idea of divine union and how you can create more communion with yourself, the divine, nature, art, and everything else I've discussed in this chapter. You are meant to feel that unity, and when you are fully aligned, you will.

EMOTION: Think of it as "energy in motion." You can only feel it in the body—without a body we would have no emotions. Blocked emotions repress movement and restrict flow. What emotions need to move? Where are you getting stuck emotionally and hanging on? What anger, frustration, resentment, sadness, or grief do you need to release? How would that free you up to feel more pleasure and be open to more connection in your life? How can you feel more joyful and alive in your daily life? When in pleasure, you relax and open. Pleasure helps us expand and open to new consciousness.

ORGASM: Probably the most powerful way to open your second chakra is to have an orgasm. Orgasms will activate second chakra energy, especially the big juicy ones that come from that intense place of ecstasy, desire, and pleasure. Have lots of those orgasms (either with yourself or others) born out of intense desire and deep connection to yourself. Those are nurturing orgasms, and your energy can be directed from inside out with an orgasmic experience. Every orgasm can be a prayer. Sex educator Annie Sprinkle teaches people to dedicate our orgasms. It's a lovely practice. Dedicate your orgasm to world peace, to a person you love, to someone's healing, to the well-being of children, to something you are working toward. Practice making your orgasms a sort of prayer—"This one is for living my life joyfully every day!" It's your orgasm—dedicate it to whatever you really want to give energy to in the world. If you have not yet experienced an orgasm, the path to learn is part of the opening.

MOVEMENT: Play with movement and dance, moving "out of your constrictions" to create more freedom in your body, allow emotions to move through you, and feel pleasure. Squat, practice yoga, and use movement to physically open the second chakra. In your life as a whole, as you get clear on new desires, move toward them.

BREATH: Learning to connect to your breath more deeply is a good way to connect to your second chakra. What does it feel like to breathe all the way down to your genitals? How does that feel? How does it enliven you? What does it shift in your body? There are hundreds of ways to breathe, and transformational/ecstatic breathwork is an incredible way to shift your energy, open up your chakras, and experience deeply profound release, ecstasy, and joy. I teach many of these practices to the women in my programs—learning to breathe this way is one of the fastest ways to juice up your body and energy and to replenish your well. Breath can bring desire right to the surface, sometimes accompanied by tears.

LISTENING TO YOUR BODY

If you learn to listen, your body tells you what you need to know. Your genitals respond to sexual and nonsexual events around you. The muscles might contract or you could feel a throbbing in your genitals. Sometimes you might even feel a shooting pain or jolt of some sort that wants you to pay attention. Sometimes they will open, flood with fluid, and become aroused. An overall aliveness can take over and you feel like you are vibrating from your core with everything around you. Pay attention to the signals they give you. Your body is full of wisdom, and the more you align with that wisdom, the more guidance you have and the more you are fully connected, present, and in your desire.

I recently attended a wedding of two people in my life who are polyamorous and reflected the expansiveness of their love in their ceremony, making vows for themselves, to each other, and to the vision they had for the impact of their love in the world. The ceremony was so powerful and we witnesses were all deeply moved by their vibrant love and the commitment they made to outrageous love. At the end, I walked up to light my candle in the fire ritual. I was vibrating in that powerful love energy, and just as I walked out of the ceremony area, I literally felt a huge gush of fluid. It was not my period and I was not peeing my fishnets. I creamed all over myself because I felt so alive and such a part of that love. I shared it with the bride and groom and they were ecstatic that my body reacted so powerfully. Listen to your body. It has an amazing voice.

SEXUAL PRACTICE

I'm not sure I can pinpoint when my sexual practice began or how I learned to nurture my own desire. It could have been the art I made when I was younger and had more time, or all the time I spent in nature, running around naked and doing ritual. It could have been my love for music and how it moved my body, sometimes to orgasm all by itself. It might have been my lusty masturbation practice. Maybe it was my active sex life or the time it dwindled down to a slow ember in my long-term relationship and our therapist prescribed a weekly sex date.

What I can tell you is that I've made sexuality a priority because I want to feel that alive and vibrant. All of the raw material is there inside us. The creativity begging for vision and birth. The flirtation that wants to abandon inhibition. The desire that allows itself to exist and boldly answers "Yes!" You have to claim your own desire.

I believe that developing a sexual practice is an important way to keep your sexuality on the front burner. I think of a sexual practice the way one might think of a spiritual practice. It's something you choose to do daily to bring attention to your sexuality and keep the well in working order. A sexual practice can be simple and quick, or it can be more involved and take time. There are endless possibilities.

You could use some affirmations or a meditation on your sexual self. Movement works well for many people. I've known women who have a daily dance practice. Some people have a masturbation-meditation practice and dedicate their orgasms as blessings. You could use some kind of breathwork or yoni massage. One of my sexual practices is that I greet my body and thank it every morning by running my hands over every part of it, starting at the crown of my head. This awakens my skin, makes it tingle, and is a way I can connect to my body every day as part of my meditation. My client Sandy named this practice "The Two-Minute Tingle."

It's important to choose something that feels meaningful to you and to where you are with your sexuality. This daily attention keeps desire activated and keeps your sexuality a priority. For people who are frustrated that sex/sexuality seems to sink down to the bottom of the priority list, this is a great way to keep that from happening and to stay present to your sexual self.

CREATE A SEXUAL PRACTICE

Choose a part of your sexuality you want to bring attention to, engage more, learn about, or heal. Maybe you want to be more connected to your body or love your body more. Maybe you want to experience more pleasure or develop your desire. Maybe you want to overcome sexual shame or feel more connection. Choose something, and then develop a practice that relates to this part of your sexual self. For instance, if you aim to love your body more, do something that involves your body being more activated and physical. Choose something or a series of things that you spend between five and thirty minutes doing each day. Choose a time of day that works best for you and begin to practice. Over time, your practice might shift or evolve, and that's fine. Just choose something to begin with and allow yourself to see what opens up for you when you show up for your sexuality daily.

AN ALTAR TO SEXUALITY

I have kept altars in my home since I was a teenager and learned to keep a special place for meditation. I always keep a main altar as my sacred place where I sit to be quiet, to meditate, to connect with my self and spirit. I enjoy making it a beautiful, intentional space. I keep art, special objects, candles, and representations of the elements on my altar. I change it with the seasons, with my moods, or what I am focused on in my life. I use cloth and color and I have a special round table I have used for years for this altar.

I've built altars in my kitchen, in my office, outside, and in other parts of my house. They are fun to create and are a place of beauty—an offering to something. Over the years I have asked the women in my programs to build an altar to their sexuality, to their sexual self, or to their desire. It's a great way to bring attention to what you want to keep in the front of your mind, to envision what you want, and to keep sexy afoot. The women get very creative in how they make their altars. They might put in images that make them feel sexy, pictures of themselves, photos or lists of their ideal future lovers,

BUILD AN ALTAR FOR YOUR SEXUALITY AND DESIRE

What do you want to honor? What would make it come alive? What objects or images will make you feel connected to your sexuality and your path of sexual growth and empowerment? What do you desire that you could represent on your altar? Put it in a special part of your house, maybe your bedroom. Keep it as sacred—don't rest drinking glasses on it or let others play with the things on it. It's for you. This can be an excellent place to perform sexual practices or ritual if appropriate to the space.

collages, sex toys, fruit, water, or other objects that relate to whatever they are growing in their sexuality.

RITUAL

The element of ritual is very important for most people's sexuality, and using ritual consciously to invoke things we want, create meaningful experiences, and bring attention and intention to various parts of our sexuality is important. It's also tremendously underused. We are used to big rituals like weddings, but rituals can go way beyond ceremonies of love to seal marriages between life partners.

The key to ritual is to set an intention and take some sort of action around that intention. Ritual can help you actualize a desire. There are so many possibilities for how you can "intensify" your desires and the things you want to create through ritual. We have all sorts of dating rituals and rituals of seduction: lighting the candles, turning down the lights, putting on the music, and making yourself smell nice before your date comes over. Putting on sexy lingerie and primping in anticipation of a date. These are all rituals. I often assign rituals to my clients when there is something they need to release, invoke, or make peace with in their sexuality. This could be everything from releasing a past lover, forgiving themselves for an abortion, or setting an intention for how they will love and embrace their body with pleasure. Rituals can also be part of how we bring in what we want. I provided a ritual related to loving the body in the last chapter and I've put a few rituals in the online portal for you to use if you feel moved.

There are endless ways to do ritual. Use the elements, baths, writing, dancing, making written or verbal commitments, doing things that symbolically resonate with what we are intending—anything goes! I find ritual to be an immensely satisfying creative activity. I do rituals alone, with lovers, and in groups, and all have power to move energy, shift focus, and help you align with what you desire.

Rituals and sexual practices ideally should help you become aligned with and begin to experience your highest sexual and spiritual good. As you are tapped into your own core energy, connected to your desires by taking conscious action to express your sexuality from an authentic and aligned place, you become more empowered sexually. Taking conscious action and making clear choices about your sexual expression and invocation are clear ways to feel empowered. We always feel more empowered when we are doing something for ourselves that feels right and that meets a self-need. Ritual and practice accomplish this.

DREAMS AND FANTASIES

You are meant to create. Nothing comes into being in the world without first a vision, a dream of its becoming. You have dreams and visions. You can choose to make them realities. In the sexual realm, we call dreams "fantasies." What do you imagine yourself doing? What fantasies do you see in your mind? Which ones get you most excited? Which ones do you see over and over?

Sometimes we have fantasies that we would not necessarily want to experience in the actual world. Our fantasies could involve some big risks or absence of safety, and that's part of what makes them so very hot. You do not have to feel guilty for your fantasies—they are part of the canvas of your mind's art. Your fantasy might be of the husband, the white picket fence, and two well-behaved children, or it might be for anonymous mind-blowing sex with an attractive stranger. Or a hot sexual experience with another woman. Go for it. Fantasize without censorship. Go for what you really do want and stop judging yourself for the content of your wants or fantasies, or for your desire itself.

HOW TO EXPLORE FANTASY

When people are not in touch with their fantasies, there is a whole aspect of their sexual potential they are not using. Your brain is a powerful sex organ. If you are not actively using it, you are seriously limiting your potential for pleasure. Your brain is an essential sexual tool activated in pleasure and orgasm. Exploring what's in there and what creates excitement for you will help you get more of what you want and to feel more pleasure. If you do not know what's sexy for you, how will you explore it?

Many women get nervous about fantasy because they really don't know what they desire. Some of the women in my women's sexuality program asked me for a list of sexual things they could do or try because they don't know what to ask for and are confused about desire. How do you order something if you don't even know what's on the menu? We developed a list of things (which can always be supplemented) and added it to the *Woman on Fire* portal for you.

If you've never really had a strong fantasy life, there are many good ways to engage it. Many women seek ideas from others because they don't know what their fantasies are. Expose yourself to stories and ideas and see what turns you on. Pay just as much attention to what doesn't turn you on as what does, and why. This helps you figure out the elements that really work for you. Read magazines, advice columns, or erotica, watch feminist pornography, erotic films, or other media designed to arouse. Talk to other people about their fantasies to open up possibilities. Chat rooms and advice columns are particularly interesting because they are real people's stories, and sometimes out of nowhere one will really turn you on or give you an idea for something that feels super sexy for you that you never thought of before.

You want to explore. Your sexual fantasies don't need to be original; someone has already thought of just about anything you might ever think of. You can take a scenario and put any type of person into it or you can start with someone you find hot and build a fantasy around them. It's about letting yourself play! Sexy daydreaming!

Playing storytelling games with a partner is particularly fun. Tell a story. One person starts it, then the other adds to it, and so on. It's a great way to share your erotic thoughts and find out more of theirs. Do what works for you in order to inspire, motivate, and expose yourself to sexual energies and images so you can figure out what you like and what you don't!

KEEPING IT JUICY

Once you have a sense of what moves you toward desire, take action! Knowing is one step, doing is the next. It doesn't mean you have to live out a whole fantasy, but you might masturbate to it, write about it, or share it with a lover. As you do, you activate more of your own desire and sexual energy. The more you activate your energy, the more vitality, aliveness, juiciness, and vibrancy you feel. This is why it's important—not because you need to live in a fantasy world; rather, as you connect to what makes you feel sexy, desirable, sexual, and desirous, you light your sexual energy up like the flame it is.

When your flame is lit, you choose how you direct the light. You might use it to spark a sexual liaison. You might take it into your art studio, dance piece, kitchen, writing, or whatever creative project it might fuel. You might just express yourself with more passion and enjoy life a bit more. Sexual energy is creative energy. It's all sourced from the same well. Keep that well fed.

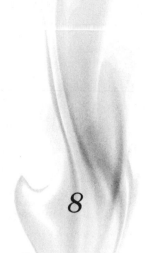

Element 6:

PERMISSION

GIVE YOURSELF PERMISSION TO BE EROTICALLY AUTHENTIC

In order to be sexually free, you've got to give yourself permission. Permission to be who you are. Permission to love. Permission to show up fully, to stop hiding the unseemly parts. Permission to explore sexually. Permission to like what you like, even if other people won't like it or might judge it. Permission to claim your own desires and to go for them. Permission to be and become who you really are. The act of self-permission opens up your sexual potential more than just about anything else. It is a self-loving act. Once a woman gives herself permission, the proverbial chastity belts come off and her sexuality can feel like it is fully hers.

WHY DO I NEED PERMISSION?

One of the biggest things I do in my work with women is give them permission to explore their sexuality, to have desires that are outside of typical cultural norms and to embrace their whole, authentic sexual selves. And that gives them permission to give permission to themselves. We all learn to hold back from others and from ourselves for self-protection, fear of what might or might not happen, not wanting to be "too much," not wanting to be disappointed, fear of not being able to do it or of being inadequate, feeling guilt or shame about likes or wants, or deep feelings of unworthiness. Sometimes the quickest way through some of these mental blocks is just to say "Why not?" and to go for it. Because none of these blocks are good reasons not to. They are fear- and shame-based.

If you've been told your whole life you didn't have permission—that the real decisions for what you were allowed to do or be sexually lay somewhere else (with the church, your family, your future mythical husband, your girlfriend, your father, your mother)—it's really hard to give yourself permission to do something out of bounds. What it requires is claiming your own agency over your decisions and getting clear about your own boundaries. It means exploring your limits and your "yeses." It means having the freedom and safety to explore and discover what is really authentic—that is, true—for you.

I have regular conversations with women in which they tell me all that they deeply and truly want sexually and how frustrated, sad, or angry they are that they are not getting it. Sometimes I'm the first person they've revealed these thoughts and desires to in full, and the act of speaking them and feeling heard is a first step to their own sexual freedom.

You will never know what you really like if you don't explore it. There is a vast terrain of sexuality, but if we take on the ubiquitous mainstream cultural idea about it, we just see it as penis-in-vagina, monogamous heterosexual sex. This narrative is so limiting and so boring it's astounding it has gotten so much play for so long. I'm not saying that monogamous heterosexual intercourse is wrong; just that it leaves out a whole array of erotic activity, identity, and expression that are part of feeling sexually whole—and many of us want more. Most of us don't see the fullness of our desires and experiences represented in the media, and that limits our ideas of what we can have and who we can be.

You can create your own narrative. You have an erotic orientation that is yours and just yours that is waiting to be discovered. To discover it, you have to go toward it, you have to have experiences, you have to allow yourself to think about sex differently and to be open to new ideas. Give yourself permission to approach sex in new ways, ways that are right for you.

RAIN'S STORY, PART 1

When Rain, a forty-nine-year-old counselor from Virginia, came to work with me with her husband, she knew what she wanted and she wasn't getting it. She was at her wits' end, having been in a nearly sexless marriage for eighteen years. She had acquired a whole drawer of sexy lingerie, had bought toys, and had even done plastic surgeries in an attempt to make herself more desirable. Nothing had seemed to work. She had poured energy into the relationship so she could have the sex life she desired. She was a sexual being and was determined not to waste another month or year in a marriage where sex was dead, and yet she really wanted to be with her partner, so they came to me to work on their sexual life as a couple.

I felt for her and understood her anger and sadness at feeling rejected for so long. I also felt for her husband, whose sexuality was so stuck, he just couldn't meet Rain in her place of desire. I sensed he had felt emasculated by her anger and that he was at a loss for what to do. He wanted to please her and to be a good lover, and he knew he was letting her down.

Both of them needed permission in so many ways: they needed permission to talk openly about this situation; he needed permission to be vulnerable about his erectile difficulties and to talk about how that shut him down in sex; she needed permission to want what she wanted and to make decisions that were in line with her desire. He avoided sex because he felt so bad about it and felt he couldn't "perform." He needed to see that sex could look many ways and that his erectile issues didn't need to be a show-stopper as they had been for years. She was the initiator and she was run-down from the repetitive rejections she had experienced while trying to advance her marital sex life. Because she had had "till death do us part" ingrained in her as a value system, she had stayed for years and years, unfulfilled. Additionally, both Rain and her partner were HIV positive, and so exploring with other partners felt tricky after being monogamous with each other for so long.

I think the biggest barrier that I faced was my Catholic upbringing and the solid, firm, conservative sexual identity of my mother. Most of the messages that I had were instilled while I was still young: Sex was 'shameful,' 'bad,' 'degrading,' outside of a monogamous marriage. I needed to release those messages in order to move forward as a sexually empowered woman. I needed to give myself permission to be honest about my sexual desire in a way that wasn't shameful, degrading, or wrong. I want to change. I want to be better than I am. I want to be more than I am. I deserve to have more than I have. I've limited myself because of the way I was raised and the trauma I've experienced.

RECLAIM PERMISSION

Rain wanted more sex; however, most women have had the experience of being the sexual gatekeepers—that is, to determine when there is sex and when there is no sex in a relationship. Women often create the limits and pace around sexual activity. It can be a lot of pressure to be that gatekeeper. In couples there is usually one person who initiates sex. If it's not you, then you risk being perpetually passive—responding to what comes or what is offered rather than going for what you want. Very different approaches. Often the one who waits is unhappy because she is not going for what she really desires. Women often need permission to ask, approach, and go for it because we've been socialized to be "good girls" who wait to be asked. And if you initiate and are rejected repeatedly, as Rain was, that can impede your willingness or ability to keep initiating. It feels deflating.

Many women have also had some experience of their sexuality or sex being "taken" by someone else against their will. Someone took it without your permission. They claimed the agency. You were rendered powerless.

This kind of sexual experience and conditioning adds to the difficulties many women have in speaking up for themselves sexually about what they want or don't want. If you've actually been judged for your sexual expression or if you have been shamed for being sexual, it can be hard to give yourself permission to like what you like, particularly if it's outside of the mainstream norms we are taught we "should" want. For every woman to step into her own sexual power, she must discover her "yes" and her "no" and exercise both with full agency in herself and her sexuality. Give yourself permission to stop trying to please others, claim your authentic response, and use your power.

FIND YOUR "YES" AND YOUR "NO"

Many women have spent a lot of time following other people's desires—most likely the desires of men and the ones the culture tells you to follow. Now it's time to follow your own. It is essential that you give yourself permission to first explore new things and to have new experiences, and then as you find your big "yeses" and your clear "nos," you can stand in them with confidence. This gives you permission to want what you really want and to set limits around what you don't. That is powerful.

People who know their boundaries and who can clearly state their "yes" and their "no" are more trustworthy. If I ask you to go see a movie with me, I only want you to go if it's going to be fun for you. I don't want you to go because you feel obligated or because you can't say "No, I'm not into that kind of film" or "I'm not up for it to-night." If I know you can assess and express your boundaries, I'm going to be able to trust that you will take care of yourself and leave me to take care of me. You won't do something you really don't want to do. Then we can both feel more at ease and more in our own place of strength and personal power. This is even more important sexually because we are more vulnerable and emotionally invested in sex than we are in a movie.

If you are not used to saying no or you haven't really explored your sexual limits and expansion, then the exploration is the path to your own authenticity. If you take the time and spend energy to fig-ure out what your likes, your kinks, your dislikes, and your "maybes" are, then you can be clear in yourself and with others. One rule that is promoted at Cuddle Parties, devised by Reid Mihalko and Marcia Baczynski, that can be a helpful guideline is that a "maybe" is not a "yes." Maybes are places where people become muddled, have a hard time being clear, and often end up regretting later. Try this: when you are in a place of "maybe," it remains a "no" until or if it becomes an actual wholehearted "yes." "Yes" can only be a true "yes," an authentic "yes." Start relegating "maybes" to "no" and see how different it feels to be that clear. It cuts out a lot of confusion.

BEING EROTICALLY AUTHENTIC

Erotic authenticity means that in all of your sexual experiences and erotic endeavors you are engaged only in what is clearly aligned and desirable for you. You are not succumbing to outside influence, creating an erotic persona that is not really who you are, or agreeing to things you do not really want out of a desire to please others, fulfill a role, or be what you think you *should* be. You are being and doing what you truly want from your own internal desire. Give yourself permission to identify how you want to explore and with whom and to take it at a pace that feels right for you.

I've spent time in lesbian and bisexual women's communities, queer communities, and other communities of sexual outlaws, with people who express their erotic selves differently and have lots of permission to explore. I have often taught at kinky events where there are workshops and opportunities for nearly any kind of play under the sun within the confines of what is "safe, sane, and consensual." What I've seen in many of these alternative sexual communities is that because there is such a wide-open playing field, it can be almost overwhelming to newcomers. Sometimes there is a feeling that one has to like everything just because everything is possible. That is not what it's about. It's about figuring out what you really want and not fearing or judging sexual expressions that might be different from your own. What is wonderful about these communities is how people can be exposed to all kinds of play—the menu you are ordering from is so much bigger. There are so many ways to explore and expand erotic terrain. Just showing up at such an event is giving yourself tremendous permission to explore, grow, and learn more about what turns you on and what just doesn't do it for you.

The BDSM motto of "safe, sane, and consensual" allows for honest negotiation and creates a positive context for exploration. All play must be safe and not cause permanent harm to another; it must be sane, which means it should be sober and participants should be clear-headed; and it should be consensual, which means everyone is a big "yes" to the play they are engaging in and that mutual consent is clear. There are safe words that players pre-negotiate so that they can slow things down or stop if the play goes somewhere that they don't like or that is too much. You can always change your mind. You let your partner know by using the safe word that there is something to address without totally interrupting the play or taking yourself out of it. The word/phrase acts as an alert.

Imagine how people's sex lives would change if everyone adopted these ideals. Whether you are engaged in kinky play or more conventional sex, we can all use a safe word to change course or have a check-in, and consent should be clear. Consent is hot. Even if I see someone engaging in sexual or kinky play that I wouldn't be interested in for myself, just knowing that they really like it and are playing in their "yes" zone is sexy.

HOW DO I KNOW WHEN I'M NOT BEING EROTICALLY AUTHENTIC?

Your body is really good at giving you signals for what it likes, wants, or fears. Your thoughts can be helpful and they can also steer you off-track because of all that preconditioning we spoke about.

This idea of erotic authenticity is a foreign concept to most people. It requires a tremendous dose of self-awareness, self-reflection, and assessment. It's easy to be influenced by outside forces about nearly anything. With sexuality, outside influence is more potent and potentially harmful.

It's more possible to be inauthentic sexually for several reasons.

Most people worry about their "normalcy" when it comes to sex, which leaves them constantly comparing themselves to others. The more you live in a place of comparison, the harder it is to determine what's really right for you because you are always basing your ground zero on something outside yourself.

For instance, if your friends tell you they are having sex every day of the week and you are having sex once a week, you might feel wrong in how you are doing it. If your peers claim that a certain kind of sexual act is undesirable or judge that it makes you a "slut," and you don't want to be viewed as a slut, you might do your best to avoid it or pretend that you don't like it when in fact you might like it very much. (Everything from sex on the first date, to anal sex, to bondage could be judged.)

So many roles and cultural and gender norms are attached to sexuality that to wade through it all to get to a place of what feels right for you can be very challenging. It's so easy to be influenced by outside forces, and many people are overly determined by them. In fact, it's nearly impossible to go through life without cultural influence and the temptation to compare. With all of that at work, how do you know when you are being erotically authentic?

If you live in a culture that teaches you that because you are female you should wait until marriage to have sex, yet you really want sex before marriage or you have no interest in marriage, you are apt to feel conflicted. Or if you learn that to be gay is undesirable, you may fight against your authentic same-sex desire in an effort to fit in. There are thousands of examples of ideas that you learn from your culture, and it is often so convoluted that it is a challenge to distinguish your true desires from what has been ingrained in you. To some degree, it's impossible to be truly free of these cultural ideas, but you can unlearn them and recondition yourself.

Perhaps the best gauge is how a particular act or belief makes you feel. You can feel like you betray yourself when you put yourself in a situation you know you don't want to be in. Doing things sexually because it's expected of you feels pretty disempowering. On the other hand, doing something sexually because you really, really want to feels powerful, delicious—even joyous, because you are in alignment. The goal is to feel this way about your sexuality. It should make you feel alive and full of joy. Sex can be a huge joy producer.

SOME QUESTIONS TO ASK YOURSELF IN ORDER TO DETERMINE WHETHER YOU ARE DOING SOMETHING THAT IS INAUTHENTIC ARE:

… What emotions do I feel? (If you feel angry, sad, resentful, afraid, or other discordant emotions, that's a sign you are out of alignment.)

… Does it bring me joy and pleasure?

… Do I feel at peace with it or do I feel conflicted?

… Do I want more of it?

… Do I find myself fantasizing about it or thinking about it with a smile on my face?

… Do I wonder how someone else is thinking about me because of it?

… Am I afraid to talk openly about it?

… Am I wary, afraid, or skeptical about it happening again?

… When I am in it, do I feel alive?

… When I feel scared, is that because it's new and I am challenging myself and pushing up against my edges or is it because there is some real fear coming up that I need to pay attention to?

Sometimes you need to take inventory about your sexuality, and these are great questions to use for a quick inventory check about how authentic you are being in your sexual expression.

RAIN'S STORY, PART 2

While working with me over the course of a year, Rain separated from her husband, moved out with her children, created a new home and a new dynamic with her husband, and began to date and fully enjoy exploring her sexuality in the ways she had wanted to for years.

I think one of the biggest struggles I have had is accepting the fact that I am desirable as a woman, and that it is okay to be desired. Amy Jo helped me come to terms with the fact that I was "okay" as I was and with what I wanted and needed in my sexual life to feel fulfilled as a woman.

I am finally in a place of understanding that desire is a healthy, normal part of the human condition and that denying it can have devastating consequences . . . and while, as a society, some desires are considered immoral, illegal, etc., feeling a particular desire isn't necessarily wrong.

I found that my sexuality has evolved a lot since I started working on myself and allowing myself to move past my personal history and the limits that my parents and the church forced on me when I was a young person. I am working hard to make sure that I don't pass down the legacy that my mother handed down to me by giving my four children a different take on what is "normal and acceptable" in the realm of sexuality. I don't want my children to go through the struggles I've gone through. I want to be a better role model to my own children, and that has been one of the core pieces of the work I have done in the last year. My work has allowed me to be open, honest, and forthright with them about being non-monogamous, and hopefully that will be in their best interests as they grow themselves and they won't get caught in the same trap I was in for years.

Rain needed permission to explore her sexuality with multiple partners, to explore desires that were outside of the norm, and to be free in her sexual expression. She realized she could not do any of that in her marriage, and she finally felt permission to make her sexual life important enough to pursue it in the way that felt fulfilling to her. She was very interested in exploring what it might look like to be polyamorous, and she began to make that dream happen for herself. She healed many of her hurts and blossomed as a sexual being who was reuniting with herself.

> *I currently have two male (and have been with one female) partners, who are all open and accepting of my history, my sexuality, and my future, and are willing to hear about what I imagine my sexual life should be. All three have been willing to help me explore my sexual boundaries. I think that sexual fulfillment involves exploring all the possibilities, the boundaries, and my own personal limits and comfort zone . . . it is a fluid, lifelong learning process.*

LEARN YOUR EROTIC LANGUAGE

If you've been on the planet long enough to form a bond, you have already developed parts of your personal erotic language. The more experiences you have in relationships, the more you develop the language about what works for you, what doesn't work, what you need, and how you like to be loved and to give love.

Oftentimes couples experience big challenges because they have different love languages. One likes to be shown appreciation through gifts and the other by spending time doing certain activities together. One likes to be approached sexually in bold, direct, flirtatious ways, the other needs subtlety and a lot of buildup and anticipation. One likes a lot of affection, the other does not or has lots of boundaries about how they want to be touched. One likes rough sex and the other likes tender touch.

No one is wrong. No one has to be one way. Sometimes you need to learn the language of your lover literally like you are learning to speak "Cedric" or "Chris," "Sam" or "Tina." If you care about being able to connect and communicate, you will take time to learn each other's authentic language. Otherwise it often will not work and you end up with two frustrated people who are not getting their needs met. Mismatched couples do it all the time.

Consider what your language is for the following aspects of your sexuality:

FLIRTATION: How do you like to flirt and to be flirted with? Do you like a lot of eye contact, a lot of verbal exchange, bodily proximity? What turns you off? Some women are wary of flirting because it can feel like giving someone else permission for sexual acts. What if you just give yourself permission to flirt and be sexy without taking responsibility for others? It doesn't have to mean anything beyond the fun of the flirt, and flirting grows confidence.

AFFECTION AND TOUCH: Affection and touch are really important. How much and where do you like to be touched? Are you a snuggler? A hugger? A hand-shaker? A hand-holder? PDA (public displays of affection) averse? Do you like to kiss in public? How do you like to be approached for kisses? Is making out exciting for you? Under what circumstances? Do you like backrubs? Massages? Rough hands? Rough touch? Tender touch? How do you like to explore your lover's body with touch? How do you like them to explore you?

CONNECTION: How do you connect with friends, lovers, and family? Do you need to connect by regular phone conversations? Do you like to write or receive letters or cards? Sharing via e-mail or text? Do you like to share ideas? Do you like to do things together? Do you like to cook and eat together? Do you like compliments? Do you like to play music or share in creativity? Do you like to be quiet together? Do you like sustained eye contact? How do you like to connect with people you love?

COMMUNICATION: How do you address problems? How do you ask for what you want? How do you like to listen? How much time do you spend communicating about issues that come up? How quickly do you address issues of concern? Do you like to mull alone first or process immediately and nip it in the bud? How do you like to get feedback? Where is your communication skill level? Have you developed active listening skills? Do you know how to use clean communication without blame or shame? What makes it easier for you to say or hear things that are challenging? How do you take and give criticism?

HOW YOU SPEND TIME: How do you like to spend time with people you love? What do you like to do? What environments do you like? Do you like to stay home or go out and be social? What kind of people do you like to be around? Do you like one-on-one time or the more the merrier?

APPRECIATION: How can people best show you appreciation? What makes you feel good? How do you like to show you appreciate others? What do you like to do for them? What kinds of gifts do you like? Which ones don't you like? Do you like to get cards? Verbal appreciation? More time together? Acts of service?

SEX: What is your preferred language of sex? Slow, soft, tender, rough, fast, hard, active? A lot of buildup and anticipation? Or do you like to get right to business? Do you like to take the lead? Do you like to be led? Seduced? Asked? Surprised? What sexual approaches work for you? What turns you off sexually? Notice how your language of power, appreciation, connection, touch, and flirtation all play into what you like sexually. If you bundled all this up into one package, what would be your ideal sexual experience? Its really not as much about the particular sex acts you like, but more about how all of these aspects of sex create a feeling and an experience that works well for you.

EXPRESSION OF NEEDS: It's critical that you learn to respectfully make requests and express your needs. If you have worked on developing your communication skills and discovering what your needs are, then you should have success in getting your needs met unless you are asking someone who really lacks skill in this regard. This is no small part of the equation. Many people have tremendous lack of personal awareness and emotional skills, and your relationship with these folks will always be limited unless they are also working on developing those skills. You have to not only be able to express your own needs, but you must be honest about what the person you are in relationship with is actually capable of.

To effectively express your needs you first need to identify what they are. For many women this is a difficult step because no one has ever asked or they've never thought they could really have sexual needs. You've got to identify them first, and then say what they are, or you'll never get your needs met. If you identify a need but are having a hard time saying what it is out loud, then say that. "There is something I want to ask for, but I'm having a hard time asking." Or set up a time to check in about your sexual life with your partner. "I'd like to check in about how our sex life is going. Can we make a time to do that?" Make it when you are doing something neutral, like taking a walk or cooking a meal, when you can talk in a relaxed atmosphere about how sex is going, what you like, and what you want to ask for. Regular check-ins about sex with any sexual partner are important.

POWER: How do you want to exercise your power in a sexual context? Do you want to dote on them? Do you want to be chased? Do you want to do the chasing? Do you want to control your lover or be controlled? Do you want to seduce them or be seduced by them? Do you want to be looked at or be the voyeur? Are you the fucker or the fuckee? The dom or the sub? The sadist or masochist? Do you want to run the fuck or gladly follow the direction of your partner?

Often couples are completely mismatched when it comes to how they work with sexual power. Power dynamics are an essential element to explore so you can find a balanced and synchronistic match. What if we identified attraction and sexual orientation not based solely on typically binary ideas of gender but rather took into account power, roles, dominance, and submission? It could be a much better way to organize our sexual relationships because these dynamics of power and desire are so important. If you get excited by being doted on or chased and you have a lover who is not oriented to chase, you'll be regularly disappointed. If you enjoy being dominant and express your power by a dynamic of domination and you try to create that dynamic with a partner who is not interested in submitting, it will never work. These are parts of your sexual power or desire orientation.

People in the BDSM community are used to the idea of seeking partners who are a match in this way. But most of the rest of the world is not. We too often default to gender-based roles of men (or the more masculine partner) being dominant initiators and women (or the more feminine partner) being submissive caretakers—there to meet the needs of others and not ask for too much. I've heard countless stories of how women have had trouble expressing their needs and asking for what they want with male partners because it ends up backfiring: they are seen as too demanding and not ladylike, "bitches," or some other uncomplimentary judgment about who they are as women and as sexual people. We are affected by this only if we buy into these roles and expectations.

The truth is that powerful heterosexual women have challenges before them in finding suitable mates. My experience is that it is hard for the vast majority of men to uphold and honor powerful women. They want them to be a bit powerful, but not "too" powerful, because then somehow their masculinity and dominant role could be destabilized. Many men continue to buy into these traditional roles because they have more to lose than women do. So even when these roles do not match a man's authentic self, it's hard to change what they've been taught their whole lives: Dominate. Run the fuck. Yet that is also unfulfilling for many men.

It's impossible to remove all of the ingrained ideas about gender, power, and sexuality. If we could, we'd all be able to self-inquire and more authentically investigate our own relationship to and yearnings about power. It is within this cultural structure that has molded us and made us to believe many ideas about power, sex, and relationships that we figure out our own orientation.

The best way to figure it out is to explore it, step into it, enjoy it, see what it feels like. What does it feel like to dominate someone else? What does it feel like to totally submit to someone? This type of exploration obviously requires trust and a safe context for exploration. That might be with a lover, a friend, or a professional. Sometimes the latter is best and provides a more level playground for you to push your own boundaries and take some risks so you can learn about yourself. At the same time, understanding how you move with power within certain relationships is also valuable information, and a loving, connected, intimate relationship is a great place to explore the things you haven't yet reconciled.

If you are in an existing relationship and you want to explore sexual power dynamics, you could begin to do that by taking turns being total initiator and guide for an entire partner-sex session. Especially if that's not something you typically do, see what it feels like to choose the time, place, and type of sex you want and to direct your partner. You could ask nicely, direct them with your body, or just tell them what to do. You choose how you want to play it. Or try all three approaches.

One fun game is to blindfold your partner, and even tie them down, and then play with them. Surprise them with sensation from ice or by feeding them sweet, salty, or spicy foods. Use textures and toys on their body. Use sound. Think about all five senses and how you could give them a sensory experience. And have them do the same ritual to you. Ask yourself what feels good to you: being tied up and blindfolded or doing the tying up and blindfolding. Or both. It's fun to play with power, control, sensation, and permission. Let yourself be creative in the way you offer control to your partner, or take it on.

YOUR SEXUAL IDENTITY

We all have a sexual identity. As I discussed in chapter 2, people take on all kinds of identities based on many aspects of the sexual self and the things they desire. Some identities are very important to people—they help them place themselves in the world, find like-minded kindred spirits, form communities, engage in social, political, and cultural activities, and find lovers who are sexually compatible. Your identities have a built-in sense of permission because they become clear areas of exploration and self-expression for you.

Your sexual identity is an important part of who you are and of how you use your power. No one else chooses your identity—that is for you to do. Others might label you correctly or incorrectly, but only you get to discover and choose how you want to identify yourself in the world. Give yourself permission to identify your sexuality the way *you* want to.

Your sexual identity can be based on many things.

Here is a partial list of some of the identities people take on as they name who they are:

SEX/GENDER/GENDER IDENTITY: cisgendered (someone who identifies as the gender/sex they were assigned at birth) man or woman, intersex, trans*, transwoman, transman, female-to-male (FTM), male-to-female (MTF), butch, femme, boi, genderqueer, genderfluid, non-binary (does not identify as man or woman in terms of binary gender) . . . hundreds of identities fall under sex and gender.

SEXUAL ORIENTATION/ATTRACTION BASED ON GENDER: lesbian, gay, bisexual, heterosexual, heteroflexible, pansexual, queer, dyke, fluid, just sexual

ORIENTATION TO SEX: vanilla, slutty, kinky, pervert, stone (can mean a person is averse to sexual contact with their own genitalia and/or sexual satisfaction is rooted in giving rather than receiving sexual pleasure)

SEX ACTS: There is a whole bandanna color system based on what people like to do sexually that has been used for decades in gay men's, queer, and kinky communities to help people find a match. Taking a cue from this strategy is helpful for anyone. Some people like anal, some don't. Some like to spank, some like to get spanked. Some just don't like spanking. Some like threesomes, some don't. You get the picture. There are so many sex acts people can put on high rotation.

RELATIONSHIP STYLE: monogamous, poly or polyamorous, various degrees of open, non-monogamous, married, single, fluid-bonded (who you share body fluids with or practice unprotected sex with), mono/poly (a monogamous partner with a poly partner), swinger (heterosexual couples who play with other couples), monogamish (mostly monogamous with some play with others)

POWER ROLES: dominant, dom, dominatrix, daddy, mommy, little girl/little boy, sub, submissive, bottom, top, service top, service bottom, masochist, sadist, doer, doee

FAMILY ROLE: partner, lover, playmate, husband, wife, caretaker, primary lover/partner, girlfriend, boyfriend, co-parent, fuck-buddy, FWB, companion

I have witnessed many people have incredible breakthroughs in their sexual and relationship lives when they discovered an identity that worked for them. Having a way to talk about and name who we are feels good and is another source of personal power and fulfillment. For instance, I've known several women who came to an identity of "lesbian" or "queer" later in their lives, thirties, forties, fifties even. As they were able to take on a queer/lesbian identity, they were able to embrace a whole new part of themselves in a big way. That new identity then opened up many doors to create LGBTQ community and/or to find other women or queer people to love.

We all have multiple identities, and this makes us complex creatures. I know queer married-to-men moms, gay dads, trans heterosexuals, vanilla queer people, kinky monogamous folks, and a range of other complex combinations. There are endless possibilities. Identities can be very fluid and may change many times during our lives depending on what is important to us at each phase. Sometimes we take on a new identity as we explore and develop a part of ourselves that was previously unacknowledged or less important, and that opens up a whole new area of erotic terrain.

GIVING PERMISSION

You might be wondering how you begin to really give yourself permission if you have taken in messages that have kept your sexual life and sexual expression contained in a particular way for your whole life. There are several ways to begin to change your relationship to permission so that you can have more of it, which means more leeway to explore and more possibilities to stretch yourself and figure out who you really are as a sexual being.

> *Every perfect action is accompanied by pleasure.*
> *By that you can tell that you ought to do it.*
> —ANDRÉ GIDE

There are several ways to practice giving yourself permission:

1. Remind yourself as often as you need to. Use the phrase "I give myself permission to . . ." and then do it.

2. Decondition yourself. Deconditioning is a process of removing the conditioning you have experienced around your sexuality and replacing it with new conditions, ideas, values, rules, or beliefs. Hopefully reading this book is helping you to decondition. It's a process and takes time. Be patient with yourself.

3. Practice saying yes to things you want or *think* you want to explore. If someone offers you something you would like, say "Yes, thank you." Stop the patterns of denial that keep you in a "no" vibration and learn to be in a "yes" vibration. Learn to say yes to what you really want, whether it's a second piece of cake, a beverage, a favor, being accompanied somewhere or driven home, or anything small or big that you truly want. Start with small things: "I'm a yes for lunch with that colleague today," or "That's a no for me—I actually don't feel like being social." "I am a yes for cuddles and some kissing." Or "I don't actually feel like being touched tonight. I need some personal space." Just practice saying yes and no without apologizing, kicking your feet, or ho-humming all the way there.

4. Say no even to little things on a daily basis—if the food you order isn't right, send it back kindly and ask again for what you want. Don't settle for a steak that is cooked medium when you ordered medium rare. Practice your "no" when it's not a full-hearted "yes" as often as you can.

5. Be the first to say what you want when negotiating with a group of friends where to eat, what movie to see, or in making some other decision. Take your place at the table by making your choices and preferences known. Stop waiting for others to express opinions that you can then only react to. Be proactive rather than reactive.

6. If there is something you currently want sexually or want to try, give yourself permission to ask for it.

7. Likewise, give your partner permission for things you want—don't wait for them to try something or to figure it out. Examples might be: "I want us to have a date where we . . ." "I'd love to be awoken by oral sex sometime." "I like when you touch me or make comments about my ass when I don't expect it." "I'd love to be taken by surprise

when you come home, thrown up against a wall, and fucked silly. Just want you to know that if you felt moved to do that, I would love it." "I'd love to be told what to wear for a date, and to meet you as if we are strangers and have hot, first-time, one-night-stand sex." "I'd like to put you over my knee sometime and spank you."

8. Initiate sex. If you have not made a practice of being the sexual initiator, since many women learn to wait and be chased rather than to initiate what they want, practicing being the initiator will be a powerful way to own your own desire, give yourself and your partner permission, and have the sexual fun you want to have. Partners who are always in the top or initiator role usually appreciate it.

9. Be dominant. It can be very powerful for women to step into sexual dominance because we are not socialized to play a dominant sexual role. Learning to "top" sexually is also a powerful way to build your confidence. Most partners will appreciate the initiative and guidance. If you gave yourself total permission to "run the fuck," what would you do? Be demanding. Be bitchy. Be a queen. Be a femme fatale. Be a wild woman. Be a seductress. Play.

ROLE-PLAY GIVES YOU PERMISSION

Stepping into a role is a great way to give yourself permission to explore a side of yourself you've never explored before or that you keep under wraps because it feels unsafe or unsavory. In a role, you can spread your wings of fancy and go for it. Choose a role you'd love to play sexually and costume up—play it full-out. As long as you get permission from your partner(s), go all the way. Have fun and play all in. Make your cowgirl, French maid, policewoman, faery goddess, schoolgirl, or teacher absolutely believable. Bonus points if you go out in public in role.

GETTING PERMISSION

In order to give yourself permission, you also need to practice getting permission from others.

SOME THINGS TO CONSIDER IN GETTING PERMISSION:

1. Communication and negotiation go a long way to set up the fun. Negotiate with your partner, ask a lot of questions, and get clear so you can really go for it. Knowing the boundaries of the playing field allows you to play full-out because you know the parameters of play.

2. Have a safe word. It helps because if something goes over a limit, or a limit shows up that you didn't realize you had, you can reset and find your way back, and so can your partner. This is far preferable to the typical reaction, which is to shut down and not tell your partner what is going on or to keep going with something you don't want. A safe word can be anything that you wouldn't normally say during sex, like "coffee" or "rain." Some people just use a simple "red" for stop, "yellow" for warning/slow down, and "green" for more, more, more! ("Yes" also works, and it's way hotter than "green.")

3. Giving permission is expressing consent. Consent is hot. "Yes" is hot. When you're in it, it's appropriate to check in if you're unsure. "Is it okay if I do this?" "Do you like this better, or *this*?" "How does that feel when I touch you like this?"

4. "No" is healthy. It's clear. It allows you to trust a relationship. Really listen for the ways your partner might say no. It's not always direct. If they seem to be avoiding sex, dodging questions, or focusing elsewhere, ask them about it. Help them define their "no" if they seem to be having a tough time saying it. It will feel better for you both.

5. Permission helps you explore and learn about your partner—this is a huge gift. "Can I massage your body?" "Can I go down on you?" "Would you like to hear a sexy story?" Or just "What would you most like for our sexy date tonight? What do you know you don't want?"

EROTIC AUTHENTICITY AND
EMPOWERMENT

The more you explore these various aspects of who you are as an erotic being, the more self-understanding you have. Your self-knowledge allows you to choose a place of truth in your sexual expression. If you are used to pretending to be something you know you are not in order to please others, hold on to a relationship, or attract a particular lover, it needs to stop. If you are role-playing, fine. But when you are pretending to be something you are not, it does not serve you—it disempowers you. When you know who you are, you can be more authentic with how you walk in the world and in your relationships. So you have to give yourself permission to be you.

You are not a clone of your friends or your partner. You are a unique sexual being with an entire erotic language that is yours to creatively express and explore. No one can take that from you or make you be someone else without your permission. And why would you willingly submit to that?

We often do it unconsciously. It's wise to examine your relationships and see if there are places where you are not being the real you. Who are you molding yourself for and twisting who you are because you think it will please them? It is not only harmful to you when you people-please; ultimately it is also harmful to others because they believe you to be something you are not and eventually that ends up being duplicitous and hurtful.

Yet when you know who you are and you express yourself from that place, you feel empowered, authentic, aligned, and right where you need to be. From that place you will draw to yourself experiences and relationships that you really want and that are aligned with the life you want. Stop wasting your life trying to get what you want from people who are incapable of giving it, like Rain did.

If I hadn't signed up to work with you, I would be stuck and still in the same old rut, crying myself to sleep at night, begging my husband for sex every six months, locked into the ideology that I'm married and stuck where I am at, believing it's not okay for me to want more or to expect more and it's not okay for me to challenge the status quo, locked into that cultural norm. I am more content now. Another part of me is still frustrated. I feel like I have to shelter Mick from the fact that I am moving on. I've done a lot. I have reorganized my life. I've come a long way.

And truly she has. Since we first met, her life has transformed and so has she. A big part of our work was the permission giving—me to Rain, and Rain to herself.

I've given myself permission so many times since my college professors modeled it expertly for me by telling the class to go home and masturbate. I gave myself permission to explore my own body. Permission to find my way to orgasm. Permission to say what I want. Permission to flirt. Permission to be sexy. Permission to scream louder. Permission to fuck myself silly. Permission to buy sex toys. Permission to have anal sex. Permission to bring a woman into my bed. Permission to be boyish. Permission to dress in drag. Permission to be feminine. Permission to submit. Permission to dominate. Permission to explore naughty things and to like them. Permission to play out fantasies. Permission to watch porn and read sexy stories. Permission to have more than one lover. Permission to be proudly single. Permission to not want children or marriage. Permission to have sex in risky places.

I could keep going—and I will. I hope you will too. For the permission you give yourself directly correlates with the amount of exploration you get to experience. Sexuality and exploration together light you up, help you live fully and without reserve, and help you to find out who you really are as a sexual being.

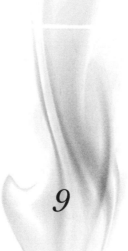

9

Element 7:
PLAY

DEVELOP SEXUAL SKILLS AND REMEMBER HOW TO PLAY

Play is the exultation of the possible.
—Martin Buber

So much of what gets in the way of sexual freedom is how seriously we take sex. Well, it *is* serious—*and* it's meant to be playful. Most of us lose some of our ability to play as children. We have our desire for play and our unhinged imagination squashed by overly serious adults who want us to be something other than what we naturally are. Then we grow into adults and want to get back some of that pure joy of play and authenticity we had when we were children before someone told us we were wrong for it.

"Quit horsing around!" my father would snap. I was the oldest child and had more serious responsibility in my family early on than my younger siblings. Somewhere I learned to be annoyed when my two younger sibs would play, joke, and laugh. Partly I might have felt left out because I was finding it hard to let myself play like that. And partly, well, they were just annoying younger siblings. As the oldest, most mature child, I thought that being grown up meant being more serious, which is where most of us land sexually.

I didn't really re-embrace play until early adulthood. Sexuality was a doorway into play, into imagination and creativity and getting back some part of myself I might have lost when I was little. By allowing myself to play and explore sexually, I allowed myself not to take life so seriously and to have more fun. No one ever thinks I am my age because my playful self, style, and fashion show a side of me that is tapped into creative imagination and expression. And creativity feels vibrantly alive, not old and decaying.

We don't stop playing because we grow old,
we grow old because we stop playing.
—Satchel Paige

I never got to go to summer camp when I was a kid. My dad was just trying to hold it together to make sure he had childcare taken care of and dinner on the table each night at five p.m. sharp. Looking back, camp would have given him a much-needed break.

I always felt like I missed out on something. So I started going to summer camp as an adult. First, I started attending women's spirituality summer camps, where I taught classes, led rituals, tended the fire at sweat lodges in service to the community, and got to stay in a cabin with other women. We would decorate the cabin, add to the graffiti on the cubbies, dress in fun outfits, and leave witchery treats for the young girls who would come to camp later that summer after we left.

Then I went to adult sex camp and discovered a whole other

adult playground. There was the cabin experience and the dress-up. There were also playrooms, kissing zones, playshops, dungeons for sexual and BDSM play, wooded areas where extensive role-plays would be staged, and a pool. Talk about adult playground! If you don't know how to play, adult summer camp will teach you to let go and allow opportunities for possibility, even if it's just through being a voyeur. When do you get to see real people have sex? When do you get to explore sexual activities that range from cuddle piles to group sex to people being restrained and flogged by a dirty-talking top? You won't be into all of it, but getting exposure to new ideas and varying sexual experience is exciting and it inspires your own play. People play in so many ways, and creativity inspires more creativity. It's the law of energy at work again. Life-giving activities reproduce themselves. Sexual desire leads to more desire. Creativity to more creativity. Ideas spawn more ideas. It's like the urge to go home and make art after a visit to a museum. When you are a part of a sexual community, you learn endless ways to explore your own desires, your kinks and perversions, or your sweet spots.

MIMOSA'S STORY

Mimosa was a playful, thoughtful twenty-six-year-old woman when she came to participate in my women's sexual empowerment program. She was ready to break through all of the ways she was inhibited and keeping herself contained as a sexual person.

> *Sex was always about the other person as far as enjoyment. It was always a means to an end. Like most children, I was very curious about sex. When I was younger my girlfriends and I would kiss or touch. This was stopped after my older sister explained to me that according to the Bible, lesbians are "bad."*
>
> *Around the age of twelve, I stumbled upon my brother's porn on*

our family computer and was totally turned on. There was shame in watching, I didn't want to be caught in the act, but I couldn't stop. I wanted to know what all of that felt like! But no one in my family talked about masturbation, and sex had been painted as dangerous and something to be saved. So even though I was curious and my body was saying, "Let's play!" I knew my will and modesty were the only things that would keep me safe.

I didn't give myself permission to explore myself sexually until I was twenty-three years old. Once I shed my shame of being attractive and embraced my beauty, I was able to appreciate those elements in others and step into my full form. I cut my hair and wore different clothes; I danced on stage in lingerie and learned how to wear makeup. I invested in my own jewelry. It has allowed me to appreciate the beauty around me rather than feel threatened by it. I have more authentic connections with both men and women.

Remembering that life is abundant with opportunity has helped me free myself to play. I used to worry about how I would be perceived by a person based on one interaction. With abundance comes permission to mess up because there will be another chance to do it again. It's funny, but within that safe space of making mistakes is where my true authentic nature comes out to play. I have learned that life can be light and meaningful simultaneously. I have learned that you can have powerful sexual experiences without it being serious.

One tangible activity that helped me come to this place was participating in a literal play, specifically a cabaret. Playing different roles in different scenarios has proven to me that I am infinite. That each moment is another opportunity to re-create myself. That I can become whomever I want to be whenever I want to become it. That who I was yesterday does not need to dictate who I am right now, and who I choose to be now does not determine who I will be tomorrow.

I made friends with people who would play with me. I went

to an open improv comedy class where all they do is play games. Probably the most helpful was the home-play through Amy Jo's Women's Sexually Empowered Life Program and Confidence Tele-class, which gave me a reason to try interacting with my world in a different way. The confidence class encouraged me to change my question from "How did I look?" to "How much fun did I have?" That simple question put into motion a different intention, which was incredibly powerful.

Maintaining a perception of abundance allows space for mis-takes, which emboldens me to try new things and ask questions that I wouldn't have asked before. Playfulness also changes my approach to masturbating. When I employ the question "How can I make this fun?" it becomes less about my orgasm and more about exploring, trying new things. It invites a curiosity that leads to self-discovery of things I like and things that I'd rather not do again anytime soon.

FINDING YOUR PLAYGROUND

We evolved through play. Our culture thrives on play. Courtship includes high theater, rituals, and ceremonies of play. Ideas are playful reverberations of the mind.
—DIANE ACKERMAN, DEEP PLAY

If we evolved through play, sex certainly did! Play always has a place where it happens—a playground, someplace familiar, a new wonder-land ready for exploration, a sacred (as in special or exalted) place. I believe we can make a playground just about anywhere if we choose to. There usually are some etiquette or rules of engagement for play in any playground. As part of my women's sexual empowerment pro-grams, I provide lots of opportunities for women to play. We play games, we form puppy piles, we dress up, we create worlds where unusual things can happen. When being faced with the opportunity for play, some women get uncomfortable and choose to sit on the sidelines watching the action rather than going for it and being in it. And that is okay—it's where they are. Often this is because many of us have had the urge and freedom to play conditioned right out of us, sometimes to the point where it can be triggering. Some people will shut down, withdraw, or go into fear about how their way of playing might be judged. We can feel too embarrassed to let others see us be silly or bring out other parts of the self. When I witness that, I know those are the same fears or patterns that will come up for a woman when she is in sexual situations. We can create our own prisons so adeptly, and the one where you have to do everything perfectly and you have a deep dread of rejection and judgment, so you don't do anything outside of the box and you try to fly under the radar sans participation—that prison is torture.

There are so many ways into play. Play is engaging with the things, places, and people you love, are curious about, or want to explore. Play is for its own sake. In our busy adult lives, we are so over-scheduled that we might have a hard time setting aside play time. Yet so many people report they are unhappy doing what they are doing in life. Play does require setting aside time for it, like anything else you care about. Yet just wearing a fun outfit to do housework is play (outfits always make it better). You can make mundane things fun too. We *all* need play. It's an essential part of life and of your sexuality.

How and where do you play? What opens you up to have experiences without needing to have a specific outcome? What allows you to let go and be in a moment without the mental tape running ruminations in your head about what everyone else will think of it? Not thinking about how the critics will receive it—whatever "it" is? What allows you to shut those voices down and just be present to creativity, discovery, imagination, and revelry? To the pursuit of ecstasy?

Consider your current favorite playgrounds. Perhaps you love to play in the kitchen, concocting delicious treats, beverages, and sumptuous meals in an alchemical explosion of culinary art. Or maybe your art room, your camera, or your writing is your playground, where your creative self gets to play and your artistic imagination gets to run with the muses. My partner and I used to go on photo dates, where we would walk around our Brooklyn neighborhood and choose things we wanted to take photos of. Then each of us would get to take one photo of each thing. It was fun to look at our different perspectives in the photos at the end of the day. Maybe your playground is a court, a stadium, or a baseball field where you play in your body and with opponents. Perhaps your playground is the tree in your backyard, the woods where you grew up, your favorite beach, or a mountain you love to hike and explore. Nature is an

WELCOME TO MY PLAYGROUND

1. **Name one to three places you currently experience as a playground on a regular basis**. What makes them playgrounds for you? What excites you and lights you up about these places or experiences? Make a list of at least five to ten words/phrases/descriptors that describe what you love about each of these playgrounds.

2. **Next, think about where in your life you'd like to be more present and playful, and identify two to three new playgrounds you want to explore.** If you look at the descriptors for the playgrounds you already have, can you see possibilities for how to make these new playgrounds resonate with those qualities? What would you need to do to take the leap and jump into exploring these new playgrounds?

amazing play partner. Play can happen in your ritual circles and in ceremony as you create something inspired with a group of people. Maybe you play with your imagination when you read fiction. Maybe play happens in your office (I hope so), your business, or your area of study, where you are excited about what you are learning and creating and the new ideas you are working to understand. Or play might happen in your meditative practice, your yoga, your risk-taking adventures, or on your travels. Animals and children make impeccable play partners. They bring you right into the present and into exploration and fun. Pure glee. I hope your sex life is one of your playgrounds, but if it is not currently, you can inspire yourself to change that right now.

FREEDOM TO PLAY

The idea is to take life less seriously, to make time for fun or for less-structured events where discovery can happen. If you can do that in life, you can do it in sex. You bring your sexuality into your play-grounds, that creative juice that fuels imagination.

Play is pleasurable and by nature requires freedom: giving yourself the freedom to be silly or to take a risk, to try new things, to use your imagination and to not give a second thought to what anyone else thinks. The thing I hear the most from people who come to me to work on their sexuality and sexual lives is that, in a word, they want *freedom*. A good way to begin your journey toward the freedom you want is to give yourself freedom to play, knowing there are new things you are meant to discover as you allow yourself a process of presence, fun, and deep engagement.

Sometimes I talk with women who had a "phase" of exploring their sexuality and feeling that freedom when they were younger or in the beginning of a relationship, and then they let that part go because they "grew up" and started to act the way they thought they "were supposed to." They find themselves missing it, thinking they can't have it again.

One woman said to me, "I want to be in that frame of mind of feeling completely free. It feels good to be so free. [Sex] was more about the freedom before. Now whenever I have sex, it's more of a 'should.' Not for my enjoyment. A part of me thinks it's not possible to get back there. To have desire . . . I would love to be able to crave sex. I wish I could enjoy it or want it. I miss the relationship that my husband and I did have."

If your sex life is not currently one of your playgrounds, today is a new day. Add it to your list. Sex is so much more fun when you don't know what's going to happen every second, when it is not predictable that it will happen the same way it happened on Tuesday, last week, and last year. When you approach sex with the curiosity of "What can I discover today?" about yourself, about your lover(s), and about the relationships involved, you are at play.

FLIRTATION IS PLAYING

Flirting is play. Flirting is giving energy, playful attention, and focus to something or someone. It can be a compliment, a tease, an energetic exchange of glances or sexy body language. When you flirt, you are allowing yourself to be seen, to make an offer, to invite another to connect with you. There is something special in that kind of exchange when it is reciprocal. It's the most fun when you are actually in your body and it's coming from a real place rather than a false put-on.

And because there is an exchange, it makes you feel engaged with life. When we are in true exchange, whether it's money for our service, service for our time, a mutually caring friendship, or a great flirtation, we are dancing in the energy of life. That dance helps us to feel aligned and whole in our beings. That dance is why we are here. That dance is the sacred dance of life itself.

Sometimes a flirt comes out a bit unintentionally, like the other night when I said to a male friend after making a goof, "You can give me a hard time. I can take it." We both laughed at the unintentional double entendre. Intentional flirting is a fun, creative game that taps into the part of ourselves that is connected to another person in the moment.

I've worked with so many women who are terrified of their power of flirtation. Their minds weigh in heavily, a constant barrage of internal questions about how far they can or should go, what it means, whether it's okay, whether it could lead someone on, forever the gatekeepers of sexual action and progression. Then comes a heavy modification so they don't spin out of line. That's a heavy burden on something meant to be fun.

What if we let go of all of that and just allowed ourselves to flirt with the world, with life, with friends, with strangers, with the wind and the sky? What if we were free to be fully sexually expressed without taking on the responsibility of what someone else might think? That responsibility is theirs, not yours. However, the fear that many women have about how much to flirt relates to their concern about being able to maintain their own healthy sexual or emotional boundaries. Where does the flirting stop? The best flirts often have excellent boundaries and can generate them in an unbounded situation so it doesn't feel risky or like they will lose themselves.

In getting your flirt on with the world, I don't mean be inappropriate, like flirting with coworkers or in situations where it would not be okay. But with clear boundaries in environments where flirting is allowed and even welcome, flirting can enhance and liven up your day. Sometimes a great moment of flirtation brings a total smile and kick to your day. One of the best ones I've heard in a while was one my team member Elise got from a stranger: "Wow, you make your planet proud, Earth Girl!" How can you not smile at that? It made her day. It's fun to make someone else's day, and more important, it feels good to flirt with life.

How do you suppress your desire for flirting? Flirting as play is totally harmless in the sense that it is done for fun and it is about being in the moment, not about taking us away from someone we care about. People are sometimes threatened by their partner's flirting and sometimes there is no threat at all. People who are in a relationship and support their partner's flirting and do not feel threatened by it are likely in a good place of balance and secure in the relationship. They don't make up stories about what the flirting will lead to or that it will be something more than it is. The flirting in and of itself can be harmless fun and it can be a great sexual energy builder for a relationship, whether the flirtation is with your partner or with someone outside of the relationship. Of course, if you are looking to bring someone into the relationship for a threesome, foursome, or moresome, you'd better learn to get your flirt on, because they'll likely need heavy cues.

Sometimes people are not comfortable with their partner being flirtatious with other people. There may be something you need in your relationship that is important. If you are in a relationship and that relationship and commitment is clear, then it's obvious to outsiders or flirtees that you are flirting. When there is ambiguity in what the relationship is, people outside of it can get confused or get their feelings hurt when you flirt with them.

It's important to be aware of the culture or subculture you are in and the context of flirting and what it means. Consider national, ethnic, or racial cultural norms, or norms around age or the norms in a LGBTQ or kinky community. For instance, older adults can flirt in ways that might be more acceptable than they would be for younger people. In kinky queer communities, people flirt and can be really direct as part of a cultural norm. It is understood that you will ask and negotiate if you want the flirting to lead to something more. That's one of the many beautiful parts of kinky communities: people are alive and vibrantly sexual. You get to be flirty and it doesn't mean you want to have sex or play with someone. Pay attention to cultural norms and, in case it's not, make it clear to people if it is just flirtation.

Sometimes people turn off their flirtation like a faucet when they get into a relationship, and then they turn around years later wondering where all the sparks and excitement went. Turning off your flirt is like turning down your own energy. Keep that energy sacred, amped, and clear, even if you choose to flirt only with your partner. Keep it in full expression. Flirt with the sun, with a tree, or a bird. It's an essential part of the fun of life and a cornerstone of play.

SEDUCTION

While flirting hints at sex, seduction is an invitation to sex. There are several phases of any sexual encounter, though sex shouldn't be an invariable three-part act. Elements of anticipation, planning, and seduction make sex hot and turn up desire. Sexual encounters have so many flavors: exciting, anticipatory, flirty and playful, soft and gentle, rough and fierce, hungry, languorous, boring, monotonous, dreamy, transcendent, electric, wild. Your seduction of a lover—or of yourself—sets the tone. Are you ready for a feisty romp? An intense connection? A lighthearted fling? A juicy fun evening? Set the tone with your seduction techniques and be inviting.

You could fire up the candles, turn down the lights, and put on some sexy lingerie. Or you could show up for your dinner date with a short skirt, no underwear, and a remote-controlled vibrating toy. Or in a suit and tie, looking dapper. You could write your fantasy to your lover prior to your date (where you will carry it out) and make some requests or demands. Provide instructions for what they should come prepared to do or what to bring or wear.

What about seducing yourself? What's sexy to you? I encourage my clients to have "masterdates"—where they will have a solo sex date and they can do any number of things to make it juicy. Do it out in nature. Take a candlelit bubble bath. Masturbate in the mirror. Make love to yourself.

PLAY WITH YOURSELF: HAVE A MASTERDATE

Plan a night of lovemaking with yourself. How can you pamper yourself? What will get you "in the mood"? Wear a sexy outfit. Get the treats you want, try out some new toys, and if you are feeling bold, masturbate in a long mirror and enjoy watching yourself get turned on. Enjoy making love to yourself. It's one of the most powerful sexual experiences you can have—to be in full sexual expression at your own hand and to take in your image, your voice, your taste, and your smell. If you have never done this, it is a must. This is a threshold to pass for anyone who wants to know themselves fully. It's a bold way of tapping into your sexual expression and erotic potential.

If you are not using seduction as part of your sex play, delight is just outside in the waiting room. Seduction that's fun just because it's fun can teach you to play, regardless of outcome. Many women avoid seduction because they are insecure or fear rejection. Think of how many things you would do if you let go of insecurity and fear of rejection. They are the biggest play killers there are. If you decided you were just not going to care what the response is, or whether your playful seduction was returned and you just did what you felt guided to do and decided to be inviting, how much fun could you have?

It can be hard to keep flirting or playing in the seduction arena if you have felt rejected, so it's helpful to remember that the "no" or lack of response is usually about them and not you. It's about the person's own insecurities or not knowing how to flirt back. It's about something going on inside of them. They are taking care of themselves. Remind yourself of this and make a pact to yourself that you won't allow your sexuality to be dimmed by someone else's boundaries, insecurity, or projections. If you don't take risks, you can't garner the benefits. Seduction is a certain kind of risk—a playful one, so if you think of it as play that isn't overfocused on outcome, you can sometimes enjoy it more. What is "overfocus"? Not enjoying the playful seduction because you are thinking about how it will end.

ROLE-PLAY

Role-play is such a fun way to play sexually—and it's a way to ensure that sex doesn't become rote. Role-play is a way to not take rejection so personally. Put on a role and it frees you up. Taking on a persona allows you to tap into parts of yourself that you might not have experienced before. You become transformed by an outfit and ready to be bold. I've seen that transformation many times: a person can't tap into something in real time, but when they take on a role, they turn into that person and a whole new side of them comes out. It's why we love Halloween so much and why cross-dressing is the most common Halloween costume. People want a chance to be something or someone different for a few hours.

There are rules of engagement within a role-play. You have parameters for who you need to be or what would be in character. You can do things when in role that would feel more risky as yourself. Some people have special props they use when in role. A particular pair of boots or stilettos. A sex toy. A hat or piece of jewelry they wear. The skirt they only break out for schoolgirl scenes. It's fun to have the special Pavlovian prop that calls attention to the role you are stepping into, helping you to leave behind the outside world and go into the place of discovery in your playground.

PLAYING LEADS TO SKILLS

Sex that is based in play does not want a particular outcome; rather, it is important purely for the act itself. You are showing up and allowing yourself to move with erotic energy, to create something, to let go.

Opening up to play allows you to open up to developing skill. If you learn to allow yourself to play and give yourself the freedom to move and open up to imagination, you hone in on what you want to be able to practice so that you can, in turn, learn to do it well. You hit on something really fun and you want to do it again. And again. And again. And soon you get better and better at it. It becomes a skill and a proclivity that sticks.

Sex is one of the greatest playgrounds adults have. If we embrace play, we can embrace playing with new skills and trying on new things. Play is trying something new just because. How could you tap into your playful side and invite new experiences?

SEX IS A SKILL

I made my students repeat aloud "Sex is a skill" as I would begin the sexuality module in my college courses, their collective voices paired with uncomfortable grins. I am always amazed at how many people do not realize that, yes, *sex requires skills*! Contrary to unfounded popular myth, sex does not come naturally. Nothing does, except maybe involuntary breathing. When we come into this world, we don't know how to do anything—not even eat. We have breast-feeding consultants to teach us that fundamental skill. Babies need to learn how to take their mothers' breast into their mouths and suckle, and new moms need to learn how to teach them!

When we are infants, we don't know how to drive a car, play Frisbee or soccer, cook a turkey, dress ourselves with style, or use an iPhone, even though Apple insists that it's intuitive. All of these things must be learned. And so must sex. Yet we have all these romantic notions that somehow sex is natural, it "just happens," and it's perfect with "the one you love," right?

I teach people the skills of sex and relationships. People love to argue about this. Invariably, someone will say, "Well, sex is instinctual. We are guided by our sexual instincts and we just know what to do." My bullshit meter spikes. We *have* instincts, yes. Instincts are at work. But sex is not instinctual. Quite the contrary. It is learned—we learn how to do it, what's appropriate, what's expected, what makes it pleasurable, and we act based on messages that are instilled about sex from the time we are born.

This is why most people's first sexual experience is typically not a super-positive one. It tends to be fumbly, awkward, and rarely involves mutual orgasm. Imagine if you had never played soccer but you knew a little bit about it, yet you'd never really seen anyone play. When you "came of age" you were thrown out onto a soccer field with a ball and some other players and told to play! What do you imagine would happen? You might know to kick the ball when it comes to you. You'd probably get bonked in the head a time or two and be confused about which way to run. You wouldn't know how to interact with the other players. You'd have no rules of engagement. At best, you'd make it out with all your bones intact, but you sure wouldn't play a great game of soccer. You might have fun, but you'd most definitely have a lot of anxiety about not knowing the game you were playing.

That's how sex goes for people when they've got no training, education, or knowledge about what they are doing. This is how many people experience their first sexual experience. They have no clue what to do. They have some feelings inside they are working with. We do feel desires, attraction, and instincts about what we want. We know if something feels good or doesn't feel good. But we don't necessarily know how to explain what we want, make something better, or extend an orgasm. We don't know how to have safe sex or much about our options for sex. We might know very little about how the other person feels. We set out in the dark on a sexual expedition without a map.

Why is it that we leave people to figure out on their own one of the most important, sacred parts of their life? We have so many questions about sexuality and typically have no idea where to get them answered. And if we did, we would have to know how to ask. And most people never learn that either. What a mess!

We have a powerful cultural myth that in sex we should just know what to do. That if we love a person, the sexual part will just fall into place. How many virgin brides approach their wedding night with terror because they have no idea what to expect or what they will be required to do? So many cultures do not even support virgin brides and grooms-to-be to discuss consummation prior. A little pre-negotiation would go a long way for a playful wedding night.

Most of us experience awkward, unsexy, muffed early forays into sexual pleasuring with a partner. I certainly did. In a culture like ours, where we place so little emphasis on teaching sex education, we are all left to fumble about and try to figure it out on our own. Sometimes we have a happy accident and learn something new, and pleasures, even orgasms, happen. Cheers for happy accidents! That is play at work. But by and large, if we don't take some time to learn and perfect the skills of sex and relationships, the quality of our sexual lives will reflect that lack of emphasis.

My first significant boyfriend taught me so much about how to love, how to be in relationship. He was an extraordinary teacher, and I was blessed to learn from such a loving, present sexual partner when I was still in high school. I clearly remember my long, painstaking path to learning to orgasm. He did his very best, he brought enthusiasm and A+ willingness to try. But I had to learn my own body and what I liked and be able to convey it to him. Women's bodies can be complicated. There is a lot to learn—for yourself and your lovers. You can't expect someone else to just know what to do. It's not instinctual, it's not obvious, and they are not mind readers. I think most guys who care about their female partners care about their pleasure and want to do their best but often don't know where to begin. You've got to develop your own skills—not just the *Cosmo* kind: "How to give a great blow job" or "How to blow his mind in bed" . . . I'm talking the skills of your own body's pleasure. How to get yourself off like a rock star. Then you can begin to teach your lovers and improve your experience of sex exponentially.

ADULT SEX EDUCATION

What does it take to be good at something? Practice, of course! All skills require practice to become good at them, and sex is no different. So since most of us had no sex education or limited education that focused mainly on prevention of unwanted consequences, we have to roll up our adult sleeves and do the work to learn the language of erotic pleasure. When you take time to develop your sexual skills—everything from sexual techniques, breathing and breathwork, anatomy, sexual functioning, communication, how to create deeper intimacy and relationships, develop awareness of desires, or how to be playful—you reap the rewards of a more satisfying sexual life, bigger orgasms, and deeper sexual connection and intimacy. What sexually active person wouldn't want that?

I remember the lover I had a long-distance relationship with who taught me how to talk dirty. I got master's-level practice in our five- and six-hour marathon phone calls long before Skype existed.

Then I got into kink, and there was an endless collection of skills to learn that could make my kinky desires possible. I continue to learn new things all the time. I'm not even close to complete. I learn them by playing with them, seeing what is fun, and then continuing to explore the things that light me up, the places I want to keep visiting.

Imagine if we grew up going to school and each day as we went to language, math, and science classes, we also went to life skills class, where we learned real skills and information that would help us to have meaningful intimate relationships, take care of our health and body, make conscious, healthy decisions, and live fulfilling sexual lives. Imagine! How different our lives would be.

Sadly, our culture does not treat our sexual life as something worthy of learning and teaching about. We are still stuck in so many taboos about sex that we will let our children watch people be violently murdered yet we will cover their eyes when the sex scene comes on. This is ludicrous given the importance of our relationships, our experience of our bodies, and our pursuit of pleasure. That pursuit is so essential that the founders of the United States put it into the first drafts of our Constitution. So it's up to each individual to develop sexual and relationship skills that will assist us to live the life we want to live. Yet most people *never* do.

The vast majority of adults will never take a sexuality class, read a meaningful sexuality book, or work with a sex coach or therapist. Just the fact that you are reading this book puts you way ahead of most people.

SAM'S "PRIORITIZE SEX AND PLAY PROJECT"

Sam is a professor in her forties who identifies as queer and is into BDSM play. She started attending classes I taught in New York City, and for four years in a row she came to my annual "Manifesting the Sexual Life You Want New Year's Ritual." I distinctly remember the year she had began her "Prioritize Sex and Play Project" and I asked the group a series of questions to assess where they were. One question was whether they currently had as much sex as they wanted in their life. Sam was the only person who stood for that one, with cheers and awe from others in the room full of people. She had taken an intentional approach to creating more play and sexy fun in her life when she realized she'd gotten into a relationship where she was unhappy sexually and had lost her own sexual drive and energy. She took matters into her hands and started to do something about it. Each year at the ritual, we got an update about how it was going. Here is how she approached it:

> *I had always thought of myself as a very sexual person, as a sex-positive person, as sexually adventurous. Yet my life did not reflect that. It started to bug me because it messed with my identity, with my sense of myself. In hindsight I do think it was in part the play that I missed. As I reflected on my life I decided that the reason I did not feel sexual was because my life was not sexy! So I decided I needed to start putting myself in sex-positive and BDSM or 'play' environments. I started announcing to close friends and random people at parties that I had embarked on a "prioritize sex and play project."*

Sam involved her partner, who was trans* and identified as queer.

> *First off, let me say that I told my partner about the project from the outset and asked for his support. One of the things that made him fall in love with me was my sexual adventurousness and openness and the way I brought that to our relationship, so I think he knew that me not even feeling sexual was indeed something worthy of addressing. Few people who know this part of me currently would believe that I ever had a period of not feeling sexual—it wasn't just*

that I wasn't acting on my sexual feelings, I just really felt nothing in this area, barely even masturbated.

I wanted spaces to explore and play with people. I started to pursue opportunities that presented themselves. Going to workshops allowed me to see kinky folks I hadn't seen in years and meet new people. I remembered how much it energizes me to be the one spurring on provocative conversations. Well, something began to shift during the Prioritize Sex and Play Project! One, I signed myself up to top a friend of a friend. We negotiated over steamy e-mails for probably close to a month and then somehow I agreed to have our first date at one of the largest women's play parties our city had seen in a while. Really? Wow. Yes.

Really, that night I was topping myself! What if I wasn't using the cane correctly? What if it wasn't hot? What if I couldn't read my bottom? Somehow I went for it—and really I thought I was going to die *and made my friend attending the party swear upside down and sideways not to watch. I survived. I jerked off thinking about it afterward, and then I kept sending steamy e-mails and signing myself up for another date of topping and another, and another, and at some point I just hit my* groove. *It was definitely faking it till you make it. In the beginning it was a little like taking vitamins. I just trusted it would be good for me some way. And it was interesting. And fun. And sometimes when I'd check later I'd discovered that my cunt was* soaking *wet.*

Seven years later, and let me tell you I have been having the time of my life sexually! Wow. Today I just feel so alive *in this area. I have sexual connections of various sorts, and this is a thriving part of my life. It feeds my work and everything else I do. For years I sat frozen in the face of desperately wanting the group play I saw at parties and even at the prospect of having threesomes like those I had organized several times in college. After literally wanting my whole life (it seemed) to be a part of an actual orgy or those group gang-up and spank someone scenes I had witnessed, I finally got to be a part of some group fun! One of the things that emerged is that now I am solidly a switch. In my late twenties' exploration I was decidedly a bottom. And I have wholeheartedly embraced my sexual-initiator and -instigator side. I have become very comfortable with initiating and with topping as well.*

Play. I was looking for a playground. I was looking to feel sexual again, and these lovely people gave me that. Created it with me. And now I have an energy for it that seems self-perpetuating. I have a community that celebrates that. I take regular joy in giving to others through my instigating based on my own desires, my lovers' fantasies, and oftentimes just because I can, just for the play of it. It propels me, energizes me, enlivens me, leads me to all sorts of discoveries. And it is just good fun.

Sam not only created a lot of fun and play in her life; she developed her sexual skills, expanded her identity, and learned about a whole array of new things she liked as she deepened her relationship to her own sexuality and brought the play and fun back. Whether you are into BDSM and group sex or something different, take inspiration from the intentional approach Sam took in making her sexual life "a priority."

HOW YOU DO ANYTHING

How you do anything is how you do everything.
—Zen koan

I think growth and people who actively seek it and value it are really sexy. A desire to be better, do better, develop yourself more. This includes the realm of skill and living your sexual life in an intentional way.

If you are someone who typically does just enough to get by, learns just enough to pass, and does not seek to excel in many areas of your life, you probably will be lazy about your sexual skill as well, and you'll learn enough to pass, have okay sex, and maybe satisfy your partners on a basic level, but you won't experience anything particularly extraordinary. There is a cliché that really attractive people, though desired by many, are actually the worst lovers because they don't have to be good at sex to get sex. They just rely on looking good. We all have to put in effort to get a return.

Deep down, you know you haven't put your heart into it. You know you could dedicate yourself to a more committed and powerful sexual practice. A lot of women get upset at their lovers for not providing more for them sexually. They want a deeper sexual life, but they are not doing it for themselves. You have to take action, as Sam did. Your life will not transform if you do not. You must lead. You are taking the reins as you begin to identify the skills you need in order to have a more empowered sexual and relationship life.

WHAT SKILLS DO I NEED?

SKILL = COMPETENT EXCELLENCE IN PERFORMANCE;
EXPERTNESS; DEXTERITY

The equation looks something like this:

EDUCATION **+** PRACTICE **=** SKILL **→** SATISFACTION & PLEASURE

It's satisfying and pleasurable to do something well. The same is true for sex, and competence is a fantastic confidence builder.

There are many skills required to have healthy intimate relationships and powerful sexual experiences and to live a fulfilling and emotionally deep life. Here are some examples of skills you might pursue to enhance and improve your sexual life, play, and relationships and other areas of your life:

EMOTIONAL SKILLS

Shifting negativity, unhealthy thought patterns, and unproductive storytelling

Coping skills

Expressing emotions in a healthy, effective way

Managing difficult emotions like anger, loneliness, and depression

Overcoming fear, doubt, and worry

Managing defensive patterns

Using emotional release techniques

Expressing love and compassion

Practicing self-care

COMMUNICATION SKILLS

Active listening

Speaking with power and without blame or shame

Asking for what you want

Setting limits and boundaries

Speaking with compassion

Giving constructive feedback

Negotiating effectively

Disagreeing with grace

Broaching difficult topics like improving your sex life or the possibility of ending the relationship

SEXUAL TECHNIQUES

Body knowledge and awareness: sexual anatomy and functioning and how it impacts pleasure

Manual stimulation: female and male genitals

Oral skills: kissing, necking, fellatio, cunnilingus, analingus

Intercourse: helpful positions, ways of dealing with various anatomy for maximum pleasure, working with injuries, health issues, or disability

Anal sex: safety and pleasure, anal anatomy, technique

Stimulation: breasts, testicles, other body parts

Role-play: how to design and execute a role-play

Particular fetishes: foot or toe sucking, rope bondage, spanking, and so on

BDSM (Bondage, Dominance, Discipline, Submission, Sadism, Masochism) skills: There is a huge array of activities that fall under the umbrella of BDSM. This could include learning how to play with sensation and body impact (spanking, flogging, caning, wrestling, electricity, cold/hot, needles) and/or how to play with power and control (dominating/submitting, master/slave play, age play, humiliation, service-oriented play).

ORGASMIC/PLEASURE SKILLS

Erotic touch

Flirtation and seduction

Techniques for deepening pleasure and prolonging and expanding orgasm

Use of sound and movement

Conscious breathwork

Muscle strengthening and control

THE KING OF SEX SKILLS?

I have spoken with several women who own woman-centric sex toy shops committed to providing sexual skills–building education. I hear the same thing over and over: they feel frustrated that their most consistently well-attended classes are the ones they offer on "How to Give a Great Blow Job."

Now, I'm not saying blow jobs aren't a skill worthy of learning. You'll be able to make many partners happy with this skill. That's great for them and good for your confidence.

But my question, and the thing that frustrates these feminist shop owners, is: Why aren't women flocking to the classes they offer about women's bodies and pleasure or some of the classes people (like myself) come to teach about sexual empowerment and healthy sexual power? Too many *Glamour* articles focused on how to be a blow job expert? Why aren't women interested in building their sexual esteem in other ways? Why is the focus on a sex act that is historically at the epicenter of sexual inequality and female submission in the bedroom? Many women have experienced deep-seated messages of subordination by serving men with blow jobs. Many women have experiences of feeling obligated to perform oral sex on their male partners and feel perpetually frustrated that it's not reciprocated.

This is not to say that some women don't just love to suck cock. Some truly do—it gives them immense pleasure. Expand your ideas of what you can learn. Sexual proficiency and skill go way beyond being able to give a good blow job.

ASSESS YOUR SKILLS

In order to figure out the skills you need to learn, begin by assessing what's not working.

> ... Do you have a lot of poor, confusing, or difficult communication?
>
> ... Do you struggle to ask for what you want and end up disappointed?

… Do you ask for things sexually that your lover fails to deliver, which means you have to show them?

… Are you unable to orgasm?

… Do you feel a lack of pleasure in your sex life—or life in general?

… Do you feel like you always have the same old sex and need to expand your repertoire?

… Have your breakups gone badly in the past?

… Is there turmoil with your former lovers?

… Do you constantly feel sexually unfulfilled?

… Do you fantasize about experiences you don't believe you will ever have?

… Do you question what your fantasies are?

… Do you want to explore something new? (Role-play, threesomes, open relationships, BDSM . . .)

3 QUESTIONS FOR IDENTIFYING AND DEVELOPING SEXUAL SKILLS

1. What isn't working?

2. What skills would help it work better?

3. Where could I learn these skills?

YOUR ASSIGNMENT: WHAT SEXUAL MUSCLES DO YOU WANT TO WORK ON?

Make a list of the top five or ten sexual skills you'd like to learn or improve on. Then research where and how you could learn those things.

... What books can I read?

... What classes can I take?

... What teachers, healers, coaches, or other practitioners specialize in these skills?

... What teleclasses, webinars, or other events could help?

... What community resources might be useful?

... What lover might explore them with me?

... How can I practice these skills and with whom?

Your sex life, sex skills, and relationship skills will not magically get better or materialize out of nothing. They will develop out of your consciousness and commitment to grow them. Have fun with this! We are talking about learning to do things that are pleasing.

SET OUT ON THE PATH

A couple years ago, in my New Year's intentions I decided I wanted to have ten sexual firsts, and I surpassed my goal. Last year I made that commitment again. This year I've upped the ante and chosen to have fifteen. On New Year's Day alone I had two, so I started out well on my way. It's fun to figure out what's next, and it's fun to be surprised. I've been teaching sexuality for more than twenty years, I know more about sex than 99 percent of the general population, and there is *always* room for me to grow, just like you. That's the great thing about sex . . . learning and growing is endless, and like other areas of life, consistent growth is what keeps it interesting and passion-filled to the end. It doesn't hurt that I am poly and kinky, which does open up a lot of possibilities, but everyone can learn new things. I've put a list of potential sexual firsts in the *Woman on Fire* online portal if you need some help jump-starting ideas.

If you want to evolve as a sexual person, it is imperative that you examine your skills and where you need to develop, and then set out to do it. It won't happen by itself—it's up to you. Once you've identified what you need, you need to commit to seeking it out and learning it. You are guaranteed to grow if you make this commitment. If you don't, you'll probably remain right where you are, knowing you are stunting your own growth by not making it a priority. That is most definitely *not* sexually empowering. Skills are malleable. This is really good news for all of us. You can build on what you know now, learn new things, and become the best possible lover you can be, to yourself as much as anybody else.

Please take time to design your own statement of commitment so as to solidify how you will build your own skills. You can find it in the online portal. And then play: unabashed, full-on, dreamlike, fantasy-in-hand, clits-out *play*. Play and find your interests. Play and awaken your desire. Play, revel, and enjoy. Play and open up. Play and find the skill sets you want to pursue, and you'll be on your way to being the sexual ninja or sexual wise woman you are capable of being—becoming sexually intelligent.

10

Element 8:
HOME

BUILD SEXUAL CONFIDENCE AND
COME HOME TO YOU

*And you? When will you begin that
long journey into yourself?*

—Rumi

The element of home is not about a place; it's about a
state of being. Home is what happens when you stop
leaving yourself and giving away your power. It's the
freedom that emerges when you are comfortable in
your own skin and you stop needing to control everything or be liked by everyone.

Being comfortable in yourself means you get to
be free: more authentic, more joyful. When you come
from this place of being at home in yourself without
all of the mitigation and self-patrolling you used to
do, without constantly filtering your thoughts, reac-

tions, and feelings so other people will like you, that's when you become the real you. When you show up as the real you in relationships, not only do the relationships become more honest, but you stop getting so much of what you don't want and start getting what you *do* want. That means you're happier. If you are happier, your relationships are happier, and that's what makes life better every day.

If you've been living in a "broken" home or seeing brokenness as home, that ends here. You are not broken, and you are every bit as capable of creating this sense of home within yourself as anyone else. You can create a whole and rich home no matter your background, your struggles, your oppression, your trauma, your past beliefs, or your doubts. You are doing your work, and in that work you are creating the home you really want, where it feels safe, nurturing, comfortable, confident, at ease. We all need a homecoming.

WHY WE ABANDON OURSELVES

We learn to abandon ourselves for so many reasons. We don't think we are likable, lovable, beautiful enough, worthy enough. We tell ourselves stories of how much we don't deserve and then feel bad every time we actually get something we want. Our wanting doesn't stop, but we get in the way of our actual enjoyment of all we have. If you are in a place of self-loathing, beating up on your body, your psyche, or your tender heart, you are abandoning the person who needs your love most. If you don't like you, you will leave you and go to other people to try to get validation that you are not as unlovable as you thought. That is the leaving.

As a child who experienced the abandonment of a parent, I have studied abandonment in my life and have abandoned myself. I became accustomed to leaving myself without even knowing it. Many of us go through an abandonment as a child, whether one or both parents actually left, or were so drunk, high, sick, unpresent, neglectful, or abusive that we felt alone and abandoned even in their presence.

PATSY'S HOMECOMING

Patsy's story (in Element 2, Release) is a good example of someone who learned to leave herself. She had to take care of her mother, even though she was abused by her father and very much needed her mother to be present for her. She took on the burden of caring for her mother and never got to be cared for in the way she needed. She was so accustomed to caring for others and being overdetermined by their needs, thoughts, and wishes, that she completely lost the inner knowing of what she needed until she decided to do the work to come home. She was truly a changed person when she did.

It took a lot of time to realize that I spent much of my time living in other people's lives. I was consumed by what other people thought of me, or might think of me, to the point where I didn't ever feel truly alone. Even by myself, I was listening to my projections about other people's thoughts. It took a lot of work to notice the extent to which I heard these voices, to realize they were me projecting my own fears onto others, and begin to believe that my voice was most important.

To change my emotional patterns around sex and everything else, I had to admit how much of my power I gave away. It was so easy to feel like a victim—it was much easier to blame others for not meeting my needs than it was to acknowledge that I was actually preventing myself and others from meeting them.

Stepping into my own power has been uncomfortable. My fear has fought me every step of the way, crying out that I am asking too much, that I will be hated, abandoned, alone. Yet every step has proven this false. That fear still exists in me, and I still have more power to reclaim, but the work I've done so far has drastically improved my quality of life. I can easily give voice to things that would have eaten me alive in silence a few years ago, all because I have faith that my needs are worth meeting.

For me, coming home to myself has been a challenging process. It's taken courage to really look at myself, to truly face the things about me that make living inside my own head uncomfortable. Cleaning out the dirt and cobwebs that accumulated while I was busy neglecting myself will take time, and it can be hard to just be in my own dirty, imperfect self. And it has been so rewarding. I feel so much more grounded and centered than I ever have. Even my worst days are so much better than before, because I am so much more solid in my own self. Coming home to myself has meant I am more authentic, more genuine, in every single thing I do.

Patsy's determination to change these patterns and be more powerful is inspiring. She saw that something wasn't working, and she set out to change it. She knew that her sexual abuse was a part of it, but she didn't see the whole picture until we began to uncover all the patterns she had learned in order to survive.

I myself had to go through a divorce to come home to myself. I hope you can do it without a dramatic event that battle calls you home. But it might take something big if you don't start to realize that when you leave home, you can't really be present to the relationships and the deep intimacy and sex you want because something really big is missing: *you.* In a homecoming, you will start to show up fully and in love with yourself, which will attract others who are at home in themselves, which is where the magic of true intimacy happens.

THE WAYS WE LEAVE

There are so many ways we leave home. How do you know when you're not at home? You become overly concerned with others, steeped in judgment and criticism—which takes you outside of yourself. You don't say no when you really mean no. Or you say no and can't stop feeling guilty for it. You spend too much energy taking care of someone else. You fail to take care of your own needs while you people-please everyone else. You stuff away your true feelings and pretend they aren't there. All of these things disconnect you from your core self.

You merge with someone else who doesn't allow you to be self-reliant. I often speak to women who routinely have "duty sex," or "receptacle sex," with their partners: this is when they don't want to have sex but have it because they feel it's their obligation to do so as wife, partner, or girlfriend. This deep self-betrayal hurts them, and it hurts their partner because anyone who really cares about you won't want you to have sex if you don't really want to. I've met many women who don't like sex (or don't think they do) because they have only ever had experiences that were controlled by others and never felt their own agency around sex. Bring your sexual agency home. Have the kind of sex you want, when you want it. That means exploring with a new slate and discovering what really turns you on apart from what a partner or other people want from you.

Sometimes facing what is inside you feels too hard—the pain, confusion, trauma, or emotions are too much to handle, and you run away from yourself so you don't have to deal with those feelings or memories. But they will be there when you sober up, when you are alone with yourself and walk through the door of your own internal house. Eventually you will have to face the parts of yourself you've been running from. And it will free you. If you know you've been leaving, it's time to call yourself back and find your way. This is your hero's journey. The call is made, and the warrior or priestess must answer the call. The journey home to yourself is the way. You are standing there with wet clothes, uncomfortable, wanting the beauty you know is possible on the other side of the mountain, and the only way out is through—you've got to walk that mucky path out of the soppy swamp, over the hill to the new vista.

TAKE BACK YOUR POWER

Women are literally conditioned to leave home—to give up our power to men, to take care of anyone else but ourselves, to chase attention and validation, to work hard at being "nice" and likable, to put everything and everyone else first. You have to be first in order to really be there for anyone else. Often I ask women, "Will you choose yourself or your partner/husband/relationship?" Sometimes that is the choice. I sit silently, waiting for their answer, hoping they will choose themselves, and I hear how hard it is for many to take the risk to be first in line. They will choose to stay in an unhealthy or dysfunctional relationship with someone who is not willing to grow rather than leave and be free to become who they are really meant to be. You've heard the cliché airplane mask analogy. It's popular because it's true. How can you be unwilling to put on your own oxygen mask before tending to others?

Women give away their power in myriad ways. When I say "You are giving away your power," people don't always know what I mean. Let's get really clear about what that looks like in different parts of your life in the words of women.

When I've asked women at my workshops how they give their power away, some of the things they say are:

EMOTIONALLY

... I don't get angry because women should not get angry.

... I don't let others see how I feel; no one sees me cry.

... I'm afraid of being judged.

... I take things personally.

... I'm afraid of what will happen if I set clear boundaries.

... I avoid confrontation, so I forgive negative behavior too quickly.

... I'm not in touch with my emotions until it's too late.

... I feel guilty and selfish when I assert myself.

... I keep others happy at my expense.

PHYSICALLY

... I push myself too hard; I don't rest enough or eat well.

... I stuff my emotions by overeating when I'm upset.

... I stop eating and deny myself pleasure to punish myself.

... I go to bed too late or get up too early to avoid my partner.

... I'm embarrassed by how I am aging.

... I feel powerless when I light a cigarette.

... I hate the way I look.

... I won't let anyone see me naked, so I can't have a true
relationship.

SEXUALLY

... I have sex when I don't want to in order to please my
partner.

... I hold back during sex because I doubt that I'm desirable.

... I can't reveal myself during sex; I'm afraid of being
vulnerable.

... I don't tell my partner what I do and do not want.

... I dissociate during sex; I'm so checked out I let
my partner do what he or she wants.

... I use sex as a tool to get what I want.

... I'm scared because I want to explore and my partner
does not.

... I worry that I'm too difficult to please and take too
much time to climax.

... I'm afraid of being judged as dirty.

… I play dumb.

… I defer to others and lessen the impact of my own intelligence.

… I play forgetful to get what I want.

… I always second-guess myself.

… I do not risk speaking what I think.

… I don't feel qualified to have an "expert opinion" because I don't have enough education.

… I tell myself I don't have anything important to say.

There are ways we give away our power financially and even spiritually as well. Personal power has to include the whole package.

HOW DO YOU GIVE AWAY YOUR POWER?

There are so many ways women give away their power. You might relate to many of them. Take a moment to check off the ones you do, and then make a list of the additional ways you give away your own personal power. Think about the things that take you out of your center, your own deep knowing, your own confidence, making powerful decisions and directing your own life. Think about the ways you avoid taking responsibility for all parts of yourself and your life. If you are not in a place of full responsibility, there is a victim at work who thinks that responsibility is someone else's, and that means you've left your center, you've left home.

Once you have made your list, pick out the top five to ten things you want to stop doing and begin to work on those. Every time you come home, you get more comfortable there, and after a while you will find yourself actually living there. Keep working these muscles.

YOUR NEW HOME

Have you ever bought a new house? Searched for the sanctuary that would make every day better, the place that you could live in, grow in, love in, and share with the people you share your life with? The home that will anchor you, the place you will come home to after long trips and feel at ease, surrounded by the comforts that bring you joy, the environment that makes you feel good? Think about how much energy you put into finding the right house or place to live. Think about how much goes into finding the special space that will nurture you and create the right conditions for your life. You've probably done that searching.

Now you are building home on the inside—and it requires just as much of you, but it's a different kind of work. To be at home in yourself requires independence, self-efficacy, radical self-reliance, a healthy relationship to self and others, self-clarity, self-intimacy, confidence, responsibility, and true power. At home you allow yourself to be in a process of evolution because you trust yourself to lead. You can grow, change your mind, expand your desires, and want new things. You are not who you were. You have to give up those old pieces of who you were—the ones that kept the real you away—so you can come home and be at peace. Give up the "I'm broken" and the "I don't deserve." The idea that you have to suffer. The ways you prevent yourself from feeling at peace within yourself. When you know you can take care of yourself and you take responsibility for it, and when you know who you are and express it with confidence, you have come home. You are in your true power when you cease to look to others to decide for you, and when you stop thinking that giving everything to them is what gives you value. You are valuable because you are. Like a huge eucalyptus tree that stands in its own glory and doesn't have to prove itself. You are your own eucalyptus. You are enough. At home in yourself, you stop running these stories about having to be something you are not. You expand into the confidence of being you—all of you. You stop trying to be what everyone else wants you to be.

Sexually, being at home in yourself means you can enjoy being in your body and experience sex more deeply. Sex with yourself becomes an exchange between you and the universe. You build up your internal fire as you fan the flames. You accept all of who you are and express it with the passion of being rooted in your own truth. When sex is not about being overly concerned about how much and how well you please someone else, and instead it's about being present and creating a mutually enjoyable space, it is a completely different experience. At home in yourself, you can be open to receive, to feel pleasure, to give what you want to give and to say no to what you are not open to without guilt or other feelings that take you out of the present moment. The anxiety and nerves quiet so you can enjoy what is revealed, create what you want, explore something new, and hear your partner's requests. You can let go of the spectatoring that keeps you watching yourself and your sexual interactions from the outside, critiquing your body and "performance" in favor of being in your body and in the exchange. Home is the centering you feel from this vantage point, and it frees you to be who you really are. When you can do this sexually, you can do it in every other part of your life.

There is no more self-abandonment, which means you no longer need to fear the abandonment of others. You love yourself and you mother yourself where you didn't get mothered or parented enough. You know you will never be alone. You follow what is true for you, regardless of what outside influences say or want. This doesn't mean you don't need other people. It means you invite the ones into your life who respect your boundaries and create a nourishing reciprocity. You allow yourself to have support because you are anchored inside.

MURPHY'S HOMECOMING

When I first spoke with Murphy, she was a thirty-one-year-old wilderness guide from Vermont who was frustrated and in a place of not having what she wanted financially and sexually. She had not been able to create sexual relationships in which she could express the full range of her desire and she felt trapped in low-paying jobs. She was keen to look at her patterns that had held her back around both sex and money and to begin to allow herself to have more in her life. As she stepped into her authentic sexual self, she learned to stand strong in her own worth, and she began to make choices based on her deep desires. She came home and stopped engaging many of the patterns that kept her in a place of abandoning herself and trying to be what other people wanted her to be. Her work deepened her most authentic expression of sexuality and gender and allowed her to break through the limiting beliefs that were holding her back.

Embracing my butch gender expression has been a long journey. It took many years for me to even become comfortable with my lesbian identity, and becoming butch felt even more transgressive. I've gone from being a shy, fairly femme, quite passive person who suppressed her sexual desire out of fear of hurting others, to being a confident butch lesbian who isn't afraid to flirt and express her desire in the world. I was really afraid that women wouldn't find me sexually desirable if I had a butch gender expression, because I myself was much more attracted to femmes than butches . . . but I finally figured out (with some help from my friends!) that I needed to stop dressing like the women I was attracted to and start dressing like the woman I am inside. As soon as I made the shift . . . bam! I started to meet beautiful femme women who were really attracted to butches in general and me in particular! Now I get way more sexual attention and flirtation than I ever did before the shift, probably because I walk with a kind of confidence, authenticity, and brashness that I didn't have before.

I know I am not empowered when other people's reactions to me trigger insecurities about my self-worth and when I make decisions about my romantic relationships that compromise what I desire in exchange for security or validation. I've grown much more confident and self-directed in all realms of my life. I've started my own business and transformed my relationship with money, both of which wouldn't have been possible before I got in touch with my own internal sense of desire. When I operate from that internal compass, I can steer a true and accountable path for myself. My relationships feel so much lighter, more free, more fun, and more truthful because I don't come to them with a strong need for validation; I come to them just for the joy of connection and to build experiences that are bigger and richer than I can create in isolation.

I feel empowered when I flirt with people I'm attracted to. It's fun when they flirt back, but I think I feel even more empowered when they don't respond and it feels totally fine—that my sexual empowerment is not dependent on external validation or the results of a particular interaction; it's something I carry within me and experience internally as a deep truth.

I have a strong drive to please my partners and honor them as sacred sexual beings, making love to them with a sense of devotion that excites and inspires us both. Learning to be confident in that was the easier half of the equation. I also have a deep yearning to be completely vulnerable and open in letting my partner pleasure me. That has been harder for me because it feels much scarier. It takes trust in my partner, but perhaps a deeper trust in myself, that I will be enough, that I deserve it, and that I will be fine if I have an amazing experience but then lose access to that person or circumstance in the future for some reason. Many thanks to the femmes who have encouraged me and shared their desire with me on this road!

Murphy's story is a great depiction of how important it is to be who we really are sexually, and how much more attractive authentic sexuality is. She stepped into herself as lesbian, butch, and as a polyamorous person, and so many experiences opened up for her. Her homecoming was intrinsically related to embracing her sexual identity. Stepping into those authentic identities and expression created a newfound confidence in her that helped her to change and dramatically improve her life.

CONFIDENCE IS SEXY

One of the most universally sexy traits in a person is their confidence. Over and over in my workshops when I ask women to define sexual empowerment and name qualities they need in order to feel sexually empowered, confidence comes up as the one women most want. Everyone wants to feel more confident as a sexual creature. Somehow women know that confidence holds a key to unlocking their greatest sexual potential. When you are authentically confident, you are at home in yourself.

Confidence is having the ability to do the things you want to do in life without holding back and second-guessing yourself. Confidence expression is different for different people. Some grow confidence through their ability to do things, developing their competence. Some through their friendliness and ability to approach and talk to just about anyone. Some with their power of oration and ability to inspire people. Others build it through making people laugh and being funny.

I believe that there are many different expressions of confidence, and they show up sexually in different strengths, vulnerabilities, and needs. Confidence isn't something you have or you don't: it looks different for an unstoppable Power Player than it does for a flirty Enigma or a shy Wallflower. Many people think that if they don't have "it," they will never have it, and I don't think that's how confidence works. I think we each have a Confidence Type.

When we can see the particulars of how we most effectively build confidence and that it's not a one-size-fits-all scenario, we have the ability to be truly successful in building our confidence. At its root, it's an inside job, whether you are a shy Wallflower, a sassy Skeptic, a mysterious Enigma, a warm Connector, or a fierce Power Player. To explain each one is beyond the scope of this book, but you can get more information on the five types and learn yours online. It's also a helpful system for understanding what drives your coworkers, family members, lovers, and friends so you can work better with them to create win-win situations.

MAPPING YOUR CONFIDENCE TYPE

I have observed how confidence works in people over the years, and I have mapped out a system of five Confidence Types, or styles, with their strengths, deep fears, challenges, emotional tone, abilities, and personal needs. I invite you to take my Confidence Types Quiz at amyjogoddard.com/ confidencequiz to identify your dominant and secondary Confidence Types.

You'll get an audio class that details the five Confidence Types so you can go deeper in understanding how to best work with your own confidence style and build on your natural abilities.

As we discussed in the previous chapter, one of the best ways to increase confidence is to build skills. When you feel assured that you are capable of performing any task to your best ability and to a high standard, you will absolutely feel confident to do that task again and again. Committing to developing your sexual, emotional, and relational skills is the surest way to feel more confident sexually and more self-assured when going after what you want. And because confidence is sexy, you will open yourself to even more success as you build on that foundation of confidence!

As you identify some of the foggy spaces or gaps in your knowledge, and expand yourself with new skills and knowledge about your sexual body and sexuality, your world begins to open up. It's exciting to crack the code. That excitement creates an exuberance and a zest for living, which compels you to seek additional excitement, more new fun abilities, and the next thing you know, you are living in a state of playful desire. As you use your desire to add to your knowledge and skills, you begin to create a craft of your sexuality. Your knowing in your body increases and your sexual expression matches it. You know something inside, and that inner knowing is expressed on the outside as confidence, a sense of self-assurance, and knowing you have the ability to follow your desires to a pleasing outcome. There is a new confidence in you about your ability to meet your own needs. That's hot.

I've seen this process so many times with my clients. They come to me wanting to work on certain outcomes and we identify skills they need to work on. As they do, they have more success in the world, which means more fulfillment. They build their confidence, start going more for what they want, and ultimately they transform their lives. It's so satisfying to be a part of and to witness. There is no end to this process. There is always more to learn. The turnoff comes when sexual confidence swings into an arrogance that prevents you from thinking you still have something to learn. Not sexy, not fun, and not even good for you because then you stop growing (not to mention that arrogance pushes people away). Confidence is good, and it is a dance to express and consistently experience it with all the challenges life sends your way.

HOMECOMING

The greatest thing in the world is to know
how to belong to oneself.
—MICHEL DE MONTAIGNE

You are gathering the pieces of yourself that have scattered, fled, or been lost. This is your homecoming. There are always more desires. More wanting, more moving away from your center—leaving home again. You come home. You leave. You dive deep and you fly back out. Homecoming is a repetitive process. We do it over and over. Even when we have come home, we sometimes stray and we need people we feel at home with to anchor us and to remind us to come back. We need to learn to anchor ourselves and bring ourselves back. You might come home again and again until it becomes the place you want to be, the familiar place you know and are most comforted by.

As you develop your own sense of sexual empowerment and intelligence, you come home to yourself more often and more easily, until you get so adept with your insights and get so intimate with yourself that you stop leaving home at all. You stay with yourself, and that makes you the best lover. If you are fully present to yourself and your own needs and wants and if you develop the skills required to express them in healthy ways, you will be honorable and present to your sex partners.

This state of home is mobile. It's portable. It's connected to your body, your spirit, and your psyche. You can be at home in yourself no matter who is around you or where you are on earth by reminding yourself of your truth, checking in with your honest desires, standing up for yourself emotionally, physically, and sexually, and ceasing forsaking yourself by standing in your love for yourself regardless of what is going on around you. One of my women's program participants commented on how valuable it was that our weekend retreats happened in multiple places because she got to see how we are capable of creating home anywhere.

Learning to be at home in yourself is essential for your empowerment. You cannot be in your own power if you are busy leaving yourself. You are not at home when you live by doing things for others out of obligation rather than a real desire in you to do them. You are not at home when you are chasing compliments and validation from the outer world. You are not at home when you play roles that are not who you really are. Home is the antecedent to all that had you feeling broken.

When at home, it is safe to be all of who you are. It is a loving and supportive place. You don't have to start from that place in order to create it. If you have been leaving, you can come home to yourself now. This home is the whole you, the unabashed "I'm damn proud to be me" place of self-possession, joy, and rich self-love.

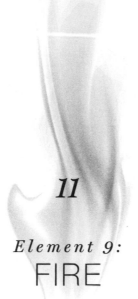

11

Element 9:
FIRE

USE YOUR DYNAMIC SEXUAL ENERGY
TO LIVE VIBRANTLY

You have unpacked your antiquated stories and
found your voice. You've released what needed releasing and have freed yourself of the things that
block you from being who you are meant to be.
You've looked hard at your emotional patterns and
have redefined what it means to be emotionally powerful. You've reconnected to your body and learned
new ways to love and accept it. You've tapped into
your desire and explored what you really want. You've
given yourself permission to want what you want, to
experience pleasure, and to have the sexual life you
dream of. You've found your enthusiastic "yes" and
your honest "no." You've set your boundaries. You've
asked for what you desire. You've assessed your skills
and gained confidence in your sexual art and craft.

You remembered how to play, which opened you up to exuberance and joy and way more fun. You are coming home to the authentic *you* that knows she is enough, she is worthy, she is whole. She doesn't have to leave herself and go outside to get what she needs anymore. She likes how it feels right here at home.

You are on fire. What lights you up with passion? What do you want to set aflame? What nourishes the seeds you have planted into full-blown creations? Your fire is your core sexual energy we talked about in chapter 2. It is the genesis of all you create, inside and out—*from* the inside out. Your fire is your own personal fulfillment generator. What does fire need in order to flare its flames? Oxygen. What does orgasm need in order to be expressed? Breath.

There is a thermal energy at the center of the earth, like there is a thermal energy in the center of you. Nurture your inner fire. Nurture that which lights you up and sets you ablaze as a kinetic force of nature.

BLAZING A TRAIL

After I'd finished grad school in my late twenties, many of my dreams were coming to life. I was being mentored by radical sex pioneer Betty Dodson and featured in her *Viva la Vulva* educational video, and I was meeting sexual luminaries who I admired. I was in love with sexy powerhouse New York City, surrounded by the most brilliant sex-positive feminists on the planet. I had written, performed, and produced my play: *Vulvalution, Her Lips Speak*. We produced a sold-out several-week run at an off-off-Broadway downtown women's theater. I had taken major risks with this work, entwining education and performance with seeming success. In *Vulvalution* I had shown larger-than-life photos of real vulvas to my unassuming audience. My activism was art. I was also hosting a women's sexuality program on the very first "Internet television" streaming network when the World Wide Web was in its infancy, and I was on the verge of publishing my first book. My creativity was on fire.

No small surprise, my sex life was too: I was in the most exploratory, expansive sexual relationship I'd ever had, with someone who could really *meet me* where I was. I was exploring the terrain of my expanding desire with a woman I trusted to guide me to places I'd not been before, and with her skilled prompts, I was becoming the true architect of my own fantasies, desire, and pleasure. I was exploring BDSM and figuring out what it was about it that turned me on. I was claiming my polyamorous life and choosing to live differently from most people I knew long before there were poly social groups, dating sites, and TV programs. I was stepping into my own identity as a queer femme and exploring gender as a drag king in the burgeoning 1990s New York City drag king scene. In short, sexuality was not just my profession, it was my art form.

I can remember walking down Houston Street in Manhattan one night with my BFF and partner in crime for many outrageously fun adventures, saying to her: "I absolutely *love* my life. I love everything about it, everything I do. It's like the best movie I've ever seen, and I can't wait to see what happens next!"

That was a moment when I recognized the quickening of my own desire, my flame being lit up—that was me, the explorer who set off into the wilderness of New York City in her early twenties, ready to take risks, push her limits, and to experience vibrant life. That was my desire on fire, the inside of me being met expertly and precisely by the outside world. I was a woman on fire.

Several years later, after I turned thirty, my path shifted as I developed a partnership with a woman I grew to love deeply. I created a home with a partner for the first time. I was loved in a way I'd not been loved before, and it expanded my ability to love. She and I began to travel the world and we lived a beautiful life together, surrounded by circles of artists and musicians and people who were doing meaningful and beautiful things with their lives—people who were also lit up with passion. Our relationship was revered and respected by friends. The way we lived our values and loved each other inspired others. I know because I was told so many times by members of our close chosen family.

I experienced an amazingly loving nine-year relationship and I spent my thirties learning and studying love, intimacy, and partnership—things I needed to understand in order to do the work I do now. In the beginning of that relationship there was a lot of sexual passion. We explored sex wildly, and our sex was connected, passionate, pleasurable, and fulfilling. I brought my fire to the relationship in so many ways. Slowly, I began to concede sexual desires. The quality of our sex was high throughout the relationship, but the frequency and level of exploration dramatically decreased. My frustration about this rose to the surface, and I found myself in couples therapy for the first time, trying to understand why we were where we were, and how to move out of it, or beyond it, back to that place of fiery passion meets loyal love.

We were in that muddy space for several years. It's that in-between heart-sink place, like when coffee goes from being just warm enough to still be enjoyed to just cool enough to be disappointing. On the eve of my fortieth birthday, the coffee was cold, and we split ways. After I got through my grief and picked myself up, I began to get excited again. Why? Because there *I* was again, with my internal desire as my compass, ready to re-create my life—or get it back on the trajectory I'd subconsciously aborted some years before. And that meant stepping into my power as a woman, as an entrepreneur, as a free agent, and as CEO of my own life in a way I never actually had. It meant being totally single for the first time in my life since age thirteen when I first started dating. It meant me dating myself. It meant getting back my fire.

And guess what? I found myself back in that place I can remember so vividly, as the one who loves her life and enjoys the popcorn while the story unfolds, ever more magical than I could even imagine—and my imaginings are pretty sparkly and sexy.

There were plenty of times when I had that in my marriage. There were times when I was alight with excitement for how we were living and loving and all we were creating together. We both were. Yet slowly I had begun leaving myself in various ways. I was not marching true north. I had to get back to blazing the trails I knew I was here to ignite. And now I can't allow myself to demand less at any time.

Kiki, a thirty-four-year-old woman from New York City, participated in one of my first women's programs. She explains so eloquently what it meant to have her fire lit up:

> *I now stand more grounded in who I am as a sensual being, swing my hips with more awareness of my body, flirt with more confidence, speak to my lover with a deeper and more honest intention, pray with a bit more attention, make love more deeply/wildly/softly/without walls, or sometimes I retreat back to where I was before, yet I'm more mindful about it. It is an everyday (sometimes extremely hard) journey, no doubt. However, the tools and energetic fuel I have gained from the workshops keep me mindful and intentional and capable of saying yes every day, no matter how quiet or loud! I wholeheartedly recommend this journey to all women wanting to live a fulfilled life in every way and are willing to accept the challenge to do so.*

BEING POWERFUL

To get clear about sexual power, let's talk about sexual energy. When your energy is strong and you are aligned with it, you have a focused way of attracting the things you want. This is an ideal state.

This core sexual energy is essentially your gas tank; it keeps you going, but it's not mere fuel. There is a quality to it that is fundamental to your having a dynamic, orgasmic life.

When your core sexual energy gets depleted, it impacts you on multiple levels. You become dulled to life, sometimes even depressed. The joy, poetry, and allure of everyday life dissipates. You find it harder to appreciate your life and the details that make it gorgeous and worth living. The colors become muted and everything is less shiny. You forget the power you have to bring into your life the people, relationships, experiences, and things you want. In a word, you stop experiencing pleasure.

Most people do not work with their sexual energy consciously. An essential step in living a sexually empowered life is to acknowledge that this energy is there, consistently nurture it like the friend it is, and increase it. Then you have more fuel and power to experience pleasure and desire and to express your sexuality with the fervor that makes your life vibrant and joyous.

Your core energy is your life force. The hot thermal core. It is the fire. It's that part of you that tingles with excitement and spreads through your body when you orgasm. You can keep it for yourself and you can share it. You can funnel it in many different directions. The power and strength of your fire comes from developing the tools we have been talking about in this book.

I hope that by now you are comfortable with the idea of your personal power, and that you are excited to exercise it ever more adeptly so you can enjoy your life more profoundly. It is your power-within. When you use it to connect to others and to co-create, it is power-*with*. No one needs to take power away from someone else in order to experience themselves powerfully. That is a harmful myth and a story that gets played out in films, on television, and in books over and over; that somehow if you own the fullness of who you are as a woman, it diminishes someone else. This myth keeps us carefully avoiding being "too powerful." It also keeps women in competition. And that is not the world I am here to co-create. I want all of us women on fire to unapologetically step into it fully, fires blazing, and make a better world. You harm no one by being strong and solid in your own personal power. You only inspire. We are a reflection of one another.

What specifically makes you feel powerful?

MY TOP 10 PLEASURE LIST

Think about what makes you feel vibrantly alive and fully expressed. What activities do you love so much that you lose track of time while doing them? You feel so connected to yourself and your own power and life force that you get lost in them. What things bring you the most pleasure?

Make a top ten (or more) list of the things that you love doing more than anything. It could be simple things like giving hugs or smiling at strangers. It could be more involved like art-making, sex, or dancing naked. It might be related to nature or the people you love. What makes you feel on fire?

Then look at how much time you are spending doing these things. To live a vibrantly pleasurable life, you've got to be doing things on this list each day. At least one. If the time you spend in your life on this top ten list is small, what adjustments can you make? Remind yourself to engage with what you actually love, with what brings you unrestrained joy.

THE ABUNDANCE OF SEXUAL ENERGY

Sexuality is, by nature, abundant. It is built to breathe and expand and invite all that is possible into your experience. Its energy is transcendent—it allows you to reach expanded consciousness that connects both physical and spiritual in a way no other energy can.

You are meant to be big. You are not meant to be small. None of us are. Yet we make ourselves small for so many reasons. I frequently work with clients on this—all the ways they sabotage and diminish the fullness of who they are. I see women diminish themselves so they don't intimidate men, leaving themselves again so they can take care of someone else. I see how so many women struggle to be in their full sexual expression without apology. They dim their own fire. No need to dim. You can bring your energy in close for safety or move with stealth in the world as a way to consciously take care of yourself and simultaneously remain firmly in your power.

You are not meant to be diminished. You are meant to live an abundant life, full with connection, sexual vibrancy, and all the love, caring, attention, joy, and money you need. You are not here to never have enough. There is enough for all of us, and as you develop and strengthen your core sexual energy, it impacts many parts of your life.

JILL'S STORY: AWAKENING SEXUAL EXPRESSION

When I met Jill at age fifty, she had recently gone through a divorce, was working as a business coach, and raising her teenaged son. She was at peace about ending her marriage, yet she was having a hard time figuring out how to reclaim her sexuality because she'd felt unfulfilled for so long.

I was so stuck, and I had been for years. I didn't have a path or a way out of it. I was stuck around my sexual expression. I was holding it all in and repressing it all because that was my way of dealing with it. I was trying to figure out what I wanted it to look like now, and what was healthy for me. My hope was that this women's sexual empowerment program would be an avenue to prod my sexuality into unstuckness.

I was shaming my desire. I needed to give myself permission to have desire, to have my desire be what it is, and to really understand it. I opened up my curiosity to really understand what my yeses and my nos were. A big yes was about who I am attracted to and who I wanted to be with even though it's not culturally the norm, and being okay with that. The yeses helped me clarify what I wanted to create, even though it wasn't what sex was supposed to be. It meant a non-monogamous relationship. It meant having a physically based relationship without all of the romantic ideals around it. Those were stretches because they were not what I was told it was supposed to be. I'm fifty years old and I'm hot-to-trot for twenty-year-old guys, and I had to get that voice out of my head, and not go to a place of shame around it. I had to trust my desire and see where it led me. Well, it has led to the best sex of my life with a twenty-two-year-old.

At one of our women's weekends, I shared a fantasy I had, and someone said, "Oh, that's doable." I thought, "Yeah, that's doable. I'm tired of this. I'm going for it." Literally within two days of being home from the weekend, the possibility showed up in my life, and then the reality showed up! It took me two or three days to get my head around the fact that I was really going to do this, to have this fantasy come true. I was learning about the power of asking and allowing. I felt like the universe and I were having this joke, like "You're fucking with me, aren't you?" but it was really "Ask, and you shall receive."

I made a huge practice of every time I'd think about a partner I wanted to be with, I'd get really clear about my intention: to share, learn, explore, and deepen my physical intention sexually. It has turned into a spiritual process. I allow myself a lot of space in my life. I meditate and pray. I have an understanding of the physical sensations in my body when I am out of alignment and I pay attention to them and ask myself where I'm out of alignment and intention. The question I ask a lot is not just "What do I want?" but "What is in my highest and best interest and how do I allow that into my life?"

*One of the things I've asked about a lot is "Teach me about inti-
macy. Help me learn about intimacy . . . and the fear and vulnerability in that." I've been blown away by how the process shows up when
I am so clear in my intention. Being willing to be with my vulnerability and fear and be empathetic with myself in it helps me to grow
my spirit and my ability to be empathetic with other people when I
see them come up against their fears and vulnerability. The power of
intention and allowing—putting it out there—is huge. Once I get
clear, it's amazing what can and does show up. I see that where I'm at
right now—this experience of my sexual self-expression is becoming
solidified and re-created in other life experiences. I can get unstuck
with my work and other parts of my life. I'm seeing it breaking open.*

*My fire feels like a passion, a deep joy, and an aliveness and a
sparkle in my eye. People keep telling me I am beaming. When I am
with my sexual partner it opens up that energy. Recently I've been
asked out on the street by four guys within minutes of meeting them
because they see it. That energy is so enlivening. Rather than trying
to capture it and hold it in my sexual relationship, I'm really getting
that it is in me and it is shared and extends to every aspect of my
life, my work, my writing, my friendships, my way of being in the
world. It's an incredible high.*

FEEDING FIRE WITH INTENTION

Your fire is the energetic source that drives and births your desire
and full sexual expression and all you do in life. It is your essential
vibrant life force, and you need to feed it and nourish it. With these
tools you can create all you want in love, sex, and relationships, and
motor your life from this vibrant force of your being.

You have been given the gift of this energy. How would you like
to spend it? How would you like to replenish your coffers when they
are low? Recognizing that it is essential to nourish and grow this en-

ergy is one of the keys to living a full sexual and creative life. It begins with your core energy. Do you want to expand or shrink? Your sexuality has the capacity for tremendous expansion—as it expands, so does your creativity, your relationships, your abundance, and your pleasure in living your beautiful life.

You can play with this energy and move it like fire. Consciously work your second chakra when you walk. Swing your hips a little. Allow the opening. Sometimes I enjoy letting my genitals lead my walk because it's less common for women to walk from their pelvis. If your genitals lead, how does that shift your energy and your movement? Try letting your pelvis lead and see. In meditation, lie in goddess pose (flat on your back, knees splayed out with feet flat against each other as close to your yoni as possible) or sit in a squat with your feet flat on the floor and say a blessing or make an intention (as Jill did) for your day or for your sexuality. Make an intention to open, receive, and connect. What a beautiful way to bring practice to your sexuality.

The vast majority of people will never walk this path. They are afraid of their own power, their sexuality, and their erotic energy. They're afraid they won't actually know what to do with all of this energy and power if they really embraced it. They're afraid to be out of control, to want too much, or to be seen as selfish. They fear they might not know how to control themselves, so they avoid the vulnerability and out-of-control nature of orgasm and sexual exposure. Sometimes it's easier to keep it in the mystery than to take responsibility for actually having it. The idea of it seems more palatable than the reality. Yet the more you clamp it down, the less able you are to pluck the unformed out of the ether and make beauty with it.

Because women are often afraid to eclipse others and avoid taking up too much space, being too big, or shining too brightly, they work deftly at managing the controlled burn. It's helpful to learn how to direct our fire to the right places. Yet sometimes life needs the wild fires. The wild woman in every one of us needs her day. She cannot be controlled, and she can be a threat because she is self-sufficient and owns her own power. She is confident and she is not afraid to follow her own compass. She is present to her fullness of being, feeling, and aliveness. She will look you deep in the eyes and seer her own image into your memory. She knows she shines among the brightest stars and she hangs unapologetically in the galaxy of possibility and dances in her own sensual world. Her sensuality is affirming of life itself.

OPENING AND ALLOWING

Sometimes it's not about the controlled burn or the wild fire; it's that you've learned to allow and be receptive. This is so hard for so many. Just let it in. Bring the unseen into creation. Be present with yourself, your lovers, your kids, your friends. Turn off the gadgets. They can easily eclipse your connection to your fire. As you allow energy to flow in, projects move, things come together with more ease, and more of those moments of feeling on fire happen until it becomes a way of life. You are feeling the pull toward all you want, you are allowing the love, the creativity, the sparks to come in. You are open to feeling good and shining ever more brightly. You've released the habit of living from a place of fear and you've begun to live from a place of desire and creation. You've claimed your birthright of pleasure. Your alignment is 360 degrees, full-on.

CREATING BEAUTY AND OPULENCE

I will not be just a tourist in the world of images, just watching images passing by which I cannot live in, make love to, possess as permanent sources of joy and ecstasy.

—ANAÏS NIN

Beauty is the highest form of spirit. Beauty inspires others. Art and music will always be needed regardless of how automated and computerized our world becomes because our spirits are deeply moved by beauty and opulence. Artists must unplug and create space to connect to the muses of their creations. They know that beauty inspires and they make it their craft. As you experience more fun, pleasure, ecstasy, bliss, and orgasm, you experience more beauty. You learn to prioritize beauty so you can experience it more deeply. Sunsets never get old. Beholding the power of the ocean or the forest or a canyon never ceases to awe because it reminds us of our place in it all and of the vastness of the natural world. It reflects back to us the opulence in nature that is in everything.

One of the best ways to refuel your fire when you feel depleted is to spend time in nature. Nature regenerates itself and reflects the process of life-degeneration-death-birth in everything. When you feel like your fire has gone, go back to nature. Walk, hike, breathe the fresh air, make love to trees, lie in the grass, swim in the ocean, behold its beauty, let nature sex you up. It replenishes your well in a way nothing else does.

Allison, a client in New York City whom I worked with over the course of a couple of years, wrote to me one day about how connected and alive she felt by getting back to nature in the context of the deep work she had done on herself:

> I just came back from Florida and made a point of being in the water often. I floated in the pool for a while just gazing up at the clouds and surrendered to the water and its flow, allowing it to wash over me and hold me up at the same time. I had a beautiful experience in the ocean yesterday. It was really windy, so the water was a little rough and choppy. I was standing about hip deep, and there were waves coming at me from all different directions, and as I stood in the swirl of water I felt an inner peace come over me. It was as if I needed to acknowledge and honor that yes, I am now strong

enough to stand in the eye of the storm and am able to stay grounded in the process, because now I have a balanced sense of self and an inner strength that is connected to the divine. And I also have been given beautiful tools and wisdom to guide me and keep myself grounded. While I was standing there I also began to feel the power of the water. Not the power on the physical plane but the spiritual power that can be given to you by the energy of the water. The current began to move through the palms of my hands and through my whole body. It was so amazing.

PLAYING FULL-OUT

What would it mean for you to play full-out? At work? In your partnerships? With your lovers? In sex? In your creativity? With your kids? With your dreams? What would it look like? What fears would you have to bypass? What confinement would you need to bust open? Exercise your leadership in sex, in relationships, in work, in creativity, and in life. Lay your claim. Make demands on yourself for high performance, high enjoyment, high fulfillment, and fun.

Life is too short not to play full-on, clits out, big, bold, brazen, and beautiful. Put the damsel who waits for her knight to rest. Stop taking whatever comes. Stop living by reacting. Quit bitching. Flirt with the one you think is attractive. You are orgasmic and full of vibrancy. Start living like it. Fire doesn't hold back. Fire plays full-out. It doesn't make itself small. It doesn't dim its light because there are other fires nearby and it might take something away from them. In fact, if they get together, they'll make a much bigger, raging pyre, lighting everything around them.

UNDENIABLE FIRE

For fifteen years, I worked as a firekeeper in a women's sweat lodge community founded on Lakota spiritual teachings and practice. I learned deep lessons by working with the fire, which "traditionally" only men were allowed to tend. I've built fires in downpours, in snow, in icy cold, in blazing heat. Each fire has its personality and each one has its needs. The fire always tells you what it needs if you listen. So I learned to listen to fire.

Some fires need a song, a prayer, a focused breath, to get going. Some just need you to stand back and let them do their thing. Any fire can catch and blaze bright when you begin with a firm foundation and all of the necessary elements: A base. A bit of kindling. Air flow. A focused caretaker. A match or a spark.

Your sexuality is like that fire. It is the force of nature itself. It is the propulsion of heat, the driver in the truck of life. The kernel in the joy. The idea in the creation. A fire doesn't know "no." "No" doesn't even compute in the world of fire. "No" is like another language. Fire is a force no one can say no to—we must reckon with it, see it, meet it, take it in, react, or run from it. Fire is. And it is more obviously, completely, and clearly what it is than nearly anything else. Fire is undeniable. If you likened yourself to the power of fire, what would change?

What would you ask for?
How would you more fully express yourself?
What would you stop limiting?
What would you stop apologizing about?
What stories would you stop telling?
What new tales would you have to tell?
How would you walk in the world?
What clothes would you get rid of?

What identities would you change?

What forgotten dreams would you put back on the table?

How would people treat you?

What would you never settle for again?

What ecstasy would you be open to experiencing?

What would be in your house of *yes*?

WHEN YOU IGNITE

What happens when you ignite your own fire? You are more creative and projects begin to move forward. Your creativity flows. You are present with yourself, your partner, your kids, your friends. You have more fun, pleasure, ecstasy, and bliss because you prioritize it and embrace it. You ask for what you want and stop taking the crumbs life always seems to dish out. You are more confident, so you go for it more often. You start living instead of self-monitoring. Criticism doesn't tear you down; it makes you stronger. You dream bigger. Work is more fulfilling. You feel powerful because you have control over your life. You make more money. You attract relationships that are healthy and fulfilling for you. You are no longer trying to be something you are not. You fully enjoy your life. You groove on the power of your body.

We live in a world that hasn't caught up with us yet. As we become our fully blazing, erotically authentic, sexually empowered selves, we are guided by this internal fiery GPS system that maps our life burn, sends us soaring from ashes, and we change the world. The world meets us in our own brilliance and light. As the tribe of women who no longer settle nor diminish our being, our desires and expression grow. As the women who demand more, we get it. We will have a world where we let go of competition and practices that tear one another down. A world where we rebuke not-enoughness and bask in the glow of gorgeous, fiery flames and undeniable creativity and ecstasy.

Woman on Fire, Embrace a New Creed:

I am a sexual being because I am human.
I am whole. I was never broken.
I am writing a story of empowered sexuality.
I have sexual rights; they are a part of my human rights.
I embrace a view of sexuality as a positive force in my life.
I am sexually intelligent.
I own my sexual power and I take life by the horns.
My sexuality and erotic energy imbue everything
I do with creative juice and lush life force.
I listen to my body.
I will never settle.
I will never forsake myself for something outside of myself.
I can be both spiritual and wildly sexual.
Sensuality and pleasure are essential life springs.
The power of pleasure enriches everything in my life.
I appreciate and cultivate beauty and vulnerability.
My passion makes my life exciting every day.
I am big and my bigness gives value to our world.
I clarify my boundaries swiftly and lovingly with grace.
I live in the delicious world of expansive yes.
My sexual empowerment and erotic energy affect everything.
I pursue the enjoyment of life and the expression of
my being without reservation.
I am deserving.
I am enough.
I am a creative being.
I am on fire.

GRACE

I am so fortunate to be able to follow my passion and to work with the incredible women who show up wanting to expand their possibilities for living and being. I am ever grateful for your spirits and hearts, which brought you into a courageous place of "yes," and for allowing me to be a guide along your paths. I am especially grateful for each woman on fire who shared her personal and moving story and allowed me to share it in this book so that others might feel less alone, more understood, and hopefully be inspired by her journey.

I have the best team I can imagine. Leonore Tjia and Elise Bish, you are generous in your spirits, abilities, and passion. Your commitment to expanding this work and helping people with their sexuality is unparalleled. I am so lucky to have you at my side in this journey, fiercely standing for the importance of this path. You have been my life support and filled in the gaps as my attention became focused on finishing this book. I am so grateful for how you have supported me and the women of our tribe.

Stephanie Tade, you are the agent I wanted; the smart and kind kindred spirit who believes in me and this book, the one who I can laugh with as a comrade and collaborator on the journey of creation and who can provide needed perspective on the work and the business of the work.

Caroline Sutton, you are the editor I sought, with largesse of vision and a sharpness that cut through the crud and got to the gold. Your critical questions and insights made this book the best book it could be. You were a true partner in birthing this child and I am ever appreciative of your strength, tenacity, and belief in the potential of this book.

Brianna Flaherty, thank you for staying atop every part of this process to ensure this book would be the artful and timely book it is. Robin Colucci, thank you for your support as both a friend and colleague and for leading me to Mark Malatesta, who helped me realize the larger vision for this book and find the rock stars who would support it as it needed to be.

I had many readers for this book who gave their time and energy to help me make it better. I am especially thankful to Cynthia Spence and Barb O'Neill, who offered critical perspectives and insights that forced me to ask bigger questions and for the fine-tuning that would make my ideas more clear. Jillian Gonzales, you are always more than a reader: you are the friend who stands with me through all the challenges and the triumphs. Thank you for always championing me. Thank you to Marcia Baczynski, Charlie Glickman, Laura Marie Thompson, and Katie Herzig, who read portions of the manuscript and offered their brilliance and expertise. I am truly surrounded by awe-inspiring humans.

Denis Faye and Elana Bell, you were each there in the meltdown moment, with your love, respect, and experiential knowing, offering help in resetting and finding the path out of the abyss and toward the work it was meant to be. Your support was golden.

I have incredible mentors who have raised me up and believed in me for years. Betty Dodson, you will always be my role model extraordinaire and you have championed me, challenged me, and cheered me on—with this book and so many other projects. Janene Sneider, your love and confidence in me have propelled me and helped me grow as a person and as a leader. ALisa Starkweather, you taught me so much about the power of vulnerability and the use of disclosure in leadership, and you have always held me up with tender, fierce support. Carol Queen, Barbara Carrellas, Pamela Madsen, and Joan Price, each of you has offered your wisdom and life experience, and your friendship in this process. There are so many other writers and sex educators who inspire me and have taught me—too many to mention here by name.

Robyn Bell, you have always been a mentor for me as a writer, encouraging and supporting with thoughtfulness. David Neagle, you were the catalyst that got me to put myself behind this endeavor full throttle and full-out. Your teachings have truly changed my life. Thank you for believing in me. Angelique Rewers, your role modeling as a businesswoman and a creative genius continues to inspire me and help me grow.

Rebecca Walker, I am humbled by your brilliance, your thoughtfulness, and your insight. You helped me structure this work with clarity and add my own voice and stories, truly enhancing the work and making it more *me*. To our writing group—Victoria, Jill, Carla, Teresa—thank you for pushing me and critiquing early chapters, for seeing the vision with me, and inspiring me with your own stories and inspirited writing.

Thank you, Dad, for being solid in your support. Whether you know it or not, it has always meant so much. I have unbelievably steadfast friends and you are each a touchstone of love, purpose, fun, heart, and comfort. Tanya Saunders, Christine McAndrews, Maria Scharron-Del Rio, Sean Wallace, Diana Adams, Beth Nelsen, and Tony Pierce, I love each of you and am grateful for your friendship. You have held me and stood by me every step of this journey. Dannette Mehalik, I will always be grateful for the delicious memories and even better stories we can now tell. You taught me more than I could have imagined.

Place is such an important element of the writing process. I wrote *Woman on Fire* in Paris, Napa, and Maui. Each place imbued the book with its energy, power, and beauty. Catherine Wallace, I am ever grateful for how you made my Paris writing adventure possible as I birthed the first draft of this book.

For every agent and editor who said no, I thank you. You strengthened me and made me even more committed to my message. As I say to the women I work with: every "no" helps me find the "yes." I am so grateful to the entire process. All was perfect.

Most of all, love to my companion Pooka, who transitioned as I wrote this book and who was my familiar for so long, offering steadfast presence, furry sensuality, needed cuddle breaks, and family in the way that only a fierce femme feline can offer. I miss you so much.

NOTES

CHAPTER ONE. THE BIG ROUND BALL

The Sexuality Information and Education Council of the United States developed a list of "Life Behaviors of a Sexually Healthy Adult." "Guidelines for Comprehensive Sexuality Education." National Guidelines Task Force. 2004. Accessed January 27, 2015. http://www.siecus.org/_data/global/images/guidelines. pdf. I wanted to espouse upon this idea of what sexual empowerment looks like for adults.

Puberty rituals. "Rituals for Girls in Different Cultures." www.miesiac zka.com. Accessed February 16, 2015. http://www.miesiaczka.com/index.php? option=com_content&view=article&id=77:rituals-for-girls-in-different -cultures&catid=5:1-miesiaczka&Itemid=62.

CHAPTER TWO. CORE ENERGY MODEL OF SEXUALITY

"Sex-positive." Hanne Blank published the most comprehensive definition of sex-positivity I have seen in *Bitch Magazine* circa 1998. I do not have the exact date of the issue of the magazine, but have used her definition in my teaching for years. As she defines it:

> The belief that all people are inherently sexual and deserve a sexuality that is safe and pleasurable to them, regardless of their sex, gender or the sex and/or gender of the person(s) for whom they express desire.

> Acknowledgement that disability or ability, race, ethnicity, religion, class, age, and other factors should not result in sexual disenfranchisement, and that when such disenfranchisement occurs, it should be challenged.

> The belief that an individual's experience of sexuality can and should be

a pleasurable experience that does not result from or in physical or psychological harm, coercion, transmission of disease, or social stigma.

The belief that sexuality can and should be represented and taught in ways that affirm and enhance each individual's ability to experience sexuality in positive ways, by their own consent and at will.

"The erotic is a measure." Lorde, Audre. "The Uses of the Erotic: The Erotic as Power," in *Sister Outsider: Essays and Speeches*. Trumansburg, NY: Crossing Press, 1984.

CHAPTER THREE. ELEMENT ONE: VOICE

Risk manager. "Shadow Work Seminars—Personal Growth Workshops and Coaching Based on Jungian Psychology, Emotional Safety, Shame-Free Containers." Shadow Work. Accessed February 17, 2015. http://shadowwork.com. The term *risk manager* is used in Shadow Work as a part of our subconscious that works to keep us emotionally and physically safe.

The Vagina Monologues. Ensler, Eve. *The Vagina Monologues*. Rev. ed. New York: Villard, 2001.

If it doesn't set you free, it's not true. Neagle, David. "Breaking Free Live Experience." Lecture by David Neagle, March 21, 2013.

The Work. Katie, Byron, and Stephen Mitchell. *Loving What Is: Four Questions That Can Change Your Life*. New York: Harmony Books, 2002.

CHAPTER FOUR. ELEMENT TWO: RELEASE

"Shame cannot survive being spoken." *Oprah and Brené Brown Super Soul Sunday Part 2: Living with a Whole Heart*. Performed by Brené Brown and Oprah Winfrey. Harpo Productions, 2013 (film).

Triggers. Abadi, Ponta. "Trigger-Warning Debate Ignores Survivors' Voices." Ms. Magazine Blog. May 29, 2014. Accessed February 16, 2015. http://msmaga zine.com/blog/2014/05/29/the-trigger-warning-debate-ignores-survivors-voices/. While the word *trigger* has become a more common term, it is not embraced by everyone. Some call it "activation" or relate it to what we know about PTSD. In 2014, a fierce debate began about the use of "trigger warnings," especially in relationship to academia and literature, which might activate students who had experienced trauma.

Dissociation. Maltz, Wendy. *The Sexual Healing Journey: A Guide for Survivors of Sexual Abuse*. New York: HarperCollins Publishers, 1991.

Breathwork. Carrellas, Barbara. *Urban Tantra: Sacred Sex for the Twenty-First Century*. Berkeley, CA: Celestial Arts, 2007. *Urban Tantra* is a great resource for learning many ways to breathe. Breathwork has also been called transformational breath, ecstatic breath, and tantra, among other names.

Defense mechanisms. Freud, Anna (1937). *The Ego and the Mechanisms of Defence*, London: Hogarth Press and Institute of Psycho-Analysis. (Revised edition: 1966, US, 1968, UK).

Defense mechanisms. Insel, Paul M. *Connect Core Concepts in Health*. Brief 11th ed. New York: McGraw-Hill, 2010.

Defense mechanisms. Grohol, John. "15 Common Defense Mechanisms." Psychcentral.com. January 1, 2007. Accessed February 17, 2015. http://psychcentral.com/lib/15-common-defense-mechanisms/0001251.

Neural pathways. Doidge, Norman. *The Brain That Changes Itself: Stories of Personal Triumph from the Frontiers of Brain Science*. New York: Viking, 2007.

"Fuck You Journal." The idea to do what I called the "Fuck You Journal" initially came from coach Joanna Lindenbaum. Personal conversation with author. www.soulfulcoach.com.

Forgiveness practice. Modified from *Radical Forgiveness*. Tipping, Colin. *Radical Forgiveness: A Revolutionary Five-Stage Process to Heal Relationships, Let Go of Anger and Blame, Find Peace in Any Situation*. Boulder, CO: Sounds True, 2009.

"Vulnerability is the birthplace." *Oprah and Brené Brown Super Soul Sunday Part 2: Living with a Whole Heart*.

We all have a victim self. Myss, Caroline. *Sacred Contracts: Awakening Your Divine Potential*. New York: Harmony Books, 2001.

"Thank you for taking care of yourself." "Cuddle Party—A Workshop and Social Event on Boundaries, Touch and Communication." Cuddle Party RSS. Accessed February 13, 2015. www.cuddleparty.com.

CHAPTER SIX. ELEMENT FOUR: BODY

Questions about the body. Cash, Thomas F. *The Body Image Workbook: An Eight-Step Program for Learning to Like Your Looks*. 2nd ed. Oakland, CA.: New Harbinger Publications, 2008. Questions inspired in part by *The Body Image Workbook*.

Radical acceptance. Brach, Tara. *Radical Acceptance: Embracing Your Life with the Heart of a Buddha*. New York: Bantam Books, 2003.

Spectatoring. Masters, William H., and Virginia E. Johnson. *Human Sexual Inadequacy*. Boston: Little, Brown, 1970. Masters and Johnson originally coined the term *spectatoring*.

Spectatoring. Trapnell, Paul D., Cindy M. Meston, and Boris B. Gorzalka. "Spectatoring and the Relationship between Body Image and Sexual Experience: Self-focus or Self-valence?" *Journal of Sex Research* 34, no. 3 (1997): 267–78.

Popularity of labiaplasty. The American Society for Aesthetic Plastic Surgery, News Release. Accessed February 13, 2015. http://www.surgery.org/media/news-releases/labiaplasty-and-buttock-augmentation-show-marked-increase-in-popularity.

Women spend thousands on genital surgery. "2013 Plastic Surgery Statistics." Accessed February 13, 2015. www.plasticsurgery.org/news/plastic-surgery-statistics/2013.html. According to this study, in 2013, $12.6 billion was spent on cosmetic surgery in the United States, an increase of 15 percent.

Betty Dodson's classic vulva drawings. Dodson, Betty. *Sex for One: The Joy of Selfloving*. New York: Crown Trade Paperbacks, 1996. Dodson drew these classic drawings based on real women and they are still unprecedented.

Full-color photos of vulvas. Blank, Joani. *Femalia*. San Francisco: Down There Press, 1993.

Line drawings of vulvas. Corinne, Tee. *Cunt Coloring Book*. San Francisco: Last Gasp, 1994.

Georgia O'Keeffe was a modern American painter known for her vulvic paintings of flowers.

Gynecological self-exam. Feminist Women's Health Centers. "Self Care—It's OK to Peek! How to Perform Self Cervical and Vaginal Examination." Accessed February 13, 2015. www.fwhc.org/health/selfcare.htm.

The vagina vs. the clitoris. Freud, Sigmund, and James Strachey. *Three Essays on the Theory of Sexuality*. New York: Basic Books, 1975.

The vagina vs. the clitoris. Federation of Feminist Women's Health Centers. *A New View of a Woman's Body: A Fully Illustrated Guide*. New York: Feminist Health Press, 1991. In response to the focus on the vagina, the Federation put forth this book, placing the clitoris at the center of women's anatomy and the primary sexual organ.

The vagina vs. the clitoris. Wolf, Naomi. *Vagina: A New Biography*. New York: Ecco, 2012. Wolf questions the way the clitoris has eclipsed the importance of the vagina in some feminist conversations about women's sexuality.

Six to eight thousand nerve endings in the clitoris. Chalker, Rebecca. *The Clitoral Truth: The Secret World at Your Fingertips*. New York: Seven Stories Press, 2000.

Vaginal orgasms are superior to clitoral orgasms. Freud, Sigmund, and James Strachey. *Three Essays on the Theory of Sexuality*.

Kegels. Ladas, Alice Kahn, and Beverly Whipple. *The G Spot and Other Recent Discoveries about Human Sexuality*. New York: Holt, Rinehart, and Winston, 1982.

Mr. Gräfenberg. Ibid. The G-spot was named the Gräfenberg spot by researchers Beverly Whipple and John Perry.

"Study Concludes That Women Who Squirt During Sex Are Actually Peeing." Accessed February 16, 2015. http://www.iflscience.com/health-and-medicine/women-squirting-during-sex-may-actually-be-peeing.

Female ejaculation is antimicrobial. Winston, Sheri. *Women's Anatomy of Arousal: Secret Maps to Buried Pleasure*. Kingston, NY: Mango Garden, 2010.

References to female ejaculation for millennia. Chalker, Rebecca. *The Clitoral Truth: The Secret World at Your Fingertips*.

"Orgasmic flush." Manderino, Amy Luna. "I F*Cking Hate Click Bait, Part Two." The Sex Evolution. Accessed April 4, 2015. http://thesexevolution .tumblr.com/post/110163847755/i-f-cking-hate-click-bait. Amy Luna Manderino of the Sex Evolution proposes we call female ejaculation an "orgasmic flush."

Cervical mucus through the menstrual cycle. Federation of Feminist Women's Health Centers. *A New View of a Woman's Body: A Fully Illustrated Guide.*

The uterus is an active part. Ibid.

Pudendal and pelvic nerve. Winston, Sheri. *Women's Anatomy of Arousal: Secret Maps to Buried Pleasure.*

Pudendal and pelvic nerve. Wolf, Naomi. *Vagina: A New Biography.*

Nerve bundles. Ibid.

Feedback loop. Ibid.

Pre-orgasmic rather than inorgasmic. Dodson, Betty. *Sex for One: The Joy of Selfloving.*

Tips on exploring the body. Goddard, Jamie, and Kurt Brungardt. *Lesbian Sex Secrets for Men: What Every Man Wants to Know about Making Love to a Woman and Never Asks.* New York: Penguin Group, 2000.

CHAPTER SEVEN. ELEMENT FIVE: DESIRE

Author's TEDx Talk. Goddard, Amy Jo. "Owning Your Sexual Power: Amy Jo Goddard at TEDxNapaValley." YouTube. Accessed February 13, 2015. https:// www.youtube.com/watch?v=m9aqVqyJlJo.

Desire disorders in women. American Psychiatric Association. *Diagnostic and Statistical Manual of Mental Disorders, Fifth Edition (DSM-5).* Washington, DC: American Psychiatric Publishing, 2013.

Desire disorders in women. Spurgas, Alyson K. "Interest, Arousal, and Shifting Diagnoses of Female Sexual Dysfunction, Or: How Women Learn About Desire." *Studies in Gender and Sexuality* 14, no. 3 (2013): 187–205. Accessed February 17, 2015. http://www.tandfonline.com/doi/abs/10.1080/15240657.2013.818854# .VSIJtougLXw.

Low sexual desire in women. West, S. L., A. A. D'Aloisio, R. P. Agans, W. D. Kalsbeek, N. N. Borisov, and J. M. Thorp. "Prevalence of Low Sexual Desire and Hypoactive Sexual Desire Disorder in a Nationally Representative Sample of U.S. Women." *Archives of Internal Medicine* 168, no. 13 (2008): 441–449.

"Spontaneous desire." Basson, R. "Female Sexual Response: The Role of Drugs in the Management of Sexual Dysfunction." *Obstet Gynecol* 2001; 98:350–353.

Maintaining sexual tension with a domestic partner. Perel, Esther. *Mating in Captivity: Unlocking Erotic Intelligence.* New York: Harper, 2007.

The second chakra. Judith, Anodea, and Selene Vega. *The Sevenfold Journey: Reclaiming Mind, Body & Spirit Through the Chakras.* Freedom, CA: Crossing Press, 1993.

CHAPTER EIGHT. ELEMENT SIX: PERMISSION

A maybe is not a "yes." "Cuddle Party—A Workshop and Social Event on Boundaries, Touch and Communication." Cuddle Party RSS. Accessed February 13, 2015. http://www.cuddleparty.com.

CHAPTER NINE. ELEMENT SEVEN: PLAY

"We evolved through play." Ackerman, Diane. *Deep Play*. New York: Random House, 1999.
"Skill." Dictionary.com. Accessed February 14, 2015. http://dictionary .reference.com/browse/skill?s=t.

CHAPTER ELEVEN. ELEMENT NINE: FIRE

Vulvalution. *Vulvalution* ran at WOW Café Theatre in the downtown theatre district in New York City in 1999. Julia Murphy co-wrote and directed it, and I co-wrote, produced, and performed in the show with an eleven-woman cast.
Top 10 Pleasure List. Jwala, and Robb Smith. *Sacred Sex: Ecstatic Techniques for Empowering Relationships*. San Rafael, CA: Mandala, 1993. This activity is adapted from Jwala's turn-on list.
"I will not be just a tourist in the world of images." Nin, Anaïs. *The Diary of Anaïs Nin, Volume 5, 1947–1955*. New York: Houghton Mifflin Harcourt, 1975.
Women's sweat lodge community. "Sweatlodge." Kunsi Keya Tamakoce. Accessed February 16, 2015. http://kunsikeya.org/sundance.html.
Lakota spiritual teachings and practice. Brown, Joseph Epes. *The Sacred Pipe: Black Elk's Account of the Seven Rites of the Oglala Sioux*. Norman: University of Oklahoma Press, 1953.

INDEX